presenting JAVABEANS

Michael Morrison

sams
net

201 West 103rd Street
Indianapolis, IN 46290

Copyright © 1997 by Sams.net Publishing

FIRST EDITION

International Standard Book Number: 1-57521-287-0

Library of Congress Catalog Card Number: 96-72398

2000   99   98   97   4   3   2   1

Interpretation of the printing code: the rightmost double-digit number is the year of the book's printing; the rightmost single-digit, the number of the book's printing. For example, a printing code of 97-1 shows that the first printing of the book occurred in 1997.

Composed in Agaramond and MCPdigital by Macmillan Computer Publishing

Printed in the United States of America

Trademarks

Publisher and President   *Richard K. Swadley*

Publishing Manager   *Mark Taber*

Director of Editorial Services   *Cindy Morrow*

Managing Editor   *Jodi Jensen*

Assistant Marketing Managers   *Kristina Perry, Rachel Wolfe*

Acquisitions Editor
Beverly Eppink

Development Editor
Kelly Murdock

Software Development Specialist
Bob Correll

Production Editor
Tonya Simpson

Copy Editors
Bart Reed
Marilyn Stone

Indexer
Bruce Clingaman

Technical Reviewer
Jeff Shockley

Editorial Coordinator
Katie Wise

Technical Edit Coordinator
Lorraine Schaffer

Resource Coordinator
Deborah Frisby

Editorial Assistants
Carol Ackerman
Andi Richter
Rhonda Tinch-Mize

Cover Designer
Tim Amrhein

Book Designer
Alyssa Yesh

Copy Writer
Peter Fuller

Production Team Supervisors
Brad Chinn
Charlotte Clapp

Production
Cyndi Davis
Paula Lowell
Carl Pierce
M. Anne Sipahimalani
Ian Smith

Overview

Contents

Dedication

To my mom, who is everything I could ever ask for in a mother. I love you, mom!

Acknowledgments

I would like to thank Beverly Eppink for keeping her faith in me when the deadlines started passing me by. Thanks also goes out to everyone else at Sams.net, who are ultimately responsible for making this book a reality.

I would like to thank my wife, Mahsheed, who puts up with my crazy work schedule and makes me happier than I ever thought I could be. Thanks for being you!

I would also like to thank my parents, who set the example for me to follow and continue to shower me with encouragement and support.

Finally, I'd like to thank my good friend Randy Weems for teaching me a great deal of what I know about software and technology in general.

About the Author

Michael Morrison is a technical writer, software developer, and avid skateboarder living in Nashville, Tennessee with his immortal beloved, Mahsheed. Michael is a contributing author to *Teach Yourself Java in 21 Days, Professional Reference Edition* and *Late Night Visual J++*, as well as the lead author of *Java Unleashed, Second Edition*. If you're ever in the Nashville area, there's a good chance you can catch Michael skateboarding at XXX Sports. Otherwise, you can reach him via e-mail at mmorrison@thetribe.com, or on the Web at www.thetribe.com.

Tell Us What You Think!

As a reader, you are the most important critic and commentator of our books. We value your opinion and want to know what we're doing right, what we could do better, what areas you'd like to see us publish in, and any other words of wisdom you're willing to pass our way. You can help us make strong books that meet your needs and give you the computer guidance you require.

Do you have access to CompuServe or the World Wide Web? Then check out our CompuServe forum by typing GO SAMS at any prompt. If you prefer the World Wide Web, check out our site at http://www.mcp.com.

> **Note:** If you have a technical question about this book, call the technical support line at 800-571-5840, ext. 3668.

As the publishing manager of the group that created this book, I welcome your comments. You can fax, e-mail, or write me directly to let me know what you did or didn't like about this book—as well as what we can do to make our books stronger. Here's the information:

Fax: 317-581-4669

E-mail: newtech_mgr@sams.mcp.com

Mail: Mark Taber
          Sams.net Publishing
          201 W. 103rd Street
          Indianapolis, IN 46290

Introduction

With Java fast on its way to becoming the standard programming language and runtime environment of choice for the Internet, many have wondered what's next for Java. JavaSoft, the makers of Java, apparently had similar thoughts after the incredible success of Java. JavaSoft realized that Java clearly had lots of potential in terms of the Internet, but it also started realizing that its benefits extended far beyond online applications. Instead of standing around waiting to see what other people could do with Java, JavaSoft seized the opportunity to assess the weaknesses of Java and beef it up with new technologies in order to make it a well-rounded software technology. One of these new Java-related technologies is JavaBeans, which is Java's answer to component software.

If you aren't familiar with component software, it is a type of software that is designed heavily around the idea of code reuse and compartmentalization. Component software is a very popular and powerful concept that is rapidly being used throughout the software industry to increase development efficiency. Software components are designed and built so that they can be accessed and used in a variety of different development and runtime scenarios. The JavaBeans component software technology is based on Java and provides a means of creating and using Java classes as software components. JavaBeans is very significant to the future of Java because many viewed the lack of a component software technology as a big weakness in Java.

JavaSoft saw the need as well and quickly made JavaBeans a high priority on its list. When assessing the initial goals of JavaBeans, the architects at JavaSoft managed to come up with a very simple mission statement that cuts right to the point of what the JavaBeans technology is to accomplish. This mission statement follows:

"Write once, run anywhere, reuse everywhere."

This statement expresses the goals of JavaBeans in a very simple, concise, and elegant set of requirements. The first of these requirements, "write once," refers to the need for JavaBeans code to be written once and not require rewrites to add or improve functionality. The second requirement, "run anywhere," refers to the need for JavaBeans components to be able to run on a wide range of operating system platforms. The final requirement, "reuse everywhere," refers to the need for JavaBeans components to be reusable in a variety of different applications and in different types of development environments.

Although the requirements of the JavaBeans mission statement are admittedly a little vague, they nevertheless paint a general picture of what the technology is to accomplish. This book is devoted to exploring the JavaBeans technology and shedding light on how this mission statement is met throughout the various parts of JavaBeans. Throughout this book you learn all about JavaBeans at a conceptual level by addressing each fundamental area of the technology. You also learn a great deal about JavaBeans from a very practical perspective by building your own JavaBeans components that can be reused in your own Java applets or applications.

Even though the main premise of this book is to introduce you to the JavaBeans technology, I think you'll be pleasantly surprised by the depth in which JavaBeans is covered. Even so, I make every effort to keep you on a level footing by balancing technical details with practical concepts. When all is said and done, I think you'll agree that JavaBeans is quite possibly the most exciting technology to come about since Java itself. I had a lot of fun working with JavaBeans during the development of this book, and I truly look forward to putting it to work in my own projects.

Who Should Read This Book?

This book covers the JavaBeans technology from a few different angles. As such, the book targets a variety of different readers with different technical backgrounds and expertise. From a conceptual perspective, this book requires little more than a basic understanding of the Java programming language and runtime system. However, Part III, "Creating Your Own Beans," delves into JavaBeans component creation and requires a definite knowledge of Java programming. If you are a Java programmer, you will find yourself right at home with this book, particularly Part III. On the other hand, if you are interested only in learning about the conceptual aspects of the JavaBeans technology, you will still find a great deal of the book useful and insightful.

Regardless of your technical knowledge or reason for wanting to learn about JavaBeans, keep in mind that at least a general knowledge of Java is required to fully appreciate the coverage of JavaBeans. This is due to the fact that

JavaBeans is itself an extension of the Java technology. I encourage you to refer to one of the many books that cover the Java programming language and runtime system if you have no prior knowledge of Java.

How This Book Is Organized

This book is divided into four parts and four appendixes, each of which takes a different approach to exploring the JavaBeans technology. Although there is naturally some overlap of material between each part of the book, the goal of each of them is to examine JavaBeans from a different perspective. Although these parts aren't entirely sequential, there is definitely a benefit to reading them in order.

In Part I, "Introduction to JavaBeans," you learn the basics about software components and why they are so important to the future of software development. You then learn about the fundamentals of JavaBeans, as well as the JavaBeans API.

In Part II, "Inside the JavaBeans API," you move into the specifics of the JavaBeans API. Each chapter in this part of the book focuses on a fundamental section of the JavaBeans API. These fundamental API sections correspond to major functional areas of JavaBeans, and consist of properties, introspection, events, persistence, and customization.

In Part III, "Creating Your Own Beans," you move from the conceptual to the practical by learning how to build your own beans. You begin by learning the basics behind general bean construction. From there, you spend the remaining chapters developing your own beans. These beans include a fancy button bean, a meter bar bean, an LED display bean, and an audio player bean.

In Part IV, "Advanced Issues and the Future of JavaBeans," you tie up loose ends by covering some advanced and future JavaBeans issues. You start off by learning how to use beans in hand-coded applications. From there, you cover a variety of advanced JavaBeans issues, followed by a look into the future of JavaBeans.

The appendixes provide vital reference information for JavaBeans, including a listing of online JavaBeans resources, a JavaBeans API quick reference, a description of what is included on the accompanying CD-ROM, and a glossary.

Conventions Used in This Book

This book follows a few basic conventions when presenting information relating to system commands and programming procedures. Text that you type and text that should appear on your screen is presented in monospace type, like this:

```
Some monospace text
```

Placeholders for variables and expressions appear in *monospace italic* type, like this:

```
Some monospace italic text
```

Beyond these type conventions, the book also uses sidebars to indicate important pieces of information. These sidebars and their respective meanings follow:

New Term

The New Term sidebar is used to indicate that a new term is being introduced into the discussion.

Note: The Note sidebar is used to present an interesting piece of information related to the discussion.

Caution: The Caution sidebar is used to present potential problems related to the discussion.

Introduction to JavaBeans

Software Component Basics

A book on JavaBeans wouldn't be of much use if it didn't begin by explaining the conceptual foundations of software components, which form the basis of the JavaBeans technology. Through its specific approach at providing a software component technology, JavaBeans enables software developers to design and create reusable pieces of software that easily integrate with each other, with applications, and even with development tools. If this description of JavaBeans makes sense to you, then great. If not, don't feel discouraged, because I deliberately jumped ahead by describing JavaBeans in this manner. Even though it lies at the heart of JavaBeans, the concept of a software component is not something you are expected to know going into this book. In fact, the purpose of this chapter is to start off the book on a proper footing by exploring software components and why they are important to the future of software.

The best place to begin when uncovering the magic behind software components is to look at the reason why they were invented to begin with; in other words, what problems are software components trying to solve? The most simple and direct answer to this question is software reuse, which is the challenge of leveraging as much previous work as possible in each new development project. Even though a variety of different software component approaches have evolved, until recently none have come far enough in offering a means to create fully reusable software. In this chapter, you learn a great deal about this problem and the fundamental concept employed to solve it: the software component. You learn how software components improve software development in a variety of ways, which enables developers to spend more time leveraging existing code instead of hacking it or throwing it away in lieu of new code. Most important, this chapter lays the groundwork for JavaBeans, which is perhaps the most exciting and promising software component technology available.

In this chapter, you learn the following:

- Problems facing the software industry
- Software component basics
- Visual and non-visual components
- Component models

The Need for Software Components

Change is embraced in the innovative world of software development probably more than in any other professional endeavor. Software enters a final commercial state for only a brief period of time, after which the next batch of enhancements and improvements is immediately planned and begun. For this reason, no other industry can more proudly boast of its products being "new and improved" than the software industry. However, all of this innovation comes at a price; that price is the stress of trying to work miracles in short periods of time. Software developers are always under extreme pressure to work faster and deliver better results. No doubt this pressure is present in plenty of other professions, but the software development community prides itself on its ability to meet seemingly unattainable deadlines.

In their quest to deliver feature-packed applications in a short period of time, software developers often are forced to cut corners in the midst of turning out applications. These cut corners typically result in code that is highly dependent on the specific application, with little usefulness beyond that particular project. Although this is acceptable in most cases, the end result is that the efforts put into a finished project offer little to aid in the development of future projects. In other words, it's back to the drawing board, or keyboard, for each new project. Wouldn't it be nice if you could somehow reuse similar features developed for one application in another application requiring the same functionality? Of course it would, but I'm getting ahead a little.

Regardless of how careful developers are about not cutting corners throughout a project's development, the mere size of a project often can lead to a great deal of problems. The most careful and thought-out design can lead to utter confusion when a project grows beyond a certain manageable size. In this situation, it becomes extremely difficult to make sense of a bloated application that has reached an unmanageable state of confusion and complexity. More than a few software development teams have thrown up their hands and started anew on projects after realizing that they were heading down a winding path of complexity with an obfuscated code base. Even if the code is well written, there simply are limits to the degree in which organization can help in making sense of things at the code level.

Lest you think I'm behind the times or just being overly negative and ignoring recent advances in software development technologies, let me say that object-oriented design methodologies and programming languages have come a long way toward improving this scenario. Even so, none of these languages has truly answered the need for a fully reusable software standard. As nice as C++ classes are, they still are inherently limited by the address space in which they execute, the specific protocol within which they communicate, and the platform for which they are compiled. In other words, programmers can reuse C++ classes only within the specific context of the applications they are developing, which is sometimes useful but nonetheless limiting. The same thing applies to Java classes, which are functionally similar to C++ classes, although they do add the benefit of being cross-platform in most situations.

New Term

A *platform* is a particular operating system and runtime environment, such as Windows 95 or Solaris.

New Term

Cross-platform refers to software that can execute on different platforms without any special modification.

OK, so I've painted a fairly ugly picture of the software world and left you feeling hopeless and desperate, right? Maybe not, but hopefully I've gotten the point across that there are some big problems with the way software is developed, and something must be done to improve things. Object-oriented programming languages are a huge step in the right direction, because they enable programmers to deal with objects instead of worrying about procedures and data. This fits in much better with the human way of thinking, because we all live in a world full of objects.

The problem is that object-oriented programming languages enforce an object paradigm only within the bounds of a particular programming model such as C++ or Java. Although this certainly enables you to reuse code easier when you are working within the same programming language on a specific target platform, it doesn't offer much for the wider view of software where there are many different programming languages and platforms. The problem is that the object-oriented idea hasn't been fully realized beyond the code level, which is a shame.

Note: It's worth noting that the issue of supporting multiple platforms has become much more important with the popularity of the Web, which brings together users of all types of computing hardware and operating systems.

The software world has been inching toward the idea of wide-scale reusability for some time, but no single technology has emerged that provides answers to the many problems inherent in software reuse. The reason is that a real solution must not only enable developers to easily reuse code within a particular application, but also across different platforms and even in a distributed network environment such as the Internet. Ultimately, a realistic software technology for the future must easily integrate into the client/server model, which has become standard in most modern computing systems.

In addition to these requirements, a long-term solution to code reuse must provide an elegant solution to the existence of multiple versions of a piece of software. As stated earlier, software is in a constant state of change, which facilitates a need for handling multiple versions. Giving software a path to grow and expand is a crucial point because it enables developers to continue their endless crusade of improving on last month's bright idea.

Software Component Beginnings

The software development community has been exploring the idea of reusable software for a while. You might have heard reusable software referred to under its more popular name, software components. In case you've missed the hype, a *component* is a reusable piece of software that can be assembled easily to create applications with much greater development efficiency. Just in case you think this idea sounds groundbreaking, it is not. You only need to look back roughly a century to see this same idea applied to a very different type of application. I'm referring to the industrial revolution, in which the assembly-line approach to developing and assembling mechanical machinery was introduced. The idea as applied to software is to build small, reusable components once and then reuse them as much as possible, thereby streamlining the entire development process.

New Term

A *software component* is a piece of software isolated into a discrete, easily reusable structure.

Although component software certainly has its merits, fully reusable software has yet to really establish itself, for a variety of reasons. Not the least of which is the fact that the software industry is still very young compared to the industries carved out in the industrial revolution. It only stands to reason that it would take time to iron out the kinks in the whole software production process. If you're like me, you'll embrace the rapid changes taking place in the software world and relish the fact that you are a part of a revolution of sorts—an information revolution.

Perhaps the hardest thing component software has had to face is the wide range of disparate microprocessors and operating systems in use today. There have been a variety of reasonable attempts at component software, but they've always been limited to a specific operating system. Microsoft's VBX and OCX component architectures have had great success in the PC world, but they've done little to bridge the gap between other types of operating systems. Weighing in the amount of work required to get an inherently platform-dependent component technology running on a wide range of operating systems, it only makes sense that Microsoft has focused solely on the PC market.

> Note: Actually, Microsoft's new ActiveX technology, which is a revamped version of its OCX technology, aims to provide an all-purpose component technology compatible across a wide range of platforms. However, considering the dependency of ActiveX on 32-bit Windows code, it has yet to be seen how Microsoft will solve the platform-dependency issue. You learn about the specific similarities and differences between JavaBeans and ActiveX in Chapter 15, "Advanced JavaBeans."

Before the explosion of the Internet, the platform-dependency issue wasn't all that big a deal. PC developers didn't necessarily care too much that their products wouldn't run on a Solaris system. Some PC developers hedged their bets and ported their applications to the Macintosh platform, but most with considerably lengthy and resource-intensive development efforts. The whole scenario changed with the operating system melting pot created by the Internet. The result was a renewed interest in developing software that everyone could use, regardless of which operating system they happened to be running. Java has been a major factor in making truly platform-independent software development a reality. However, until recently Java has not provided an answer to the issue of component software—you'll get to that in just a moment, and in fact throughout the rest of the book.

As if the platform dependency issue weren't enough, some existing component technologies also suffer because they must be developed using a particular programming language or within a particular development environment. Just as platform dependency cripples components at runtime, limiting component development to a particular programming language or development environment equally cripples components at the development end. Software developers want to be able to decide for themselves which language is the most appropriate for a particular task. Likewise, developers want to be able to select the development environment that best fits their needs, instead of being forced to use one based on the constraints of a component technology.

Therefore, any realistic long-term component technology must deal with both the issue of platform dependency and language dependency. This brings you to JavaBeans: JavaSoft's JavaBeans technology is a component technology that answers both of these problems directly. JavaBeans is implemented as an architecture-independent and platform-independent application programming interface (API) for creating and using dynamic Java software components. JavaBeans picks up where other component technologies have left off, using the portable Java platform as the basis for providing a complete component software solution that is readily applicable to the online world. Before I get carried away, let me stop and mention that you have the rest of the book to worry about the details of JavaBeans; for now, continue with software components in general.

Visual Software Components

If the discussion of software components thus far has left you a little confused, hopefully this section will clear things up. So far you've learned software components in a relatively abstract sense, which can sometimes be difficult to grasp. An easier way to understand software components is to look at a specific subset of components: visual components. Visual components are software components that have a visual representation that requires physical space on the display surface of a parent application. Parent applications are sometimes more generally referred to as containers. You learn more about containers later, in the "Component Models" section of this chapter.

> **New Term**
>
> A *visual component* is a type of component that has a visual representation that requires physical space on the display surface of a parent application.

Possibly the most simple example of a visual component is a button, which is a graphical element completely distinguishable from the application within which it is contained. Many visual design tools, or application builder tools, provide support for graphically manipulating buttons, which is proof of the fact that buttons are separate entities that can be arranged and interacted with independently of any parent application. In this way, a button functions as a discrete self-contained unit, which just happens to be one of the key traits of a software component. Even though buttons are discrete units, the real power they provide is the capability to easily integrate into applications. Using an application builder tool, a button is as easy to add as clicking and dragging the mouse. Figure 1.1 shows a button being added to a dialog box in Visual J++, a popular Java development tool.

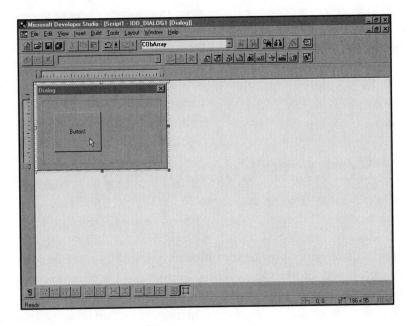

Figure 1.1.
A button being added to a dialog box in Visual J++.

The button shown in Figure 1.1 is a visual software component, as is evident in the figure. Beyond its visual presence, the button component also can be interacted with programmatically. For example, you can specify a piece of code that is executed when the button is pressed. The pressing of the button is known as a user input event, and it is normal for visual components to propagate input events to the parent application if the application is interested in knowing about the event. You learn much more about events and how they relate to JavaBeans in Chapter 6, "Handling Bean Events."

Many other types of visual components are supported in visual development environments such as Visual J++. These components include checkboxes, list boxes, and text edit boxes, to name a few. Keep in mind that the visual components used in Visual J++ are limited in that they actually are based on standard Java classes. One exception to this is the use of ActiveX controls, which provide some of the advanced capabilities required of true software components. Of course, JavaBeans components are an exception as well, but I don't want to jump ahead too much at this point.

Non-Visual Software Components

If visual components sound like the ideal use for software component technologies, understand that there are also situations in which non-visual components can be very useful. A very popular Visual Basic control is the Timer control, which is completely invisible at runtime. The Visual Basic Timer control can be set to trigger an event at periodic intervals, such as once every second. The Timer control is very useful in creating timing loops such as those that control animations. Because the Timer control is used entirely at the programming level, there is no meaningful reason to provide a graphical view of the component at runtime. The nice thing about the Timer control is that an application using the control doesn't have to be concerned at all about how the control is implemented internally; the application lets the control take care of its own business. That's the beauty of software components!

Another good example of a non-visual software component is a hypothetical spell checker component that processes text and finds misspelled words. Because this spell checker is a self-contained component, it can easily be integrated into any application that might benefit from spell checking functionality. For example, the same spell checker component could be used in both a word processor and an e-mail application. This saves the developers of each application the trouble of designing and implementing their own spell checker from scratch. Instead, they are free to purchase the spell checker component from a third-party component vendor. Or, if they so choose, they can develop their own spell checker component and reuse it however they want. The point is that the spell checker functionality is isolated into a self-contained unit, a component, that can be plugged into an application with minimal effort.

Software Building Blocks

The bottom line to this discussion is that components, both visual and non-visual, are the equivalent of software building blocks. Using components, you can build applications one discrete, functional piece at a time. To get a better grasp of why this is such a significant leap in the evolution of software design, consider some real-world building blocks. If you wanted to take up masonry as a side profession, you would first buy bricks, mortar, and a trowel. Using the trowel and a little know-how, you could start building walls without too much difficulty.

In the world of software, things just aren't that simple. First of all, you would be hard pressed to find software off the shelf that is as ready to assemble as bricks and mortar are for wall construction. More than likely, the software you find would be at a level of detail significantly lower than you had planned, and as a result you would have to spend a great deal more time developing the low-level parts of your application. The parallel in the masonry world would be if you had to create your own bricks, which is obviously well beyond the skills necessary to be a successful wall builder.

And it doesn't stop there! Back on the software side of things, most software you buy is limited to a particular platform, which means that you are often on your own if you choose to develop for a different platform. In your masonry profession, this leaves you with having to learn how to create a completely different type of brick each time you want to build a wall that looks a little different. Additionally, you would potentially have to buy a new trowel specifically designed for that type of brick.

OK, so my analogy went a little astray there, but I think you get the idea. Just as bricks and mortar form the building blocks of masonry, software components form the building blocks of software development.

Component Models

Now that you have a pretty good idea about what a software component is, it's time to look a little closer at what makes one work. At the heart of every software component technology is a component model, which defines the architecture of components and how they are manipulated and interacted with externally. The architecture defined by a component model is responsible primarily for determining how components are able to interact in a dynamic environment. Understanding component models and their related architecture is critical in seeing the big picture surrounding software components and how they work.

All software component models define two fundamental elements: components and containers. The *component* part of a component model lays the foundation for how different components are created and used. In other words, the component model provides the template from which practical components are created. The *container* part of the component model equation defines a method of combining components together into useful structures. Containers provide the context for components to be arranged and interacted with one another. For example, an application using a group of components acts as a container for the components.

New Term

A *container* is a context in which components can be grouped together and interacted with.

Containers also are sometimes referred to as forms, pages, frames, or shells, and can serve as the basis for applications. Just to confuse things a little more, containers also can be components themselves. Even though this might sound strange at first, this capability is important because it enables components to be nested within each other, resulting in complex visual interfaces. Figure 1.2 shows an example of a group box component in Visual J++ being used as a container to hold a group of buttons in a dialog box.

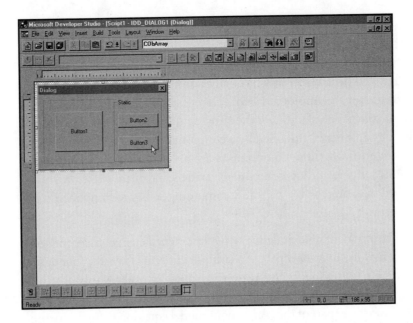

Figure 1.2.
A group box component being used as a container in Visual J++.

Besides defining the structure of components and containers, a component model also is responsible for providing a variety of services. More specifically, a full-featured component model is responsible for supporting the following six major services:

- Introspection
- Event handling
- Persistence
- Layout
- Application builder support
- Distributed computing support

Introspection

Introspection is the mechanism that exposes to the outside world the functionality of components. Through introspection, an application can query a component to find out its capabilities and then interact with the component accordingly. Introspection is one of the most critical aspects of a component model because it is responsible for dictating how a component appears to applications and other components. If you recall, one of the key requirements of a component is that it be completely self-contained. For a component to be both self-contained and useable from the outside, it must fully support introspection.

New Term

Introspection is the mechanism that exposes to the outside world the functionality of a component.

Event Handling

Event handling is the mechanism that enables a component to generate event notifications that correspond to some change in the internal state of the component. When the state of a component changes, the component generates an event notification that is broadcast to all interested parties. These interested parties can be either a parent application or other components. The event handling mechanism is structured in such a way that events can easily be caught and responded to in a consistent fashion.

New Term

An *event* is something that happens within a component that an application or other component might want to know about and possibly react to.

As an example, recall the button component mentioned earlier in this chapter, which generates an event when it is clicked with the mouse. In this case, the change in the button state is reflected by the fact that the button has been clicked. This state change causes an event to be generated and broadcast to any interested event listeners. Assume that the parent application is the interested listener. The parent application has a special piece of code devoted to handling the button press event, which is executed upon receiving the event notification.

New Term

An *event listener* is an application or component that is designed to respond to a particular event.

The issue of broadcasting and responding to events such as in the button example might seem simple in a sense that it is very straightforward. However, keep in mind that the whole mechanism of routing events to their respective listeners is something that must be outlined in detail by the component model. Furthermore, this mechanism must be consistent across a wide range of components and event types so any application or component can respond to any event.

Persistence

Persistence is the means by which a component is stored to and retrieved from a non-volatile location, such as a hard disk. The information about a component that is actually stored and retrieved is the internal state of the component, along with its relation to a container or other components. Using this information, a component can be safely stored away and re-created at a later time. Persistence is a particularly important issue in design tools, which enable developers to modify component properties to suit a particular application.

New Term

Persistence is the means by which a component is stored to and retrieved from a non-volatile location.

Layout

Another important part of any component model is its support for the physical layout of components. Physical layout really applies only to visual components, but it is an important aspect of a component model nevertheless. The layout support provided by a component model can be divided into two parts: the layout of a component within its own space and the layout of a component with respect to other components sharing space in the same container.

Typically, the spatial requirements for a component consist primarily of giving the component a rectangular area in which it can render itself visually. A parent application enables the component to render itself within this area however it chooses. Likewise, the parent application provides a facility by which the component's rectangular surface can be managed in the context of a container that houses other components. This facility is typically used by application builder tools, where a developer lays out components while constructing an application.

Application Builder Support

Throughout the chapter you've learned about application builder tools and how they relate to software components. Support for application builder tools happens to be a major requirement for component models. This support gives users the ability to graphically build complex applications out of components. The specific support required at the component model level is the capability for components to expose their properties and behaviors to application builder tools such as Visual J++. Development tools use these properties and behaviors to enable users to integrate and customize components in the context of a meaningful application.

Most application builder tools enable the user to not only lay out and edit individual components, but also to specify how the components relate to each other, both visually and programmatically. The layout support provided by a component model aids in laying out components visually, the introspection support helps application builder tools determine the capabilities of a component, and persistence enables the user to save components that have been customized. Specific application builder tool support often consists of dialog boxes that enable the user to graphically edit a component's properties.

Figures 1.1 and 1.2, which you saw earlier in this chapter, are examples of an application builder tool (Visual J++) at work. In Figure 1.1, you saw a dialog box being designed visually using a button component. In Figure 1.2, you saw a group box being used to group a set of buttons in a dialog box. In both examples, components are being manipulated in a development environment, which differs greatly from how the end user interacts with them. For example, the properties of the button component can be edited in Visual J++ by double-clicking the button. Figure 1.3 shows the visual property editor for the button component in Visual J++.

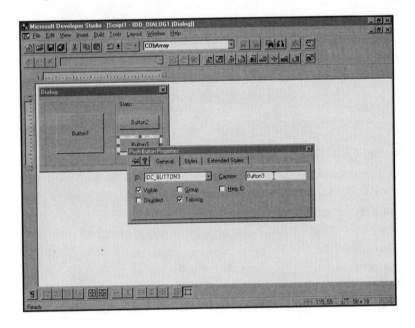

Figure 1.3.
The visual property editor for a button component in Visual J++.

This property editor is not part of the Visual J++ environment itself, but part of the button component. The code required to display and work with the property dialog box is a perfect example of the application builder tool support often provided by components.

Distributed Computing Support

The last major part of a component model is support for distributed computing, which has become important recently with the increased popularity of the Internet. It is now becoming not only realistic, but at times imperative, to build applications that are capable of executing in a distributed environment connected across vast networks. Consequently, it is important for component models to address the challenges inherent in building applications engaging in distributed computing.

Not surprisingly, distributed computing brings on a wide range of problems that aren't present in a single-system environment. Distributed systems are subject to both transmission errors and failure, along with limitations on communication speeds. The capability to handle these problems and limitations comes at no small cost; it requires significant overhead to deal with the problems brought on by distributed computing. The overhead is so significant, in fact, that adding it to an object model must be heavily weighed against the added complexity. Directly adding extensive support for distributed computing simply doesn't make sense when a developer is trying to make component models as lightweight and simple as possible.

Another option to implementing direct support for distributed computing is for an object model to leverage this support from an existing technology. With this approach, the single system component model is kept simple and lightweight, while the distributed model is still available via access to a leveraged solution. You learn more about distributed computing and how it affects a real component model in Chapter 15. For now, just understand that support for distributed computing is important in any object model, regardless of whether that support is implemented directly or leveraged from another model.

Summary

This chapter introduced you to a concept fundamental to the JavaBeans technology, software components. You first learned a little background on the state of software and why the software development community is adopting the paradigm of reusable software. You learned that the idea of software reuse is neither unique nor new, but that suitable technologies for exploiting it have only recently surfaced. The premise behind software components was then presented, with explanations of how components can provide an answer to the software reusability problem. You followed up this discussion by learning about the architectural heart of a component, the component model.

Although this chapter hinted at some things to come, it deliberately avoided getting into the specifics of the JavaBeans technology. The reasoning is that by being fully presented with the issues surrounding component software, you'll be better able to judge JavaBeans and decide for yourself how it fares as a component technology. That's not to say I won't have something to say about JavaBeans and how it relates to other component technologies such as ActiveX; I just want you to understand the big picture before jumping into the details of JavaBeans.

Speaking of JavaBeans, it's about time to move on and see what it is all about. Chapter 2, "Welcome to JavaBeans," goes far beyond the generalities of software components and covers exactly what JavaBeans is as a technology and what it aims to accomplish.

elcome to JavaBeans

When JavaSoft released the Java programming language and runtime system, I don't think it quite realized the impact it would have on the software development community. The explosion of the Web and the need for a solid way to bring it interactivity created the perfect climate for an innovative technology like Java. When JavaSoft regrouped and started realizing the full potential of Java, it began planning a host of related technologies aimed at dealing with various issues facing software developers today. One of these technologies is JavaBeans, which is JavaSoft's answer to the need for a comprehensive software component technology.

JavaBeans makes a concerted effort to address the multitude of challenges that must be overcome by a high-power software component technology. The fact that it is based on the Java environment is but one reason JavaBeans has more than a good chance of becoming a hit with the software development community. Another significant advantage JavaBeans has as a component technology is that it was developed entirely from scratch with no limitations imposed from a prior technology, except maybe from Java. In other words, JavaBeans is a completely new component technology specifically designed to deal with the problems software developers face today.

In this chapter, you learn about the following:

- The JavaBeans mission
- How JavaBeans meets its design goals
- The relationship between JavaBeans and Java
- The structure of a JavaBeans component
- Development scenarios involving JavaBeans components

The Mission

Before getting into the details of JavaBeans, it's important to understand what JavaSoft wanted to accomplish by developing a component technology for Java. You might already be thinking about the many benefits provided by software components in general, about which you learned in Chapter 1, "Software Component Basics." However, now focus instead more on JavaSoft's specific plan to couple a component technology with Java. This plan can probably best be summarized by JavaSoft's own JavaBeans mission statement: "Write once, run anywhere, reuse everywhere."

This mission statement cuts through all the complexities surrounding component software and delivers a very simple, concise, and elegant set of requirements for the JavaBeans technology. To better understand exactly what the architects at JavaSoft have in mind, examine each part of this statement in more detail.

Write Once

No, the folks at JavaSoft aren't referring to kids writing home from summer camp. They actually are referring to the issue of software development and how programmers all too often have to rewrite code when they decide to make changes. JavaSoft is suggesting that a well-developed software component technology should fully encourage code to be written once and not require rewrites to add or improve functionality. Adhering to this premise, JavaBeans should provide a practical means of adding and improving functionality in an existing code base without reworking the original code.

This goal of writing JavaBeans components once, in addition to making sense in terms of development resources, also makes perfect sense in terms of version control. This encourages developers to incrementally make changes to components instead of rewriting significant portions from scratch. The result is a steady progression of functionality, which in turn dictates a more consistent evolution of a component through increasing versions.

Run Anywhere

This statement doesn't refer to what you tell the cat after putting it outside. Instead, it refers to the capability of JavaBeans components to be executed (run) in any environment. What this statement really boils down to is the requirement for JavaBeans components to be cross-platform. You learned in Chapter 1 how a software component technology simply must be cross-platform to have a realistic chance of succeeding in the software climate of today and in the future. Fortunately for JavaBeans, cross-platform support comes easily because it is based on Java.

The "run anywhere" statement doesn't just refer to JavaBeans components executing on different platforms, however, but also to execution across distributed network environments. You learned in Chapter 1 about the importance of distributed computing support in a component model. This part of the mission statement also addresses the need for JavaBeans to support distributed computing in some way.

Reuse Everywhere

Sorry, but I don't have a cute joke for this part of the JavaBeans mission statement, so I'll get straight to the point. This part of the statement refers to the capability for JavaBeans components to be reused in many different scenarios including (but not necessarily limited to) applications, other components, documents, Web sites, and application builder tools. This is perhaps the most critical part of the mission statement because it drives home the point that JavaBeans components should be capable of being used in a wide range of situations. Furthermore, this requirement meets the primary goal of software components in general, which is code reuse.

Meeting Its Goals

Now that you know the fundamental ideas surrounding JavaSoft's drive to develop a component technology, it's time to move on to some of the specific goals it pursued in making JavaBeans a reality. The primary design goals for JavaBeans are summarized by the following list of requirements for JavaBeans components:

- Compact and easy to create and use
- Fully portable
- Built on the inherent strengths of Java
- Support flexible design-time component editors
- Leverage robust distributed computing mechanisms

JavaSoft felt it imperative that JavaBeans meet all of these goals in order to be taken seriously as a component technology. Fortunately, it accomplished these goals and succeeded in making JavaBeans a major contender for charting the future of software components. Now take a closer look at how each of these goals was met.

Simple and Compact

The first requirement of JavaBeans to be very compact is based on the fact that JavaBeans components often will be used in distributed environments in which entire components might be transferred across a low-bandwidth Internet connection. Clearly, components must be as compact as possible to facilitate a reasonable transfer time. The second part of this goal relates to the ease with which the components are built and used. Imagining components that are easy to use is not such a stretch, but creating a component architecture that makes building components easy is a different issue altogether. Existing attempts at component software often have been plagued by complex programming APIs that make it difficult for developers to create components without serious brain strain. Therefore, JavaBeans components must be not only easy to use, but also easy to develop. This is a critical requirement for component developers because it means less ulcers and more time to embellish components with interesting features.

JavaBeans components are based largely on the class structure already in use with traditional Java applet programming, which is an enormous benefit to those people heavily investing time and energy in learning Java. This has the positive side effect of making JavaBeans components very compact, because Java applets already are very efficient in terms of size. Even though the goal is for JavaBeans components to be as compact as possible, this is in no way a limitation toward creating complex and potentially bulkier components should the need arise.

Portable

The second major goal of JavaSoft in creating JavaBeans was to make it fully portable, the importance of which you learned in Chapter 1. The JavaBeans API coupled with the platform-independent Java system on which it is based together comprise the platform-independent component solution alluded to earlier in this chapter. As a result, developers don't need to worry about including platform-specific libraries with their Java applets. The end result will be reusable components that unify the world of computing under one happy, peaceful umbrella. OK, maybe that's asking a little too much—I'll settle for just being able to develop a component and have it run unmodified on any Java-supportive system.

Leveraging Java's Strengths

The existing Java architecture already offers a wide range of benefits easily applied to components. One of the more important, but rarely mentioned, features of Java is its built-in class discovery mechanism, which enables objects to interact with each other dynamically at runtime. This results in a system in which objects can be integrated with each other independently of their respective origins or development history. The class discovery mechanism is not just a neat feature of Java, it is a necessary requirement in any component architecture. It is fortunate for JavaBeans that this functionality is already provided by Java at no additional cost, meaning that no extra overhead is required to support it. Other component architectures have had to implement complex mechanisms to achieve the same result.

Another example of JavaBeans inheriting existing Java functionality is persistence, which is the capability for an object to store and retrieve its internal state. Persistence is handled automatically in JavaBeans by way of the serialization mechanism already present in Java. Alternately, developers are free to create their own customized persistence solutions whenever necessary.

> **New Term**
>
> *Serialization* is the process of storing or retrieving information through a standard protocol.

Application Builder Support

Another design goal of JavaBeans relates to design-time issues and how developers build applications using JavaBeans components. The JavaBeans architecture includes support for specifying design-time properties and editing mechanisms to facilitate visual editing of JavaBeans components. The result is that developers are able to use visual application builder tools to assemble and modify JavaBeans components in a seamless fashion, much like existing visual development tools on the Windows platform work with components such as VBX or OCX controls. In this way, component developers specify the way in which the components are to be used and manipulated in a development environment. This feature alone will officially usher in the use of professional application builder tools and significantly boost the productivity of application developers.

Distributed Computing Support

Although it is not a core element of the JavaBeans architecture, support for distributed computing is a major issue with JavaBeans. Because distributed computing requires relatively complex solutions attributed to the complex nature of distributed systems, JavaBeans leverages the use of external distributed approaches based on need. In other words, JavaBeans enables developers to use distributed computing mechanisms whenever necessary, but it doesn't overburden itself with core support for distributed computing. This might seem like some of the folks at JavaSoft are just being lazy, but in fact it is this design approach that enables JavaBeans components to be very compact. This is due to the fact that distributed computing solutions inevitably require a great deal of overhead.

JavaBeans component developers have the option of selecting a distributed computing approach that best fits their needs. JavaSoft provides a distributed computing solution of its own in the Java Remote Method Invocation (RMI) technology, but JavaBeans developers are in no way handcuffed to this solution. Other options include both CORBA and Microsoft's DCOM, among others. The point is that distributed computing has been purposely left out of JavaBeans to keep things tight while still enabling developers who require distributed support a wide range of options. You learn more about how JavaBeans relates to distributed component technologies such as DCOM and CORBA in Chapter 15, "Advanced JavaBeans."

The JavaBeans Relationship to Java

Even though I've hopefully made a clear distinction between the two up to this point, a common source of confusion about JavaBeans is the relationship between it and Java. To be fair, there certainly is some justification to this confusion. Hasn't Java been touted as an object-oriented technology capable of serving up reusable objects? Yes and no. Java certainly enables you to build reusable objects, but there are few rules or standards governing how these objects interact with each other. JavaBeans builds on the existing design of Java by specifying a rich set of mechanisms defining interactions between objects, along with common actions most objects will need to support, such as persistence and event handling.

Although the current Java component model works well, it is relatively limited in regard to delivering true reusability and interoperability. At the object level, there really is no straightforward mechanism for creating reusable Java objects that can interact with other objects dynamically in a consistent fashion. The closest thing you can do in Java is to create applets and try to enable them to communicate with each other on a Web page, which isn't a very straightforward task. JavaBeans provides the framework by which this communication can take place with ease. Even more important is the fact that JavaBeans components can easily be tweaked via a standard set of well-defined properties. Basically, JavaBeans merges the power of full-blown Java applets with the compactness and reusability of Java AWT (Advanced Windowing Toolkit) components such as buttons.

JavaBeans components aren't limited to visual objects such as buttons, however. You can just as easily develop non-visual JavaBeans components that perform background functions in concert with other components. In this way, JavaBeans merges the power of visual Java applets with non-visual Java programs under a consistent component framework.

> Note: Even though you learned about them in Chapter 1, let me reiterate what a non-visual component is: It is any component that doesn't have visible output. When you think of components in terms of Java AWT objects such as buttons and menus, this might seem a little strange. However, keep in mind that a component is simply a tightly packaged program and has no specific requirement of being visual. A good example of a non-visual component is a timer component, which fires timing events at specified intervals. Timer components are very popular in other component development environments such as Microsoft Visual Basic.

You can use a variety of JavaBeans components together in application builder tools without necessarily writing any code. This capability to use a variety of components together regardless of their origin is a major enhancement to the current Java model. You certainly can use other pre-built objects in Java, but you must have an intimate knowledge of the object's interface at the code level. Additionally, you must integrate the object into your code programmatically. JavaBeans components expose their own interfaces visually, enabling you to edit their properties without programming. Furthermore, you can use a visual editor to simply "drop" a JavaBeans component directly into an application without writing any code. This is an entirely new level of flexibility and reuse not previously attainable in Java alone.

> New Term
>
> An *interface* is a set of public methods used to interact with a component.

The Basic Structure of a Bean

At this point, you've learned a fair amount about JavaBeans as a technology and what problems it is aimed at solving. However, you haven't really learned any details about JavaBeans components themselves. The time has come to get down to business and find out some specifics about what a JavaBeans component is made of. First, let me clarify a little different terminology that is sometimes used for JavaBeans: A JavaBeans component can also be referred to as a "bean" or a "JavaBean." Therefore, from here on, note that "bean," "JavaBeans component," and "JavaBean" all refer to the same thing. (Hey, variety keeps things interesting!) Also, keep in mind that "JavaBeans" usually refers to the component technology itself, as opposed to multiple components.

OK, so JavaBeans as a technology answers a lot of hopes and expectations as a component software solution, but of what is a bean comprised? A bean, like an object in any object-oriented environment, is comprised of two primary things: data and methods that act on this data. The data part of a bean completely describes the state of the bean, whereas the methods provide a means for the bean's state to be modified and for actions to be taken accordingly. Figure 2.1 shows the two fundamental parts of a bean.

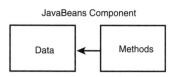

Figure 2.1.
The fundamental parts of a JavaBeans component.

Like a normal Java class, a bean is capable of having methods with different types of access. For example, private methods are accessible only within the internals of a bean, whereas protected methods are accessible both internally and in derived beans. The methods with the most accessibility are public methods, which are accessible internally, from derived beans, and from outside parties such as applications and other components. *Accessible* means that an application is capable of calling any of a component's public methods. Public methods have a unique importance to beans because they form the primary means by which a bean communicates with the outside world.

> **Note:** A bean also communicates with the outside world through events, which are generated when the internal state of the bean changes. Events are handled and responded to by interested outside parties (event listeners) such as applications.

A bean's public methods are often grouped according to their function. These functionally similar groups of public methods are also known as interfaces. A bean exposes its functionality to the outside world through these interfaces.

Interfaces are important because they specify the protocol by which a particular bean is interacted with externally. A programmer need only know a bean's interfaces to be able to successfully manipulate and interact with the bean. Figure 2.2 shows how interfaces expose a bean's functionality to the outside world.

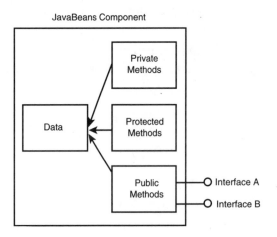

Figure 2.2.
The relationship between interfaces and methods in a JavaBeans component.

Although beans are expected to provide support for facilities such as persistence and application builder tool integration, all beans ultimately boil down to data and methods. These facilities are supported in the form of additional methods, data, and interfaces, which are themselves groups of methods. Therefore, no matter how complex a bean looks on the outside, just keep in mind that it is ultimately a combination of data and methods deep down. How simple!

Usage Scenarios

The last area to cover in this first tour of JavaBeans is how beans are used in practical scenarios. Because of their adherence to JavaSoft's goal of "reuse everywhere," beans are capable of being used in several different ways. By going through several different bean use scenarios, you'll get a better idea of how they fit into the software development process in general. The two primary development use scenarios for beans are as follows:

■ Using an application builder tool to build an applet
■ Hand coding an applet

Using Beans with an Application Builder Tool

In this scenario, JavaBeans components are used with a visual application builder tool to construct an application. The developer must purchase the builder tool along with whatever beans he wants to use. Of course, if he's crafty enough he can write his own beans or download freeware beans developed by others.

The next step is for the developer to lay out the application visually using the builder tool in conjunction with the beans. When the visual aspects of the application are all layed out and the appropriate beans are placed correctly, the developer can customize the beans. He edits the beans' properties using visual property editors supplied by the beans themselves, which are invoked by the builder tool. At this point, the developer also connects the beans to each other and the application by wiring events to appropriate handler routines. Again, this process is primarily performed in a visual fashion by virtue of the builder tool. I say "primarily" because it is usually necessary to write some code in the event handling routines. When this step is completed, the developer can test everything and iron out the kinks. When he's happy with the outcome, he simply packages up the application along with the beans and distributes them together as one physical unit.

> Note: Understand that I use the term *application* in a general sense throughout this discussion. In Java programming, an application is a stand-alone Java program, as opposed to an applet, which is a Java program that runs within the confines of a Web browser. In this discussion, and throughout most of this book, the term *application* has a more general meaning and refers to both types of programs.

To summarize, the basic steps required to build an application with JavaBeans components using an application builder tool follow:

1. Visually lay out the application, using beans where appropriate.
2. Customize the beans using visual property editors.
3. Connect the beans using builder tool facilities and write event handler code.
4. Package the application with the beans and share it all with the world.

As you can see, the entire development process described requires very little programming. Using beans in this way is very convenient because it alleviates many of the drudgeries of programming by putting a visual spin on the challenge of application development. Even though many of these conveniences are provided by the builder tool itself, they wouldn't be possible without the internal support provided by the beans. For example, the builder tool must be able to determine what features a bean provides, which is carried out by the introspection facilities of the JavaBeans component model. Also, the beans are responsible for providing a visual property editor to enable themselves to be edited and customized.

Using Beans in Handwritten Code

This scenario isn't quite as rosy as the previous one, but just as much can be accomplished. In this handwritten scenario there is no fancy application builder tool and nothing is done visually. Instead, all the code for the application is written by hand, including the integration of beans. This scenario corresponds with a developer using the standard Java Developer's Kit (JDK) provided by JavaSoft, which includes a command-line compiler and debugger. These tools are not fancy, but they are free. Even though the tools themselves are free, the developer still is responsible for coming up with beans to use in building the application; he is free to buy, borrow, or develop his own beans, just as in the first scenario.

The developer begins laying out the application by writing code to create and position the beans appropriately. With the beans created and positioned, the developer then moves on to customizing the beans by writing code that calls various methods that modify the properties of the beans. Calling these methods has the same effect as visually editing a bean with a property editor—you be the judge of which approach sounds easier for the developer.

When the beans are customized, the developer connects the beans to the application via event handlers. To accomplish this, he must write code to register each event listener with the appropriate component so that event notifications can be routed. He then must write code for the event handlers themselves. To be fair, the visual approach usually requires the event handlers to be written as well, but the event listener registration is typically handled automatically. When the beans are connected and everything is tested, the developer can package up the beans with the application and distribute the results.

To summarize, the basic steps required to build an application by hand with JavaBeans components follow:

1. Lay out the application by writing code to create and position the beans where appropriate.

2. Customize the beans by writing code that calls property modifying methods on the beans.

3. Connect the beans by writing code that registers event listeners and handles bean events.

4. Package the application with the beans and distribute them just as in the previous scenario.

This development scenario differs from the first scenario primarily in that everything is done by writing code. Although nothing is wrong with this approach, replacing handwritten code with more visual techniques generally results in a more rapid and intuitive development process. Even so, some developers still are more comfortable getting dirty in the details of handwritten code, which is perfectly fine. The beauty of JavaBeans is that it fully enables and even encourages the existence of both scenarios. With JavaBeans, there's something for everyone!

Summary

This chapter introduced you to JavaBeans, JavaSoft's software component technology built upon the rapid success and many benefits of Java. You began the chapter by learning about the fundamental criteria JavaBeans had to meet as specified in JavaSoft's concise mission statement: "Write once, run anywhere, reuse everywhere." This statement succinctly presents the ideal aspirations of any component model. The fact that JavaSoft chose this statement is testament to its desire to deliver a complete software component solution. You examined each part of this statement in this chapter and how it applies to JavaBeans.

You then moved on to the specific design goals for JavaBeans, which provide perhaps the best summary of the technology as a whole. Each of these design goals led directly to the development of a major part of the JavaBeans API, about which you learn in Chapter 3, "The JavaBeans API at a Glance." By understanding the goals under which JavaBeans was developed, you are well on your way to understanding the technology as it exists in its final form.

You also learned in this chapter how JavaBeans relates to Java, which is an interesting topic because of the way in which JavaBeans is built on top of Java. From there, you learned the basic structure of a JavaBeans component, which was probably familiar to you from the structure of Java classes. You learned that JavaBeans components are internally composed of data and methods, which is to be expected because JavaBeans is fundamentally still an object-oriented technology. You finished up the chapter by learning about a couple of development scenarios involving JavaBeans components, which gave insight into the options developers have in how they use JavaBeans.

Although this chapter didn't go into painstaking detail, it hopefully gave you a solid introduction to JavaBeans components. In the next chapter you go another level deeper by learning about the JavaBeans API and what is has to offer at the programming level.

CHAPTER 3

The JavaBeans API at a Glance

With all the neat things JavaBeans accomplishes, you might imagine that there is some highly complex system pulling all kinds of magical tricks under the hood. The truth is, there is no magic behind JavaBeans and surprisingly little complexity considering how advanced it is as a software component technology. The lack of complexity in JavaBeans is due to the well-designed JavaBeans API, which is completely responsible for carrying out all the interesting ideas about which you learned in Chapter 2, "Welcome to JavaBeans."

In this chapter you take a quick tour through the JavaBeans API to familiarize yourself with all emergency locations. No, actually the tour is meant to help you get the big picture of how the API is divided and what type of functionality each part of it addresses. Although there are a decent number of classes and interfaces defined in the API, you don't have to worry about them just yet. Being faced with a large amount of new information to process and digest is always somewhat overwhelming, so this chapter just hits the high points. This way, you'll have some perspective when you dig into more details in chapters to come.

Keep in mind throughout the chapter that JavaBeans is ultimately a programming interface, which means that all of its features are implemented as extensions to the standard Java class library. Therefore, the functionality provided by JavaBeans is actually implemented in the JavaBeans API. The JavaBeans API itself is merely a suite of smaller APIs devoted to specific functions, or services. Following is a list of the main component services in the JavaBeans API that are necessary to facilitate all the features that make JavaBeans such an exciting technology:

- Property management
- Introspection
- Event handling
- Persistence
- Application builder support

By understanding these services and how they work, you'll have much more insight into exactly what type of technology JavaBeans is. This entire chapter is devoted to understanding the basics of these APIs and why they are necessary elements of the JavaBeans architecture. Keep in mind that each of these parts of the JavaBeans API is covered in greater detail in Part II of the book, "Inside the JavaBeans API."

Property Management

The property management facilities in the JavaBeans API are responsible for handling all interactions relating to bean properties. Properties reflect the internal state of a bean and constitute the data part of a bean's structure. More specifically, properties are discrete, named attributes of a bean that determine its appearance and behavior. Properties are important in any component technology because they isolate component state information into discrete pieces that can be easily modified.

New Term

Properties are discrete, named attributes of a bean that determine its appearance and behavior.

To get a better idea of the importance of properties, it's helpful to consider some different scenarios in which properties are dealt with. Following are some examples of how bean properties are accessed and used:

- As object fields in scripting environments such as JavaScript or VBScript
- Programmatically via public accessor methods
- Visually via property sheets in application builder tools
- Through the persistent storage and retrieval of a bean

As this list shows, properties come into play in a variety of ways when it comes to bean access and manipulation. Notice the flexibility properties provide: You can access them through scripting languages such as JavaScript, full-blown programming languages such as Java, and visual builder tools. This freedom to access and manipulate beans in a variety of ways is one of the critical design goals of the JavaBeans technology. And it is fulfilled by the property management facilities in the JavaBeans API.

The next few sections cover some of the major issues addressed by the JavaBeans API property management facilities. These issues are explored in much greater detail in Chapter 4, "Manipulating Bean Properties."

Accessor Methods

The primary way in which properties are exposed in the JavaBeans API is through *accessor methods*. An accessor method is a public method defined in a bean that directly reads or writes the value of a particular property. Each property in a bean must have a corresponding pair of accessor methods: one for reading the property and one for writing. The accessor methods responsible for reading are known as *getter methods* because they get the value of a property. Likewise, accessor methods responsible for writing are known as *setter methods* because they set the value of a property.

> ### New Terms
>
> An *accessor method* is a public method defined in a bean that reads or writes the value of a property.
>
> A *getter method* is an accessor method that reads, or gets, the value of a property.
>
> A *setter method* is an accessor method that writes, or sets, the value of a property.

Indexed Properties

So far, the discussion of properties has been limited to single-value properties, which are by and large the most common properties used in JavaBeans. However, the JavaBeans API also supports *indexed properties*, which are properties that represent an array of values. Indexed properties work very similarly to arrays in traditional Java programming, where you access a particular value using an integer index. Indexed properties are very useful in situations in which a bean needs to maintain a group of properties of the same type. For example, a container bean that keeps track of the physical layout of other beans might store references to them in an indexed property.

> ### New Term
>
> *Indexed properties* are bean properties that represent an array of values.

Bound and Constrained Properties

The JavaBeans API supports two mechanisms for working with properties at a more advanced level: bound and constrained properties. *Bound properties* are properties that provide notifications to an interested party based on changes in the property value. An interested party is an applet, application, or bean that needs to know about changes in the property. These properties are called bound properties because they are bound to some type of external behavior based on their own changes. Bound properties are defined at the component level, which means that a bean is responsible for specifying which components are bound. An example of a bound property is a visibility property, which a bean's container might be interested in knowing the status of because it would need to graphically reorganize other beans based on a bean's visibility.

New Term

A *bound property* is a property that provides notifications to an interested party based on changes in its value.

The other interesting property feature provided by the JavaBeans API is support for *constrained properties*, which are properties that enable an interested party to perform a validation on a new property value before accepting the modification. Constrained properties are useful in enabling interested parties control over how a bean is altered. An example of a constrained property is a date property, where the application containing the bean wants to limit the valid date property values to a certain range.

New Term

A *constrained property* is a property that enables an interested party to perform a validation on a new property value before accepting the modification.

Introspection

The introspection facilities in the JavaBeans API define the mechanism by which components make their internal structure readily available to the outside world. These facilities consist of the functional overhead necessary to enable development tools to query a bean for its internal structure, including the interfaces, methods, and member variables that comprise the bean. Although the introspection services are primarily designed for use by application builder tools, they are grouped separately from the application builder services in the API because their role in making a bean's internal structure available externally is technically independent of builder tools. In other words, there might be other reasons for querying a bean as to its internal structure beyond the obvious use in builder tools.

The introspection services provided by the JavaBeans API are divided into two parts, low-level services and high-level services, which are distinguished by the level of access they provide to bean internals. The low-level API services are responsible for enabling wide access to the structural internals of a bean. These services are very important for application builder tools that heavily use bean internals to provide advanced development features. However, this level of access isn't appropriate for developers who are using beans to build applications because it exposes private parts of a bean that aren't meant to be used by developers at the application level. For these purposes, the high-level API services are more appropriate.

The high-level services use the low-level services behind the scenes to provide access to limited portions of a bean's internals, which typically consist of a bean's public properties and methods. The difference between the two levels of services is that the high-level services don't enable access to internal aspects of a bean that aren't specifically designed for external use. The end result is two distinct services that offer bean introspection capabilities based on the level of access required by the interested party, be it an application builder tool or a user.

The next few sections cover several of the major functions supported in the JavaBeans API introspection facilities. These functions are described in much greater detail in Chapter 5, "Introspection: Getting to Know a Bean."

Reflection and Design Patterns

The JavaBeans API has a very interesting technique of assessing the public properties, methods, and events for a bean. To determine information about a bean's public features, the bean's methods are analyzed using a set of low-level reflection services. These services gather information about a bean and determine its public properties, methods, and events by applying simple design patterns. Design patterns are rules applied to a bean's method definitions that determine information about the bean. For example, when a pair of accessor methods are encountered in the analysis of a bean, the JavaBeans introspection facilities match them based on a design pattern and automatically determine the property they access.

New Terms

Reflection is the process of studying a bean to determine information about its functionality and public facilities.

Design patterns are rules used to determine information about a bean from its reflected method names and signatures.

The whole premise of design patterns is that method names and signatures conform to a standard convention. There are a variety of different design patterns for determining everything from simple properties to event sources. All of these design patterns rely on some type of consistent naming convention for methods and their arguments. This approach to introspection is not only convenient from the perspective of JavaBeans, but it also has the intended side effect of encouraging bean developers to use a consistent set of naming conventions.

Explicit Bean Information

Even though the design pattern approach to introspection is very useful and encourages a consistent approach to naming, you might be wondering what happens if bean developers don't follow the convention. Fortunately, design patterns aren't the only option for introspection, meaning that obstinate developers are free to ignore the suggested naming conventions if they so choose. The developers who opt to cast convention into the wind must use another introspection facility in the JavaBeans API where they explicitly list the public information about their beans. They must "spill the beans," to inject a painfully bad pun.

The explicit introspection facility in the JavaBeans API to which I'm referring involves creating a bean information class that specifies various pieces of information about a bean including a property list, method list, and event list. This approach isn't automatic like the design patterns about which you just learned, but it does provide a means to explicitly describe your bean to the world, which might be advantageous in some situations.

The Introspector

Just in case you're wondering how two different introspection approaches can possibly coexist to describe a single bean, there is another service that consolidates the whole introspection process. The introspection facilities provide an introspector that is used to obtain explicit information for a bean. The introspector is responsible for traversing the inheritance tree of a bean to determine the explicit bean information for all parent beans. If at any point explicit information is not defined, then the introspector falls back on the reflection services and uses design patterns to automatically determine external bean information.

This two-tiered solution to assessing bean functionality is very nice because it first attempts to use information explicitly provided by a bean's developer, and relies on automatic design patterns only if the explicit information isn't there. The other nice thing is that it supports a mixture of the two approaches, which means, for example, that methods for a bean could be explicitly defined via a provided bean information class but the properties and events could be determined automatically via design patterns. This gives bean developers a lot of flexibility in deciding how they want their beans exposed.

Event Handling

The event handling facilities in the JavaBeans API specify an event-driven architecture that defines interactions among beans and applications. If you're familiar with the Java AWT, you know that it already provides a comprehensive event handling model. This existing AWT event model forms the basis of the event handling facilities in the JavaBeans API. These event handling facilities are critical in that they determine how beans respond to changes in their state, as well as how these changes are propagated to applications and other beans.

The event-handling facilities hinge around the concepts of event sources and listeners. A bean that is capable of generating events is considered an event *source*, whereas an application or bean that is capable of responding to an event is considered an event *listener*. Event sources and listeners are connected via an event registration mechanism that is part of the event handling facilities. This registration mechanism basically boils down to an event listener being registered with an event source via a simple method call. When the source generates an event, a specified method is called on the event listener with an event state object being sent along as its argument. Event state objects are responsible for storing information associated with a particular event. In other words, event state objects carry with them any information related to the event being sent.

New Terms

An *event source* is a bean capable of generating events.

An *event listener* is an application or bean capable of responding to events.

An *event state object* is used to store information associated with a particular event.

The next few sections cover some of the major issues dealt with by the JavaBeans API event handling facilities. These issues are explored in much greater detail in Chapter 6, "Handling Bean Events."

Unicast and Multicast Event Sources

Although most practical event sources support multiple listeners, the event-handling facilities provide for event sources that choose to limit their audience to a single listener. These sources are called *unicast event sources*, and their more liberal counterparts are called *multicast event sources*. The primary functional difference between the two is that unicast event sources will throw an exception if an attempt is made to register more than one listener.

New Terms

A *unicast event source* is an event source capable of generating events for retrieval by only one listener.

A *multicast event source* is an event source capable of generating events for retrieval by any number of listeners.

Even though the JavaBeans API supports both unicast and multicast event sources, keep in mind that multicast event sources are much less limiting in terms of practical use. In other words, developers should avoid designing beans as unicast event sources whenever possible.

Event Adapters

Even though many bean events fall under the standard source/listener model about which you just learned, the JavaBeans API provides a mechanism for dealing with more complex situations in which this model doesn't quite fit the bill. This mechanism is based on event adapters, which act as intermediaries between event sources and listeners. Event adapters sit between sources and listeners and provide a means of inserting specialized event delivery behavior into the standard source/listener event model. Event adapters are important to the event-handling facilities because they open the door for implementing a highly specialized event handling mechanism tailored to the unique challenges sometimes encountered in applications or application builder tools.

> ### New Term
> *Event adapters* are intermediaries placed between event sources and listeners that provide additional event delivery behavior.

Persistence

The persistence facilities in the JavaBeans API specify the mechanism by which beans are stored and retrieved within the context of a container. The information stored through persistence consists of all parts of a bean that are necessary to restore the bean to a similar internal state and appearance. This generally involves the storage of all public properties and potentially some internal properties, although the specifics are determined by each particular bean. Information not stored for a bean through persistence are references to external beans, including event registrations; these references are expected to be somehow stored by an application builder tool or through some programmatic means.

By default, beans are persistently stored and retrieved using the automatic serialization mechanism provided by Java, which is sufficient for most beans. However, bean developers are also free to create more elaborate persistence solutions based on the specific needs of their beans. Like the introspection facilities, the persistence facilities provide for both an explicit approach or an automatic approach to carrying out its functions. The JavaBeans API persistence facilities are described in much greater detail in Chapter 7, "Persistence: Saving Beans for a Rainy Day."

Application Builder Support

The final area of the JavaBeans API deals with application builder support. The application builder support facilities provide the overhead necessary to edit and manipulate beans using visual application builder tools. Application builder tools rely heavily on these facilities to enable a developer to visually lay out and edit beans while constructing an application. These facilities fulfill a major design goal of the JavaBeans API in that they enable beans to be used constructively with little or no programming effort.

One issue the JavaBeans architects wrestled with is the fact that application builder support for a specific bean is required only at design time. Consequently, it is somewhat wasteful to bundle this support code with a runtime bean. Because of this situation, the application builder facilities call for builder-specific overhead for a bean to be physically separate from the bean itself. This enables beans to be distributed by themselves for runtime use or in conjunction with the application builder support for design-time use.

The next few sections cover some of the major issues dealt with by the JavaBeans API application builder support facilities. These issues are explored in much greater detail in Chapter 8, "Customization: Bean Support for Application Builders."

Property Editors and Sheets

One of the ways in which the JavaBeans API supports the editing and manipulation of beans with application builder tools is through property sheets. A *property sheet* is a visual interface that provides editors for each public property defined for a bean. The individual editors used in a property sheet are called *property editors*. Each type of exported property in a bean must have a corresponding property editor in order to be edited visually by a builder tool. Some standard property editors are provided by the JavaBeans API for built-in Java types, but user-defined properties require their own custom editors. The property editors for all the exported properties of a bean are presented together on a property sheet that enables users to edit the properties visually.

New Terms

A *property sheet* is a user interface that contains property editors for all the exported properties of a bean.

A *property editor* is a user interface that enables the visual editing of a particular property type.

Customizers

The other way in which the JavaBeans API enables beans to be visually edited in an application builder tool is through *customizers*, which are user interfaces that provide a specialized means of visually editing bean properties. Because customizers are implemented entirely by bean developers, there are no firm guidelines as to how they present visual property information to the user. However, most customizers probably will be similar in function to "wizards," which are popular user interfaces on the Windows platform that use multiple-step questionnaires to gather information from the user.

New Terms

A *customizer* is a user interface that provides a specialized means of visually editing bean properties.

A *wizard* is a user interface that uses multiple-step questionnaires to gather information from the user.

Summary

This chapter took you a significant step deeper into the JavaBeans technology by exploring the JavaBeans API. This API is ultimately responsible for delivering all the functionality of JavaBeans. You learned that the API is comprised of several major functional areas that are each devoted to a particular JavaBeans service. You covered the basics of each of these areas and looked at the kinds of problems they address and the different solutions they provide.

Although the discussions throughout this chapter were fairly general and avoided too much technical detail, they still painted a pretty complete picture of the JavaBeans API, at least from a conceptual level. Armed with this knowledge, you're ready to press on to the inner workings of each of these API areas in the next part of the book, "Inside the JavaBeans API." Roll up your sleeves and get ready for more fun!

Inside the JavaBeans API

CHAPTER 4

Manipulating Bean Properties

Properties are one of the most important aspects of JavaBeans because they represent the internal state of a bean. If you recall from Chapter 3, "The JavaBeans API at a Glance," properties are discrete, named attributes of a bean that determine its appearance and behavior. Fortunately, the JavaBeans API provides a wide range of support for managing bean properties. In this chapter you learn a great deal about how the JavaBeans API goes about managing properties, including the different types of properties supported and the different ways in which properties are used.

Properties are also important in JavaBeans because they represent one of the primary means in which users interact with beans at design time. By altering property values, an application developer can customize both the appearance and the behavior of beans. This customization can be carried out either programmatically or visually, depending on the development tools being used.

In this chapter, you learn about the following topics:

- The basics of properties
- Accessor methods
- Indexed properties
- Bound properties
- Constrained properties
- Practical use of properties
- API support for properties

Property Basics

You probably already get the idea that properties form the internal state of a bean and in doing so serve as the data portion of a bean's structure. It is through properties that a bean is allowed to take on different values, which in turn impact its appearance and behavior. Properties appear as bean attributes that can be modified to enable full customization of a bean. When you are developing your own beans, properties take on an even bigger role, because you define the data part of your beans entirely through them. In other words, constructing a bean of your own consists largely of defining the different properties supported by the bean and assigning them default values. You learn a great deal more about defining properties in your own beans in Part III, "Creating Your Own Beans."

Even though properties often represent built-in Java data types such as int and long, they also can represent class and interface types. In this way, a property can really be any data type you choose, including your own custom types. If that still doesn't offer enough freedom for you, you'll be glad to know that properties also can be computed values based on other properties or pieces of information. This might sound strange at first, because you typically think of a property as being a piece of discrete information, but there is no stipulation in the JavaBeans API that a property remain independent of other pieces of information.

Along with having the capability of being dependent on other pieces of information, properties also can cause changes in the appearance or behavior of a bean any time the bean is modified. As an example, consider a user interface bean that has its background color represented by a property. If this color property is changed, it is necessary for the bean to repaint itself in order for the change to affect the bean's appearance. This is necessary because the bean must reflect its current state at all times. If the bean didn't repaint itself, it would be displaying the previous background color while its background color property would have the new value. This inconsistency is not a good thing, which is why property modification isn't always just a process of changing a simple value.

Just so you understand how important properties are in the world of beans, look at an example of the different properties that constitute a simple bean. Here is a list of properties for a hypothetical meter bar bean:

- `orientation`
- `fillColor`
- `totalParts`
- `partsFilled`

Just in case you aren't familiar with a meter bar, it's a user interface element representing a meter that graphically shows some value as a fraction of a total. Meter bars are commonly used to display the status of time-consuming operations such as loading a large file or performing a complex mathematical computation. Figure 4.1 shows a meter bar in action at 25 percent full.

Figure 4.1.
A horizontal meter bar that is 25 percent full.

Getting back to the original reason for bringing up the issue of meter bars, look at the meter bar and see if the property list makes sense to you. The four properties listed are in fact sufficient for representing the state of the meter bar. The only one you might not see the importance of right off is the `orientation` property, which determines whether the meter bar is horizontal or vertical. Just so you understand the difference, Figure 4.2 shows a vertical meter bar at 75 percent full. Moving along, the `fillColor` property simply determines the color of the bar itself. The `totalParts` and `partsFilled` properties form the fractional pair that determine how much of the meter is filled.

Figure 4.2.
A vertical meter bar that is 75 percent full.

The only remaining question at this point is how to model these properties with Java data types. Table 4.1 shows these properties with some reasonable data types.

Table 4.1. Meter bar properties and data types.

Property	Data Type
orientation	boolean
fillColor	Color
totalParts	float
partsFilled	float

The orientation property is a boolean data type because it has only two possible states: horizontal or vertical. In this case, the documentation for the bean would clearly indicate which state (horizontal and vertical) went with each boolean state (true and false). The fillColor property is a Color data type because it represents a Java AWT color. This is an example of a property representing a complex data type—in this case, a standard Java AWT class type. The totalParts and partsFilled properties are both float data types because that provides the most flexibility; you want to allow the user as much freedom as possible when using a bean. In other words, int types can easily be cast to float types if necessary, but the reverse isn't always true.

This set of properties is sufficient to represent the internal state of the meter bar bean. All you need now is a way to access them and put the bean to use. Read on!

Accessor Methods

Because properties serve as the data portion of a bean, it stands to reason that managing access to them should be of great importance. In fact, property access is one of the biggest responsibilities of the JavaBeans API. Fortunately, property access is managed through a very simple and straightforward technique: accessor methods. An *accessor method* is a public method defined in a bean that enables access to the value of a particular property. Accessor methods typically come in pairs, with one half of the pair capable of reading a value and the other half capable of writing a value. A pair of accessor methods is all that is required to have full access to a bean property.

Not all properties have a pair of accessor methods, however. There are certainly cases in which there is a need to be able to read a property but not write it. In other words, there is a need for read-only properties that change state internally rather than being writable externally. Likewise, there might also be situations in which a property is writable and not readable. Granted, this is much less likely, but the JavaBeans API nevertheless supports this type of arrangement. The point is that accessor methods can be used individually as well as in pairs, depending on the particular property requirements.

Getter and Setter Methods

Accessor methods responsible for reading a bean's properties are known as getter methods, while accessor methods responsible for writing a beans properties are known as setter methods. These names are based on the fact that reading is a process of getting something, while writing is a process of setting something. Getter and setter methods aren't just important as cute names for accessor methods, however, because they play a vital role in determining how a bean's properties are accessed externally. In fact, getter and setter methods form the interface between a bean's properties and the outside world. This brings up an important point: Under no circumstances are you ever allowed direct access to a property from the outside of a bean. You must always work with properties through accessor methods, which should give you a clue as to why they are so important. Figure 4.3 illustrates how accessor methods enable access to a bean's internal properties.

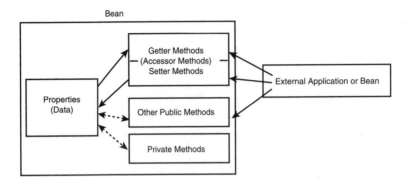

Figure 4.3.
The role accessor methods play in allowing external access to a bean's properties.

Working with Accessor Methods

Accessor methods use a simple naming convention to specify the action they perform and on which property they perform it. The two actions available to accessor methods are getting and setting a property. The names of accessor methods are based on these actions as follows: An accessor method that gets a property must begin with get, and an accessor method that sets a property must begin with set. For example, if you have a bean that has a property called depth, a getter method for the bean would be called getDepth(), and a setter method would be called setDepth(). As I said earlier in this chapter, accessor methods are a very simple and straightforward means of accessing properties. But don't be mistaken, they are also very powerful in their simplicity.

Now take a quick look at some more accessor methods just to make sure you understand how this naming stuff works. Here are the definitions of a pair of accessor methods for a bean with a color property:

```
public Color getColor();
public void setColor(Color c);
```

The property in this case is of type `Color`, and the accessor methods are responsible for providing a means of getting and setting the color property value. Notice that both methods are defined as being public, which is important because the whole point of accessor methods is that they can be accessed from outside of a bean. Also notice that the `getColor()` method returns a `Color` object, whereas the `setColor()` method takes a `Color` object as its only parameter. Matching data types among getter and setter methods is a fundamental design guideline for accessor methods, which only makes sense considering that the methods are acting on the same property.

The most obvious reason for having accessor methods is to provide an interface for applications and other beans to query or modify the internal state of a bean. Although this reason is certainly very important, there is another reason for having accessor methods—one that makes the naming conventions of getter and setter methods much more significant. I'm referring to introspection, which is the mechanism that enables an outside party to query for the internal structure of a bean. It turns out that a major part of the JavaBeans default approach to determining a bean's structure is examining its accessor methods. By examining a bean's accessor methods, it's possible to ascertain a bean's properties. This is due to the fact that accessor methods follow a consistent naming convention that fully specifies both the type and name of the property they access. You learn a great deal more about introspection and how it relates to accessor methods in Chapter 5, "Introspection: Getting to Know a Bean."

Indexed Properties

The discussion of properties thus far has been limited to single-valued properties. Based on what you've learned, you might think that the JavaBeans API only supports properties with a single value, because that's by and large what you think of in terms of properties. Not so! The JavaBeans API also supports *indexed properties*, which are properties that are very similar to arrays in traditional Java programming. Indexed properties contain several elements of the same type that can be accessed via an integer index; hence the name indexed property. Indexed properties aren't typically used as much as single-valued properties, but they serve a vital purpose nonetheless.

> Note: JavaSoft has mentioned that indexed properties might eventually enable element access via an index type other than an integer. However, in the 1.0 release of JavaBeans, integers are the only allowed index type. Keep in mind that this in no way limits the type of indexed properties themselves, just the way in which you access individual elements.

Because indexed properties ultimately refer to multiple individual elements stored in an array, the standard getter and setter methods aren't sufficient for property access. It is actually necessary to have two pairs of accessor methods; one pair gets and sets individual properties in the array via an index, while the other pair gets and sets the entire array of properties as a single unit. Here is an example of two pairs of accessor methods for a bean with an indexed property containing float values:

```
public float getMass(int index);
public void setMass(int index, float mass);
public float[] getMass();
public void setMass(float[] masses);
```

In this case, the mass property is an indexed property. The first two accessor methods get and set an individual mass element from the property array, which is evident by the fact that each method requires an integer index. The last two accessor methods get and set the mass property array as a whole, which is evident by the array brackets ([]) used when defining the property type. These last two methods are pretty powerful in that they enable you to get and set the entire array of elements as a single unit.

Just as with single-value properties, remember that bean developers are free to implement any of these accessor methods they choose. Therefore, a bean with an indexed property might or might not provide a setter method enabling you to set the entire array as a whole. For beans that do enable you to set the property array to a new one, keep in mind that this enables you to change the size of the array. In fact, this is the only way to change the size of an indexed property array.

Just as in working with standard Java arrays, it is possible to index outside the bounds of an indexed property array. When this occurs, the accessor method used to perform the indexing typically throws an `ArrayIndex-OutOfBoundsException` runtime exception, which is consistent with how normal Java arrays behave when indexed out of bounds.

Bound Properties

As if indexed properties aren't enough, the JavaBeans API goes a few steps further by providing some other, more advanced property types. One of these types is *bound properties*, which are properties that provide a notification service upon being changed. Bound properties are registered with an outside party (an applet, application, or bean) that is interested in knowing about changes in the property. Whenever the value of the bound property changes, the interested party is notified. These properties are called bound properties because they are effectively bound to outside parties via changes in their value. Outside parties can be either applications or other beans, and are also commonly referred to as *listeners*.

The mechanism by which a bound property is connected with an interested party is actually very simple. A bean with a bound property is required to support a pair of event listener registration methods: addPropertyChangeListener() and removePropertyChangeListener(). These methods are used to register outside parties (listeners) with the bean that contains properties to which they want to bind themselves. Both of these methods take an object implementing the PropertyChangeListener interface as their only argument, as the following method definitions show:

```
public void addPropertyChangeListener(PropertyChangeListener l);
public void removePropertyChangeListener(PropertyChangeListener l);
```

As you might have guessed, these two methods are responsible for adding and removing event listeners. When an interested party wants to bind itself to a property, it must call addPropertyChangeListener() and provide a suitable object implementing the PropertyChangeListener interface. The PropertyChangeListener interface is used to report changes in the bound property. More specifically, when a bound property's value changes, the propertyChange() method is called on all registered PropertyChangeListener interfaces. This method is passed a PropertyChangeEvent object, which contains information about the specific property that has changed, along with its old and new values.

If this explanation of bound property notifications was a little too much to handle in one paragraph, look at Figure 4.4, which graphically shows how a bound property works.

Figure 4.4.
The inner workings of a bound property.

Notice in the figure that the main thing taking place is the sending of a property change notification from a bean to a listener. This notification is sent whenever a change occurs in one of the bean's bound properties. The notification itself comes in the form of a `PropertyChangeEvent` object, which encapsulates all the information related to the property change. The listener is free to use this information however it chooses.

You might have noticed from the discussion thus far that I haven't mentioned a way for listeners to register themselves with a specific property. Instead, they must register themselves with the bean and then determine the particular property that has changed by examining the `PropertyChangeEvent` object sent with the notification. Although this approach technically works fine, the JavaBeans API supports another approach involving the registration of listeners with specific bound properties.

If a bean developer wants to provide listener registration on a per-property basis, she must support a pair of methods for each property of the form: `add<`*PropertyName*`>Listener()` and `remove<`*PropertyName*`>Listener()`. This method pair works exactly like the global pair of event listener registration methods about which you learned earlier, except they apply only to a specific property. Here is an example of definitions for these methods given a bound property named `numberOfLives`:

```
public void addNumberOfLivesListener(PropertyChangeListener l);
public void removeNumberOfLivesListener(PropertyChangeListener l);
```

When an interested party wants to bind itself to the `numberOfLives` property, it simply registers itself by calling the `addNumberOfLivesListener()` method. When the `numberOfLives` property changes, a notification is sent to the listener via a call to its `propertyChange()` method. This situation is no different than the one described earlier, except that the listener in this case only receives notifications for the `numberOfLives` property.

Keep in mind that per-property listener registration methods are always provided in addition to the global registration methods (`addProperty-ChangeListener()` and `removePropertyChangeListener()`). In other words, per-property listener registration methods act as optimizations to the global listener registration approach, as opposed to replacing the global approach. Even so, per-property methods can still be a nice convenience.

Constrained Properties

Another type of advanced property type offered by the JavaBeans API is constrained properties, which are properties that enable an outside party to validate a change in them before accepting the change. In other words, when you attempt to change the value of a constrained property, the value is first checked with an outside validation source that accepts or rejects the change. Like bound properties, constrained properties are registered with an outside party, but in this case the party is given the opportunity to accept or reject changes in the property. Property change rejections come in the form of `PropertyVetoException` exceptions, which are handled by the bean that contains the property. When a rejection exception occurs, the bean is responsible for reverting the property back to its original value and issuing a new property change notification for the reversion.

Because property changes take place through setter methods, it is necessary for constrained property setter methods to support the `PropertyVetoException` exception. This makes it clear to users that the property is constrained and attempts to set it might be vetoed. Following is an example of the getter and setter methods for a simple constrained property:

```
public int getQuantity();
public void setQuantity(int i) throws PropertyVetoException;
```

The mechanism by which a constrained property is connected with an interested party is very similar to the one used for bound properties. A bean with a constrained property must support a pair of event listener registration methods: `addVetoableChangeListener()` and `removeVetoableChangeListener()`. These methods are used to register listeners with the bean containing properties they want to validate. Both of these methods take a `VetoableChangeListener` object as their only argument, as the following method definitions show:

```
public void addVetoableChangeListener(VetoableChangeListener l);
public void removeVetoableChangeListener(VetoableChangeListener l);
```

Just as in registering bound property listeners, when an interested party wants to register itself as validating a property, it must call addVetoableChangeListener() and provide a suitable object implementing the VetoableChangeListener interface. The VetoableChangeListener interface is used to report changes in the bound property. More specifically, when a bound property's value changes, the vetoableChange() method is called on all registered VetoableChangeListener interfaces. This method is passed a PropertyChangeEvent object, which is the same property change information object used in bound property notifications.

Just so you can see how similar the mechanism behind constrained properties is to that behind bound properties, Figure 4.5 graphically shows how a constrained property works.

Figure 4.5.
The inner workings of a constrained property.

As with bound properties, the main thing taking place here is the sending of a property change notification from a bean to a listener. However, in this case the listener has the option of rejecting the change by throwing a PropertyVetoException exception. If an exception is thrown, the bean is responsible for handling it and appropriately restoring the original property value. Although the method that gets called is different (vetoableChange()), the property change notification sent for a constrained property is the same as that sent for a bound property, which is a PropertyChangeEvent object. This notification is the same because the same information is required to be sent: the property name, the old property value, and the new property value.

Like bound properties, constrained properties also support listener registration methods on a per-property basis. The naming of these methods is the same as for bound properties, with the distinguishing factor being the listener type passed as the sole argument to each method. Instead of taking a `PropertyChangeListener` object, the constrained listener registration methods take a `VetoableChangeListener` object. Following is a set of listener registration methods for a constrained version of the `numberOfLives` property mentioned in the previous section:

```
public void addNumberOfLivesListener(VetoableChangeListener l);
public void removeNumberOfLivesListener(VetoableChangeListener l);
```

The only difference between these methods and their bound equivalents from earlier is the type of argument they take. This is logical because the argument specifies the type of listener, which in turn dictates the type of method called for a notification. In the case of bound properties the `propertyChange()` method is called, and in the case of constrained properties the `vetoableChange()` method is called.

Using Properties

Now that you understand the ins and outs of how properties are managed under the hood in the JavaBeans API, take a step back and see how they are used in practical situations. As you learned in the previous chapter, properties reveal themselves to the user in a variety of different scenarios, a few of which follow:

- Properties appear as object fields in scripting environments such as JavaScript or VBScript.
- Properties are accessed programmatically via public accessor methods.
- Properties are accessed visually via property sheets in application builder tools.
- Properties are used to persistently store and retrieve the state of a bean.

Now look at each of these scenarios and how the property management concepts you've learned in this chapter come into play in supporting each particular type of property usage.

Properties in Scripting Environments

Scripting environments such as JavaScript and VBScript offer a powerful means of interacting with beans and using them at a higher level than pure programming languages such as Java. Although beans certainly see a great deal of use in straight Java programming, they are also just as important from a scripting perspective. JavaBeans as a technology makes a significant impact on scripting environments because it offers a simple, yet powerful approach to enabling access to custom objects (beans).

One of the key ways beans expose themselves to scripting environments is through properties. Properties are accessible through scripting as member variables of bean objects. In other words, beans appear to scripting environments as extension objects, and their properties are accessible as member variables. Now, even though it appears to the script writer that he or she is actually given free reign to directly modify the properties of a bean object, in actuality the bean's accessor methods are being used behind the scenes to handle the access. As I mentioned earlier in the chapter, no outside party is ever allowed direct access to a bean's properties. The point is that scripting environments themselves make heavy use of bean accessor methods in enabling script writers to interact with beans. So, don't be misled when you see scripting code manipulating a bean property like this (thing is a bean object):

```
thing.numberOfLives = 12;
```

Although it looks like this code is directly modifying a bean property, you know better! Behind the scenes the scripting environment is executing a piece of code like this:

```
thing.setNumberOfLives(12);
```

This might seem like a minor point, but trust me, it's not. Forcing all outside parties to use a standardized set of interfaces (accessor methods) to interact with the data parts of a bean is one of the key benefits of the JavaBeans technology. It guarantees that no property ever changes without somebody knowing about it, even if it is just a little accessor method.

Programmatic Use of Properties

Another common use of properties is in full-blown programming languages such as Java. Unlike scripting environments, Java uses no illusions to make you feel like you are closer to a bean than you really are. What I mean by this statement is that Java forces you to always interact with bean properties through accessor methods. So, going back to the example from the previous section, the following code wouldn't even work in Java:

```
thing.numberOfLives = 12;
```

In Java terms, this code amounts to you trying to access a private member variable of a class externally, which simply isn't allowed. You don't have any choice but to use getter and setter methods to work with a bean's properties in Java. This is just as well, because it helps you remember the fact that beans shield their internal properties by relying on interfaces.

Visual Use of Properties

One of the most touted features of JavaBeans as a technology is its support for the visual editing of bean properties. In this case, the glitter of editing a property through a purely visual means might have you thinking you somehow have some secret control over a bean. Not to worry, visual bean editing ultimately boils down to the same old accessor methods. Just when you thought JavaBeans was looking high-tech, I had to spoil it by telling you that the same boring mechanism is at the heart of it all!

Don't despair, because if you haven't gathered from the discussion thus far, it is this consistency of relying on the same property access mechanism throughout that makes JavaBeans so powerful. What it comes down to is that no matter how you interact with a bean property, the interaction ultimately ends up being a simple call to an accessor method. This insight should give you more cause to appreciate the simplicity inherent in the design of access methods. A more complex solution would probably run into difficulty in attempting to be scaleable to so many different scenarios.

Properties and Bean Persistence

The last area of property usage I want to touch on is that of *persistence*, which is the storage and retrieval of a bean's state. Because the state of a bean is ultimately defined by its properties, it stands to reason that persistence primarily involves the storage and retrieval of properties. And how do we store and retrieve bean properties? You got it, using accessor methods! Persistence is primarily a process of calling getter and setter methods on all the properties of a bean, depending on whether the bean is being stored or retrieved. What have you learned from this discussion? When in doubt, use an accessor method!

API Support

Having said about all there is to say about properties, I want to finish the chapter by taking a look at the classes and interfaces that make the property management facilities in the JavaBeans API a reality. Here are the classes and interfaces that comprise the property management portion of the JavaBeans API:

- PropertyChangeEvent
- PropertyChangeSupport
- PropertyVetoException
- VetoableChangeSupport
- PropertyChangeListener
- VetoableChangeListener

> Note: All of these classes are covered in much greater detail in Appendix B, "JavaBeans API Quick Reference."

PropertyChangeEvent

The PropertyChangeEvent class is used to store information relating to a change in a bound or constrained property. This information consists of the name of the property, the old value of the property, and the new value of the property. PropertyChangeEvent objects are sent as notifications from a bean to registered listeners through the PropertyChangeListener and VetoableChangeListener interfaces, depending on whether the property in question is bound or constrained. More specifically, a PropertyChangeEvent object is sent as the only argument to the propertyChange() and vetoableChange() methods, which are called on the respective listener interfaces.

PropertyChangeSupport

The PropertyChangeSupport class is a helper class for managing listeners of bound and constrained properties. It primarily handles the chore of maintaining a list of listeners and firing property change notifications to each, which is often a nice convenience to beans with bound properties.

PropertyVetoException

The PropertyVetoException class is used to notify a bean that an attempt has been made to set a constrained property to an unacceptable value. This exception is thrown by the vetoableChange() method of the VetoableChangeListener interface.

VetoableChangeSupport

Similar to PropertyChangeSupport, the VetoableChangeSupport class is a helper class for managing listeners of bound and constrained properties. It primarily handles the chore of maintaining a list of listeners and firing property change notifications to each, which is often a nice convenience to beans with constrained properties.

PropertyChangeListener

The PropertyChangeListener interface serves as the listener interface implemented by classes wanting to receive notifications regarding a bound property change. This interface consists of the propertyChange() method, which is called whenever the value of a bound property has changed on a bean for which the interface is registered.

VetoableChangeListener

Similar to PropertyChangeListener, the VetoableChangeListener interface serves as the listener interface implemented by classes wanting to receive notifications regarding a constrained property change. This interface consists of the vetoableChange() method, which is called whenever the value of a constrained property has changed on a bean for which the interface is registered. The vetoableChange() method will throw a PropertyVetoException exception if it rejects the new value of the constrained property.

Summary

This chapter took you through a complete tour of the property management facilities that form an integral part of the JavaBeans API. As you learned, the JavaBeans technology relies heavily on properties as the data portion of beans. Realizing the importance of properties and how they are managed, the JavaBeans architects took care in making sure the property interfaces for beans are both consistent and simple. This chapter explored the primary mechanism behind property interfaces: accessor methods. You learned about the different types of accessor methods and how they are used to get and set the values of bean properties.

With accessor methods under your belt, you moved on to more advanced property topics such as indexed properties, bound properties, and constrained properties. In learning about each of these property types, you saw a different piece of the JavaBeans property management services fall into place. You then moved on to looking into some practical scenarios in which accessor methods are used to access bean properties. Finally, you finished off the chapter by taking a peek at the specific JavaBeans API classes and interfaces that make all the property management facilities a reality.

If you've had enough of properties, don't give up just yet. The next chapter focuses on introspection, which is highly dependent on properties. Fortunately, you won't have to delve quite so deeply into the mechanics behind properties, so you can relax a little.

Introspection: Getting to Know a Bean

It is imperative in the design of JavaBeans that all beans somehow expose information about their public properties, methods, and events. In doing so, beans enable outside parties to learn what features they have to offer and how they are used. Outside parties in this case include application builder tools and application programmers, among others. The importance of this public exposure of bean information is that a builder tool or programmer needs to be able to take a prepackaged bean and have a consistent and automated way to find out how the bean works.

The process of analyzing a bean to find out how it works is called *introspection*. Introspection is a fundamental part of the JavaBeans API because it is the means by which beans are easily integrated into new environments. In this chapter you learn a great deal about introspection and how it is implemented behind the scenes in JavaBeans. Although introspection has often involved relatively complex schemes in other component models, you learn in this chapter that JavaBeans provides an extremely elegant and simple solution to introspection. More important, the JavaBeans approach to introspection requires very little effort on the part of beans developers. JavaBeans even goes a step further than most component models by providing two different approaches to introspection, each one suiting the needs of developers in different ways.

This chapter covers the following topics related to JavaBeans introspection:

■ Introspection basics
■ Design patterns
■ Providing bean information explicitly
■ A composite approach to introspection
■ Security issues
■ API support for introspection

Introspection Basics

The JavaBeans API provides a great deal of support for introspection, which enables any interested party to find out information about the structure and functionality of a bean. The introspection services provided by the JavaBeans API are divided into two parts: low-level services and high-level services. The low-level API services are typically used by application builder tools, which make heavy use of bean internals to provide advanced development features. This level of access isn't appropriate for application developers, however, because it exposes bean internals that aren't meant to be accessible at the application level. For developers, the high-level API services are more appropriate.

The high-level services provide access to a limited portion of a bean's internals, which typically consist of a bean's public properties, methods, and events. The high-level introspection services rely heavily on the low-level services; the primary difference between the two is that the high-level services limit access to bean internals. The end result is two different levels of introspection that offer solutions tailored to the access requirements of the party attempting to introspect a bean.

You might be wondering exactly how the introspection facilities in the JavaBeans API enable an outside party to find out about the internal workings of a bean. In other component models such as ActiveX, component developers are required to explicitly define each aspect of a component that they want to be available to outside parties. This process can get very messy and even involve learning a component definition language. JavaBeans takes a very different approach by offering a means of automatically assessing bean information from the class makeup of the bean itself. In other words, with JavaBeans it is possible for bean developers to not put forth any extra effort toward supporting introspection. This is very nice because it pushes the issue of introspection onto the JavaBeans introspection facilities, instead of saddling bean developers with the responsibility. This not only helps developers get up and running with JavaBeans development faster, but it also makes beans a little leaner and easier to work with. If JavaBeans is the first component software technology you've encountered, then you'll just have to take my word for it as far as how much of a convenience it is not having to worry about explicitly supporting introspection at the code level.

Before you start thinking JavaBeans has taken away all the fun, understand that the automatic approach to introspection isn't the only way introspection is handled. For those cases in which bean developers want to get up close and personal with bean information, there is an option for explicitly defining the information you want to be known publicly. Even this approach is much easier to use in JavaBeans than the component information schemes required in other component models. So, if you happen to be a control freak and insist on having total control over how your beans are introspected, you'll be glad to know it doesn't take too much extra effort.

The first approach of JavaBeans automatically assessing information about a bean uses the *reflection facilities* in the core Java API. The reflection facilities are responsible for analyzing the low-level structure of a bean and returning information. The introspection facilities in the JavaBeans API take this information and apply design patterns to it to determine the specifics about the public properties, methods, and events supported by a bean. You learn much more about design patterns in the next section of this chapter, so don't worry about it if they don't sound familiar.

The explicit approach to defining bean information requires a little more work on the part of bean developers. The JavaBeans API provides support classes that are used by developers to explicitly define the public information for a bean. Keep in mind that this approach is purely optional and can even be used in combination with the automatic approach. In other words, developers are free to explicitly provide some bean information and allow the introspection facilities to automatically determine the rest. It's important to note that automatic introspection is the default approach taken by JavaBeans, and is superseded only if explicit information is available. This ability to leverage both introspection approaches provides lots of flexibility for bean developers.

The Significance of Introspection

If you're new to the world of component software, you might not immediately see the importance of introspection. Although simple in concept, the idea of being able to find out information about an executable piece of software is a pretty big deal, at least in terms of components. Consider all the different applications installed on your computer. If you wanted to find out how one of them worked internally, how would you go about finding out? Give up? First off, commercial applications are always shipped in some form of executable machine code that isn't too human friendly. The only option you really have is to break out a disassembler, which is a tool that takes executable machine code and resolves it into comparable assembly language code. If you happen to be an assembly language whiz, you might be able to figure out a few things about the application after a great deal of effort. Even then, you probably wouldn't be anywhere near understanding the specific design of the application as a whole.

One of the reasons why commercial applications are so hard to reverse engineer is that their developers don't want to give away their secrets. Even if that wasn't an issue, however, you still would need to contend with the fact that executable code is virtually incomprehensible by humans. Don't get me wrong, there certainly are people capable of understanding machine code to some extent, and you might be one of them. If you are one of these people, feel free to skip the rest of this paragraph, you've earned it! For the rest of us mere mortals, machine code is just a big series of meaningless numbers. The point of all this is that executable code generally isn't designed to provide any information about its internal makeup to the outside world; executable code is designed for machines to understand, not people. This has worked out well for commercial applications, where developers typically don't want their hard work understood for fear of it being copied and reused.

Note: This discussion touches on an interesting subject related to the inability of humans to understand executable machine code. In the world of custom software development, many deals are structured based on whether source code is delivered or just an executable application is delivered. Developers charge a great deal more for source code because they know that by delivering just an executable, they still have tight control over their development efforts and aren't at risk of someone taking their code and reusing it elsewhere. In other words, outside of component software, reusability is possible only when you have direct access to source code.

Now, consider the issue of component software. A major requirement of an executable software component is that it provide information about its internal makeup so outside parties can know how it works. The problem is that components are developed and distributed using roughly the same model as applications, making them just as hard to figure out in executable form. Enter introspection. Introspection provides a means of getting around the problem of not being able to find anything out about an executable component. This explains why introspection simply must be a standard part of any component model.

Design Patterns

I mentioned that one of the approaches taken by the JavaBeans API in assessing the makeup of a bean is automatic, meaning that bean developers aren't required to add any additional support for introspection in their code. Although it's true that developers don't have to add additional code, how they structure the code for the bean itself is important because JavaBeans relies on the naming and type signatures of the methods defined in the code for a bean to determine what properties, methods, and events the bean supports for public use. In other words, the conventions used in the code for a bean is also used as a means for introspecting the bean.

This might sound pretty strange, but keep in mind that most properties are accessed through very consistent methods: accessor methods. The JavaBeans architects reasoned that it would be pretty convenient if accessor methods were used to automatically determine the public properties of a bean. This approach is hardly just a convenience, however. The automatic approach to JavaBeans introspection relies heavily on the naming conventions and type signatures of a bean's methods, including methods for registering event listeners.

At first, the whole idea of JavaBeans analyzing the methods for a bean and automatically determining the bean's public properties might sound a little mystical. You might imagine that the JavaBeans API is jumping through many hoops to pull off such behavior. In fact, the mechanism behind this automatic introspection approach is quite simple. The approach relies on design patterns, which are standardized naming conventions and type signatures that are used to define bean methods based on their function. For example, accessor methods are a specific type of design pattern that applies to properties. Likewise, there is also a design pattern for events.

The whole premise behind design patterns is that method names and signatures generally conform to a standard convention, sometimes by accident, but more often by virtue of class organization. Because most Java developers use similar naming conventions for methods, the JavaBeans architects reasoned that with a little nudging developers might be willing to adhere to a more rigid naming convention, especially if there's something to be gained by doing so. Indeed, not having to worry about explicitly adding introspection support to a bean is certainly worth the effort of sticking with a naming convention.

There are a variety of different design patterns for specifying everything from simple properties to event sources. All of these design patterns rely on some type of consistent naming convention for methods and their related arguments and types. Keep in mind that this approach to introspection is not only convenient from the perspective of JavaBeans, but it also has the intended side effect of encouraging bean developers to use a consistent set of naming conventions. Here are the three major types of design patterns, each of which are discussed in more detail in the next few sections:

■ Property design patterns

■ Event design patterns

■ Method design patterns

Property Design Patterns

Property design patterns are used to identify the publicly accessible properties of a bean. Not surprisingly, property design patterns are closely related to accessor methods. In fact, you didn't really know it at the time, but in the previous chapter you were adhering to a design pattern when you saw the sample accessor methods for various properties. It turns out that accessor methods are the means by which the JavaBeans automatic introspection facilities determine which properties a bean exposes. Basically, any time the JavaBeans introspector encounters a public getter or setter method, it assumes the property in question is a public property and exposes it to the outside world.

If you recall from the previous chapter, properties need not always have pairs of accessor methods. For example, if a property has only a getter method, JavaBeans assumes it is a read-only property. Likewise, if a property has only a setter method, JavaBeans assumes it is a write-only property. If both methods are defined, guess what? You got it, the property is a read-write property. As you can see, design patterns are amazingly simple, but quite effective.

The design patterns for properties vary a little based on the type of property. Here are the property types supporting different design patterns:

- Simple properties
- Boolean properties
- Indexed properties

Simple Properties

Simple properties consist of all single-valued properties, which include all built-in Java data types as well as classes and interfaces. For example, int, long, float, Color, Font, and boolean are all considered simple properties. The design patterns for simple property accessor methods follow:

```
public <PropertyType> get<PropertyName>();
public void set<PropertyName>(<PropertyType> x);
```

So, for a property called numBullets that is of type long, the following accessor methods would safely conform to the introspection design patterns:

```
public long getNumBullets();
public void setNumBullets(long nb);
```

When the JavaBeans automatic introspector encounters these method definitions, it determines both the numBullets public property, as well as the getNumBullets() and setNumBullets() accessor methods for accessing the property. And this takes place without you having to do anything more than conform to the simple property design patterns when you design your methods.

Boolean Properties

Although they are technically simple properties, boolean types have an optional design pattern for the getter method that can be used to make it more clear that a property is of boolean type. This design pattern follows:

```
public boolean is<PropertyName>();
```

The only difference between this design pattern and the one for simple properties is that it uses the word is instead of get in the name. It is fairly common for Java developers to access boolean properties with an is method, which is why JavaBeans supports the use of this special case design pattern. The following is an example of a pair of accessor methods for a boolean property named amphibious that conforms to the boolean design pattern:

```
public boolean isAmphibious();
public void setAmphibious(boolean a);
```

You might be wondering what happens in the event that both a get method and an is method are defined for a property. Not to worry, JavaBeans handles this by always using the is method if it is available, and the get method if not.

Indexed Properties

If you recall from the previous chapter, an indexed property is an array of simple properties. Because indexed properties require slightly different accessor methods, it only makes sense that their design patterns differ a little from other properties. Here are the design patterns for indexed properties:

```
public <PropertyElement> get<PropertyName>(int i);
public void set<PropertyName>(int i, <PropertyElement> x);
public <PropertyElement>[] get<PropertyName>();
public void set<PropertyName>(<PropertyElement>[] x);
```

The first pair of design patterns defines accessor methods for getting and setting individual elements in an indexed property. The second pair of patterns defines accessor methods for getting and setting the entire property array as a whole. You saw an example of how these accessor methods are defined for an indexed property in the previous chapter, but for clarity's sake, here's another one:

```
public Color getPalette(int i);
public void setPalette(int i, Color c);
public Color[] getPalette();
public void setPalette(Color[] c);
```

In this example, the indexed property is called palette and is an array of Color objects. The reason for the lowercase p in palette is because it is standard Java naming convention that all variables and methods begin with a lowercase letter. The first pair of accessor methods enable you to get and set individual colors in the palette, and the second pair enables you to get and set the whole palette of colors.

Event Design Patterns

When a bean's internal state changes, it often is necessary to notify an outside party of the change. To accomplish this, beans are capable of broadcasting event notifications that inform interested parties of some change in a bean. Events themselves can represent many different types of notifications, but some of the most popular ones are mouse clicks and drags. For example, when the user drags the mouse over a bean, you might want the bean to notify its parent so the appearance of the cursor can be changed. This notification is handled by the bean sending its parent an event. You learn a great deal more about events in Chapter 6, "Handling Bean Events." For now, it's only important that you understand how a bean knows what to send event notifications to.

Beans send notifications to event listeners that have registered themselves with a bean as wanting to receive event notifications. Because listeners must register themselves with a bean, it is important that beans provide appropriate methods to facilitate the registration process. The event registration methods come in pairs, with one method enabling listeners to be added and the other enabling beans to be removed. Because this method pair is sufficient for defining an event registration between a bean and an interested party, it's probably not going to come as a surprise to you that the JavaBeans introspector uses these methods to assess the events that a bean is capable of sending.

Event registration methods must conform to the following design patterns for the automatic introspection services to work properly:

```
public void add<EventListenerType>(<EventListenerType> x);
public void remove<EventListenerType>(<EventListenerType> x);
```

In these design patterns, `<EventListenerType>` refers to the object type of the event listener being registered with the bean. JavaBeans requires that this object implement the `EventListener` interface and have its name end with `Listener`. Therefore, if you want to add support for an event listener implementing the `ActionListener` interface, you would do so like this:

```
public void addActionListener(ActionListener al);
public void removeActionListener(ActionListener al);
```

The `ActionListener` interface is used to receive action events such as mouse clicks. In this example, action listeners can easily be registered to receive actions by calling the `addActionListener()` method, or removed as a listener by calling the `removeActionListener()` method.

The event registration design patterns discussed thus far are designed for beans that support multicast events, meaning that there can be multiple registered event listeners. JavaBeans also supports the use of unicast event sources, which are beans that enable only one listener at a time to receive event notifications. In other words, unicast beans enable only one event listener to be registered at a particular time. If an attempt is made to register more than one listener with a unicast bean, the `add<EventListenerType>()` method is thrown a `TooManyListenersException` exception. The design pattern for this method follows:

```
public void add<EventListenerType>(<EventListenerType> x)
➥throws TooManyListeners;
```

Here is the same action listener example designed for a unicast event source:

```
public void addActionListener(ActionListener al) throws
➥TooManyListeners;
public void removeActionListener(ActionListener al);
```

Method Design Patterns

The last area to cover in regard to design patterns is related to public methods that aren't accessor methods. These methods are completely user-defined in that they have no pre-established purpose such as getting or setting a property. Because the naming and type signature for non-accessor public methods is totally up to the bean developer, there aren't any specific design patterns governing them. JavaBeans assumes all public methods are to be publicly exported for outside use. The only difference between these public methods and public accessor methods is that accessor methods notify the JavaBeans introspector of a bean property.

Explicitly Providing Bean Information

Even though the design pattern approach to introspection is very useful and removes a significant burden from bean developers, there is nothing forcing you to follow them. What happens if you don't like the naming conventions enforced by the design patterns? Better yet, what happens if you have devised your own naming convention that you feel is far superior to the one used by the automatic design patterns? In either case, you are responsible for explicitly providing information about the publicly accessible parts of your beans. This certainly is more work than allowing the automatic introspection facilities to study and assess your beans, but it gives you total control over the parts of your beans that are made available for public use.

This explicit approach to exposing bean information involves creating a bean information class that specifies various pieces of information about a bean, including lists of public properties, methods, and events. The bean information class must implement the `BeanInfo` interface, which provides methods for learning about the public information for a bean. You form the name of a bean's information class by adding `BeanInfo` to the end of the bean's class name. Therefore, if you have a bean named `CoolWidget`, its associated bean information class must be named `CoolWidgetBeanInfo`.

Bean developers who want to explicitly provide bean information have the option of providing partial information through the `BeanInfo` interface if they so desire. In other words, it is possible to use the `BeanInfo` interface to offer information about a bean's methods but not about its events. In this case, the JavaBeans introspector will use the explicit information when analyzing the bean for methods but will fall back on automatic introspection for the bean's events and properties.

The Introspector

I have mentioned the JavaBeans introspector several times throughout the chapter, and it's time you met the introspector. The JavaBeans introspector is implemented as a class called `Introspector`. This class is used to obtain information about a bean using the introspection facilities about which you've learned. The introspector is responsible for determining whether a bean has an associated bean information class, and for using automatic introspection if not. More specifically, the introspector closely examines the inheritance tree of a bean looking for explicit information. If this information has not been provided via an object implementing the `BeanInfo` interface, then the introspector uses reflection techniques combined with design patterns to assess the bean's public attributes and behavior automatically.

This two-tiered approach to introspecting beans is provided to enable the utmost flexibility for bean developers. It is expected that many complex commercial beans will explicitly provide public bean information, but that end users deriving their own beans will probably prefer automatic introspection. The two-tiered introspection approach taken by the JavaBeans introspector enables this mixed arrangement to successfully work without any problems.

Introspection and Security

Security, which is always a big issue in regard to Java, has some relevance to JavaBeans as well. As you are probably aware, Java makes a huge distinction between whether an application is trusted or untrusted. Trusted applications include stand-alone Java applications as well as applets that have been digitally signed. Untrusted applications, on the other hand, are Java applets that have not been digitally signed. What does all this have to do with JavaBeans introspection?

One of the ways security enters the picture with JavaBeans is through the introspection of beans. The JavaBeans architects decided that internal information about a bean should be protected from untrusted applications with the same zeal as other resources, such as a user's hard drive. The reason is that you don't want an untrusted application to modify parts of a bean that they have no business bothering. To what parts am I referring? Basically, untrusted applications are only allowed access to public methods, properties, and events. This shouldn't come as a big surprise because that's how beans appear to most outside parties anyway. But not all.

A trusted application, such as an application builder tool, needs to know more about a bean than what is provided in a bean's public information. For trusted applications, the security restrictions are lifted, giving the applications the freedom to dig deeper into a bean's structure. This ultimately gets back to the discussion from the beginning of this chapter regarding low- and high-level JavaBeans introspection APIs. The low-level APIs are made available to trusted applications, while the high-level APIs are made available to untrusted applications.

API Support

None of the neat introspection features you've learned about in this chapter would mean much without the underlying classes and interfaces that make it all happen. You finish off the chapter by taking a quick look at the classes and interfaces that make the introspection facilities provided by the JavaBeans API a reality. Here are the classes and interfaces that make up the introspection portion of the JavaBeans API:

- BeanDescriptor
- EventSetDescriptor
- FeatureDescriptor
- IndexedPropertyDescriptor
- IntrospectionException
- Introspector
- MethodDescriptor
- ParameterDescriptor
- PropertyDescriptor
- SimpleBeanInfo
- BeanInfo

> Note: All of these classes are covered in much greater detail in Appendix B, "JavaBeans API Quick Reference."

BeanDescriptor

The BeanDescriptor class provides global information about a bean, including the name of the bean and the bean's customizer. You learn about customizers in Chapter 8, "Customization: Bean Support for Application Builders."

EventSetDescriptor

The EventSetDescriptor class represents a set of events that a bean is capable of generating. The events defined in an EventSetDescriptor class are all deliverable as method calls on a single event listener interface.

FeatureDescriptor

The FeatureDescriptor class serves as a common base class for the EventSetDescriptor, MethodDescriptor, and PropertyDescriptor classes. It represents bean information that is common across these classes, such as the name of an event, method, or property.

IndexedPropertyDescriptor

The IndexedPropertyDescriptor class represents a publicly accessible indexed property. This class provides methods for accessing the type of an indexed property along with its accessor methods.

IntrospectionException

The IntrospectionException class is used to bring attention to an error that has occurred during introspection, such as an accessor method with an invalid type signature.

Introspector

The Introspector class provides the overhead necessary to analyze a bean and determine its public properties, methods, and events. This class uses explicit bean information if it exists, and it relies on reflection and design patterns to automatically analyze a bean if not.

MethodDescriptor

The MethodDescriptor class represents a publicly accessible method. This class provides methods for accessing information such as a method's parameters.

ParameterDescriptor

The ParameterDescriptor class represents the parameters to a method and is mainly provided as a means for bean developers to provide detailed parameter information beyond that obtained through the Java reflection services.

PropertyDescriptor

The PropertyDescriptor class represents a publicly accessed property. This class provides methods for accessing the type of a property along with its accessor methods and whether it is bound or constrained.

SimpleBeanInfo

The SimpleBeanInfo class is a support class designed to make it easier for bean developers to provide explicit information about a bean. This class basically implements every method in the BeanInfo interface but returns a value that triggers the automatic introspection services. This enables developers to provide selective bean information by overriding specific methods, without having to implement every method in the BeanInfo interface.

BeanInfo

The BeanInfo interface defines a set of methods that can be used to find out information explicitly provided by a bean, such as lists of properties, methods, and events. Developers who want to provide explicit bean information must implement the BeanInfo interface and provide suitable information. It's important to note that any information not explicitly provided via the BeanInfo interface is determined using the automatic introspection facilities of the JavaBeans API.

Summary

This chapter took you on a tour of a very important part of the JavaBeans API: introspection. You began the chapter by learning exactly what introspection is and why it is important to a software component technology such as JavaBeans. You learned that beans would be pretty useless without some form of introspection. From there, you moved into the specifics of the automatic introspection services provided by the JavaBeans API, which rely heavily on design patterns. You saw how simple, yet powerful design patterns are in the automatic assessment of a bean's public information.

You also learned in this chapter that JavaBeans gives bean developers the capability to explicitly provide information about their beans. This is an alternative to the automatic introspection services provided by JavaBeans. It is the job of the JavaBeans introspector to balance the use of these two introspection approaches and determine exactly how to analyze a bean and find out about its public properties, methods, and events. From there, you learned about security as it relates to JavaBeans and introspection. You then finished up the chapter by taking a quick look at the specific classes and interfaces in the JavaBeans API that make introspection possible.

Now that you have a solid grasp of introspection and how it fits into the JavaBeans API, you're ready to move on to yet another API area: event handling.

CHAPTER 6

Handling Bean Events

The concept of an event lies at the heart of almost every graphical computing environment, and JavaBeans is no exception. In JavaBeans, events are used to communicate information about the changing state of a bean or user interactions with a bean. Events form a core component of the JavaBeans architecture in that they are largely responsible for enabling beans to be plugged together as building blocks in a parent application. JavaBeans inherits its event-handling mechanism directly from the event-handling mechanism built into the standard Java 1.1 Application Programming Interface (API). The primary goal of the event-handling facilities in the Java 1.1 API is to provide a powerful and extensible means of propagating event information from components (beans) to applications and other components (beans).

Java 1.1 event handling revolves largely around the concepts of event sources and listeners. Beans that generate event notifications are considered event *sources*, whereas applications and beans that respond to events are considered to be event *listeners*. Event listeners are connected to event sources via an event registration mechanism provided by the standard Java 1.1 event-handling facilities. In this chapter you learn a great deal about event sources and listeners and why they are so important to event handling and JavaBeans. You also learn about event state objects, which represent information associated with an event, and event adapters, which make responding to events a little less cumbersome.

You learn the following major issues in this chapter:

- Event basics
- Event state objects
- Event listeners
- Event sources
- Event adapters
- Delivering events
- API support for events

Event Basics

The event-handling mechanism that JavaBeans uses is directly based on the built-in event-handling facilities provided by the Java 1.1 API. The event-handling approach taken by the Java 1.1 API is very different than the one used in the Java 1.0 API. Because the Java 1.1 API event-handling solution is relatively new, I'll go ahead and cover some of the fundamental issues behind it. You are probably already familiar with the event-handling mechanism employed by the Java 1.0 API, but it's important for you to understand how Java 1.1 deals with events. Like the persistence support used by JavaBeans, the event-handling support is directly provided by the Java 1.1 API.

In the Java 1.1 API, the event-handling portion of an application is completely separate from the application-specific code. This is starkly different from how the Java 1.0 API deals with events. Java 1.1 pulls off this feat by establishing different event types; each type of event is given a unique type class that is derived from a common root event class. The Java 1.1 API also introduces the concepts of event sources and listeners, which act as the sending and receiving ends of an event notification, respectively. Event sources are capable of generating events, whereas event listeners are designed to respond to events. An event is propagated from an event source to an event listener when the event source invokes a method on the listener and passes an object of the event type generated. Although beans typically play the role of event sources, they are fully capable of being listeners, as well.

Event listeners are connected to event sources through a registration mechanism that requires a listener to call a registration method on a source. When the registration method is called, the source is informed to send event notifications to the listener. Along with the capability of being registered with a source, listeners can also be unregistered, or removed as listeners from a source. Event sources are required to support the addition and removal of event listeners through a pair of public event registration methods. You learned a great deal about the syntax of event registration methods in Chapter 5, "Introspection: Getting to Know a Bean."

When an event occurs within an event source, the source sends an event notification to any listeners that have been registered. The event notification is sent via a method call on the listeners. Listeners are required to implement the generic EventListener interface, which is how sources are able to determine the types of registered listeners. Listeners define a method for each event to which they want to respond; these are the methods called by the source when one of the events occurs.

I mentioned the fact that multiple event listeners can be connected to a single source. Although most event sources support multiple listeners, some sources are designed in such a way as to enable only one listener at a time. This type of source is called a *unicast event source*, and its more liberal counterpart is called a *multicast source*. You learn more about unicast and multicast event sources later in the "Event Delivery" section of this chapter.

Note: This discussion of event sources and listeners might sound familiar to you. It turns out that the mechanism used by bound and constrained bean properties, about which you learned in Chapter 4, "Manipulating Bean Properties," is very similar to the event-handling mechanism involving sources and listeners.

Event State Objects

In the Java 1.0 API, all of the events in the Java system are encapsulated in a single class called Event, and each different event is identified by a unique numeric identifier. The Java 1.1 API takes a very different approach by requiring each event to be implemented as a unique event class type. In other words, each event in the Java 1.1 API is a class within a hierarchy of event classes derived from a common root class, EventObject. With this approach it is possible for each event to have unique data and methods for accessing the data.

Actually, the Java 1.1 approach doesn't explicitly require every event type to map one-to-one to a unique class. It is acceptable to have a class represent a group of event types that are somehow related. For example, the MouseEvent class represents the event types corresponding to mouse moves, drags, and button clicks. In this case, the event data is the same for all of the events in the group, so it is perfectly reasonable to group them under one class. The different event types within an event group are differentiated by numeric identifiers, similar to the Java 1.0 approach.

One of the primary reasons for changing the event model to a hierarchy of classes in the Java 1.1 API was to enable the creation of user-defined events. This is a critical change in the core design of Java that was no doubt made to some extent because of JavaBeans. It would have been very difficult for JavaBeans to be as extensible as it is without this change to the event model.

The Java 1.1 API provides two conceptual types of standard events: low-level and semantic events. Low-level events are used to convey information about a low-level input or visual interface interaction such as a mouse drag, key press, or focus change. The following are the low-level events defined in the Java 1.1 API and how they are triggered for a bean:

- ComponentEvent—Triggered whenever the bean is resized, moved, hidden, or shown.
- FocusEvent—Triggered whenever the bean receives or loses focus.
- InputEvent—Never triggered directly; this event class serves as the organizational event class for input events.

- KeyEvent—Triggered whenever the bean receives a key press, key release, or special key such as the Delete or Enter keys.

- MouseEvent—Triggered whenever the bean receives a mouse button click, mouse button release, mouse move, or mouse drag.

New Term

Low-level events are events that convey information in response to a low-level input or visual interface interaction.

Semantic events convey information in response to high-level visual interface actions that relate to how a particular bean is used, as opposed to how it operates at a low level. For example, there is an adjustment event that corresponds to the value of a bean being adjusted; adjustable bean values are numeric values contained within a bounded range. The following are the semantic events defined in the Java 1.1 API and how they are triggered for a bean:

- ActionEvent—Triggered whenever a generic action occurs.

- AdjustmentEvent—Triggered whenever a value is adjusted.

- ItemEvent—Triggered whenever an item state changes.

New Term

Semantic events are events that correspond to high-level visual interface actions that are based more on the semantics of a particular bean.

Semantic events are different from low-level events in that they can apply across a variety of different beans that share a similar semantic usage. For example, buttons generate an action event when they are pressed, whereas menu items generate action events when they are selected. Additionally, a non-visual timer might generate an action event whenever its delayed time period expires.

Figure 6.1 shows how the low-level and semantic events fit into the Java 1.1 API event hierarchy. Notice that the EventObject class is the common root class for all events. Similarly, the AWTEvent class serves as the root for all the standard Java 1.1 event classes, although other classes could certainly derive directly from EventObject.

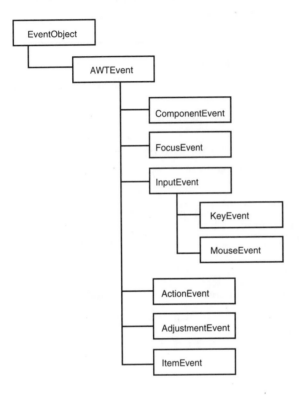

Figure 6.1.
The Java 1.1 API event hierarchy.

Note: Throughout this section I've referred to the standard Java 1.1 API event-handling mechanism in terms of how it impacts beans. Actually, this mechanism is used throughout all of the Java 1.1 API, even in the absence of JavaBeans. In fact, due to the automatic nature of most of the JavaBeans facilities, standard Java 1.1 Advanced Windowing Toolkit (AWT) components technically qualify as beans themselves. The point is that there is often a blurring of functionality between JavaBeans and Java 1.1, as is the case with event handling.

Event Listeners

The standard Java 1.1 API includes support for a variety of different event listeners. If you recall, event listeners provide a formal means of declaring which events can be caught by a particular application or bean. An event listener interface typically has an individual method for each different event type it is capable of catching and responding to. Related events are usually grouped together within a single listener interface. For example, the standard `MouseListener` event listener interface provides event response methods for the mouse entering and exiting a bean, as well as the mouse button being pressed and released over a bean.

Similar to the event classes about which you learned in the previous section, the event listener interfaces defined in the Java 1.1 API are divided into two different types: low-level and semantic. The low-level listener interfaces deal with events at a low level, such as mouse movement and bean focus changes. The following are the low-level event listener interfaces provided by the Java 1.1 API:

- `ComponentListener`—Listens for a bean being resized, moved, hidden, or shown.
- `FocusListener`—Listens for a bean focus change.
- `KeyListener`—Listens for a key press, key release, or special key such as the Delete or Enter keys.
- `MouseListener`—Listens for mouse clicks and for the mouse entering and exiting a bean.
- `MouseMotionListener`—Listens for mouse moves and drags.
- `WindowListener`—Listens for a window opening, closing, iconifying, or de-iconifying.

The semantic listener interfaces deal with events at a higher logical level, such as menu item selections. The following are the semantic event listener interfaces provided by the Java 1.1 API:

- `ActionListener`—Listens for an action.
- `AdjustmentListener`—Listens for a value adjustment.
- `ItemListener`—Listens for an item state change.

I haven't really clarified why the event listener interfaces in the Java 1.1 API are provided as interfaces rather than classes. The reason is that event listeners typically are used to provide some type of application-specific response to an event notification. This means that there really is no default behavior available for an event listener response method. Knowing this, you might think that there is no reason to even have any built-in event listener support. However, there still needs to be a standard, consistent mechanism for passing events from source to listener. Event listener interfaces provide that mechanism by defining the standard methods that are to be called by a source whenever an event occurs. Classes that must actually handle an event are required to implement an event listener interface and provide event response code in the appropriate listener method.

Note: Because most event listener interfaces provide a range of event response methods, you might be concerned about having to fully implement an interface. In other words, what happens if you want to respond to only one event, but the listener interface requires you to implement a handful of response methods? The Java 1.1 API provides event adapter classes that provide empty do-nothing versions of all the methods in an interface. Using an adapter class, you can easily override only the methods you need without worrying about the others. You learn more about adapters a little later in the "Event Adapters" section of this chapter.

Event Sources

Although the event listener interfaces are very important in the grand scheme of Java events, they provide only half of the event delivery mechanism in Java. The other half is handled by event sources, which actually generate event notifications. Event sources must provide a means for registering listeners, which is how sources know to which listeners to dispatch events whenever they occur. Whenever an event occurs, an event source must handle the details of examining its registered listeners and dispatching the event notifications.

Where the event listener methods easily distinguish event listeners from other classes, the event listener registration methods distinguish event sources from other classes. Event sources are in fact required to implement a pair of registration methods for each type of event listener they support. This enables users and application builder tools to connect listeners to sources so that events can be successfully delivered. The event listener registration methods provide the wiring for the event handling mechanism in Java 1.1, and subsequently for JavaBeans.

One of the primary reasons for using event sources and listeners is to optimize event delivery. In Java 1.0, events are delivered to all objects defined as being able to receive a particular event. For example, when you drag the mouse over a button, the button is flooded with mouse move events. The source/listener approach promoted by Java 1.1 and used by JavaBeans is much more efficient because events are delivered only to registered listeners. In other words, no events are ever generated without an object explicitly being registered as an event listener. This explicit statement is made by an event listener when it is registered with an event source.

Similar to the other areas of Java event handling, a distinction is made among event sources by way of low-level and semantic events. The event source for low-level events usually is a visual component such as a button or menu. Low-level events are tightly bound to the physical event source that generates them. Basically, a low-level source implements a low-level event listener interface, whereas a semantic source implements a semantic event listener interface. The Java 1.1 API defines low-level event listeners on the following standard event source components:

- Component
- Dialog
- Frame

These low-level sources are pretty logical because they form the core set of classes that model visual components. More high-level components implement the higher level semantic event listeners. The following are the standard event source components that implement semantic event listener interfaces in the Java 1.1 API:

- Button
- Choice
- Checkbox

- CheckboxMenuItem
- List
- MenuItem
- Scrollbar
- TextField

Event Adapters

One problem alluded to earlier in this chapter in regard to event listener interfaces is that they require a class to implement all the methods defined in the interface. Without implementing all the methods, the class would remain abstract and could not be used directly. This is not a problem in cases in which most or all of the event response methods defined in an interface are going to be used. But what about the opposite scenario, in which you want to respond to only a single event and the listener interface provides a variety of different response methods?

Because you must provide implementations for all the methods in the interface, you would have to add empty do-nothing methods for all the events you don't care about responding to, in addition to the event response method in which you are interested. This approach clearly is annoying, simply because you must add unnecessary code that is required only to adhere to the object-oriented underpinnings of the Java programming language.

There is a simple solution. The Java 1.1 API provides a set of event adapters that are convenience classes for supporting event listeners. "Convenience classes" means that event adapters enable you to implement only the event response methods you need, freeing you from the hassle of writing a bunch of useless empty methods. Keep in mind that event adapters are classes and not interfaces, which means that you must derive from them instead of implementing them. The fact that they are designed as classes is what enables you to selectively provide only the event response methods you need.

There is a unique event adapter class for each low-level event listener interface. Each event adapter implements all the methods in the corresponding event listener interface it is designed to support. You might be wondering why there are no event adapters for the semantic event listener interfaces. Well, if you look closely at the Java 1.1 API documentation, you will find that each semantic event listener interface defines only a single method. Because there is only one method in these interfaces, there is no benefit to providing an adapter class.

At this point, you might be wondering how the event adapters pull off the seemingly magical trickery of bypassing the limitation of having to fully implement an interface. Don't get too excited, because there is absolutely nothing magical about event adapters. Event adapters simply provide empty do-nothing methods for all the methods defined in an interface, just as you could provide in your own classes. As you learned earlier, event adapters are convenience classes, which means that they are there only as a convenience; they don't work miracles or do anything else other than save you a little bit of coding hassle. The following are the event adapter classes provided by the Java 1.1 API:

- `ComponentAdapter`
- `FocusAdapter`
- `KeyAdapter`
- `MouseAdapter`
- `MouseMotionAdapter`
- `WindowAdapter`

> Note: Aside from just being a programming convenience, event adapters can also be used to provide customized delivery of events. In this scenario, a special event adapter is designed and positioned between an event source and event listener so that it can enforce some kind of specialized policy on the event delivery.

Event Delivery

Perhaps the most important issue relating to JavaBeans and events is how events are actually delivered. You already understand the relationship between event sources, listeners, and state objects, but you still might not see the big picture in terms of how they fully relate to each other. On the other hand, maybe you do. If so, just bear with me a little because I'm going to hammer it home one more time. Along with covering the relationship between these functional elements, I also want to introduce a few other topics related to event delivery.

To recap a little, an event delivery consists of three functional parts: an event source, an event listener, and an event state object. The entire process begins when an event listener notifies a source that it wants to listen to a particular event. It does this by calling an event listener registration method provided by the source. When this happens, the source is ready to deliver events to the listener. Whenever an internal change occurs in the source that generates an event, the source creates an event state object describing the event and sends it out to the listener. The source does this by calling one of the event response methods defined in the listener's event listener interface.

Note: It's worth noting that event delivery is synchronous, meaning that an event is guaranteed complete delivery without interruption. However, there is no guarantee that event delivery across a group of listeners will occur within the same thread.

That summarizes the basic scenario surrounding an event delivery from an event source to an event listener. Now let's look at a few issues relating to this delivery process.

Unicast and Multicast Delivery

All of the standard Java 1.1 API components support multiple event listeners, which means that multiple event listeners can be registered with and receive events from a single event source. This type of event delivery is known as multicast delivery, because the event is being broadcast to multiple event listeners simultaneously. With multicast event delivery, event listeners can be added and removed at will via the event listener registration methods, and the source is responsible for keeping track of the current set of listeners. Keep in mind that the Java event delivery mechanism makes no guarantees about the order in which listeners receive events during a multicast delivery.

Although multicast event delivery is the most popular type of event delivery and shares the widest range of use, Java 1.1 also supports unicast event delivery, in which only one listener is permitted to listen to a source at a time. Unicast event sources can have only one registered listener at any given time. The event registration methods are designed so that an exception is thrown if additional listeners are attempted to be added to a unicast event source with a listener already registered. Even though none of the standard Java 1.1 API components are unicast sources, it is expected that some custom components (beans) will implement a unicast approach for one reason or another.

It's important to understand that unicast event delivery is a more limited form of event delivery and should be avoided whenever possible. In other words, if you are developing your own beans, make sure you have a very good reason for making them a unicast event source. Otherwise, stick with multicast and you will give users of your bean far more event delivery options.

Just so you get the picture of unicast and multicast event sources, Figures 6.2 and 6.3 show how each of them works in regard to the delivery of an event.

Figure 6.2 shows how an event is delivered from a unicast source to a single listener via an event state object. Figure 6.3 shows how an event is delivered from a multicast source to a group of listeners via an event state object. These two scenarios are very similar; the only difference is the number of listeners allowed to receive the event.

Figure 6.2.
Unicast delivery of a bean event.

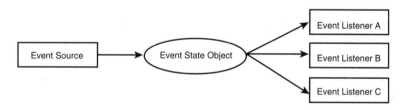

Figure 6.3.
Multicast delivery of a bean event.

Delivery Problems

There are a few different problems that can arise when you are dealing with event delivery. It is important to understand these problems and how they impact event sources and listeners. One problem occurs when event response methods throw exceptions back at an event source. The problem is, how should an event source react to an event response method when the listener throws an exception? It doesn't seem like a listener method should be throwing exceptions at the source, but the situation can technically occur. Unfortunately, there are no hard and fast rules governing what should happen in a situation like this. Java 1.1 stipulates that the manner in which an event source deals with listener-generated exceptions is entirely implementation dependent, which means that you must consult the documentation for a particular source to find out what happens.

Another problem associated with event delivery occurs when the set of event listeners for a source is updated during a multicast event delivery. In this situation it is technically possible for a listener to be removed from the source before its event has been delivered. When this occurs, it is possible for an event to be delivered to a listener that is no longer registered, which certainly seems like a problem. Again, there unfortunately are no strict rules about how event sources should deal with this scenario. It is entirely implementation specific, so you might want to refer to the source documentation if you are worried about this problem creeping up on you.

API Support

The powerful event-handling mechanism about which you've learned in this chapter is made possible largely by a simple class and interface in the Java 1.1 API. The chapter finishes with a quick look at this class and interface, which follow respectively:

- EventObject
- EventListener

> Note: This class and interface are both covered in detail in the API documentation that ships with Java 1.1. They are mentioned here because the JavaBeans approach to event handling is largely based on them.

EventObject

The EventObject class represents information associated with a generic event. This class is designed as an abstract base class from which all event state classes

are derived. The following additional event state classes are derived from
EventObject and are provided in the standard Java 1.1 API:

- ComponentEvent
- FocusEvent
- InputEvent
- KeyEvent
- MouseEvent
- ActionEvent
- AdjustmentEvent
- ItemEvent

> Note: For more information on these event state classes, please refer to Appendix B, "JavaBeans API Quick Reference."

EventListener

The EventListener interface defines the overhead required of an event listener.
This class actually defines no methods, which means that it exists primarily as
a means of identifying derived class types as event listeners. The following
additional event listener interfaces are derived from EventListener and are provided in the standard Java 1.1 API:

- ComponentListener
- FocusListener
- KeyListener
- MouseListener
- MouseMotionListener
- WindowListener
- ActionListener
- AdjustmentListener
- ItemListener

> Note: For more information on these event listener interfaces, please refer to Appendix B.

Summary

This chapter took you through one of the more core elements of JavaBeans: events. Events ultimately take on the responsibility of enabling beans to interact with each other, which is no small task. Fortunately, the event handling facilities in JavaBeans are borrowed directly from the standard event handling facilities in the core Java 1.1 API. This results in a leaner and more consistent design, which is not surprising considering the fact that JavaBeans is intended to alleviate much of the learning curve of other component technologies with minimal overhead.

In this chapter, you learned how event sources and listeners are used to manage the flow of event information between beans and interested parties. You also learned a great deal about how this mechanism works behind the scenes, which gave you greater insight into JavaBeans event handling in general. You moved on to learn some details about event delivery and some of the problems associated with it. You finished the chapter by learning about the specific parts of the Java 1.1 API that bring events to life.

With events safely behind you, you are now ready to push on into another area of JavaBeans: persistence. In Chapter 7, "Persistence: Saving Beans for a Rainy Day," you find out what persistence is all about and how it enables beans to be resurrected from the grave.

Persistence: Saving Beans for a Rainy Day

Although beans are fun to design and even more fun to use, there often comes a point when it is necessary to store a bean away for later use. The process of storing a bean in a non-volatile location for later use is known as *persistence*. Persistence plays an important role in JavaBeans because it gives application developers a way to save the changes they make to beans that comprise an application. Because beans see a great deal of use as application building blocks, it is imperative that the JavaBeans API provide some means of persistently storing a bean's internal state. In addition to being important in terms of builder tools, persistence enables data-oriented beans to store themselves for later retrieval.

This chapter looks at persistence and how it impacts JavaBeans. You learn about the specific mechanism used by JavaBeans to carry out the persistent storage of a bean's state. More specifically, you find out about serialization and how it is used to provide an automated approach to persistence. You also learn about an approach to persistence where bean developers have the freedom to control all the details of how a bean is stored. These two approaches to persistence parallel the two approaches to introspection about which you learned in Chapter 5, "Introspection: Getting to Know a Bean," where one is automatic while the other provides more freedom at the expense of some effort on the part of bean developers. You probably will be surprised to find out that the approach JavaBeans takes in handling persistence has more to do with the core Java API than with the JavaBeans API.

In this chapter, you learn about the following:

- Persistence basics
- A composite persistence approach
- Serialization and automatic persistence
- Versioning
- API support for persistence

Persistence Basics

Persistence is the mechanism by which beans are stored away in a nonvolatile place for later use. This statement, as straightforward as it is, might not give you the full picture as to what persistence means to JavaBeans. When you think about the concept of persistence, you have to consider the issue of a bean's life cycle. In other words, in the absence of persistence, consider what the lifetime of a bean consists of. To start things off, a bean first is created, probably within the context of some application or application builder tool. Then, some properties are probably manipulated and some public methods called on the bean. After seeing some degree of use, the bean will eventually no longer be needed and will be destroyed (removed from memory), never to be seen or heard from again. Figure 7.1 illustrates the life cycle of a typical bean.

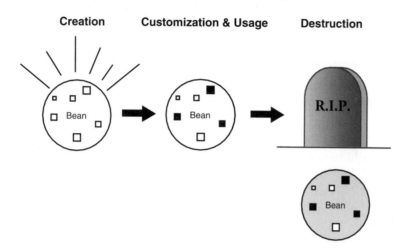

Figure 7.1.
The life cycle of a bean.

Don't worry, I'm not trying to tug at your heart strings and get you feeling sorry for helpless little beans that have met their demise. What I'm trying to do is establish that without persistence, a bean's life cycle is limited to whatever happens in the context of a particular session of an application. When an application ends, all the beans that have been created alongside it are automatically destroyed. You might be thinking that this is no big deal, considering the fact that beans are just little objects and can easily be re-created. But remember that a significant part of using beans is being able to customize them for use in different situations. And what good are customized beans if the customizations are lost after you close an application? Persistence puts a twist on the life cycle of a bean by providing a means to keep up with the state of a bean and restore it later. Check out Figure 7.2, which shows how persistence impacts the life cycle of a bean.

Notice in the figure how the bean is not required to always be created anew. Through persistent storage and retrieval, it is possible to load a bean to the state it was in during the last session of its use. Hopefully, you are starting to get an idea about how this ability to load and use a customized bean is of great importance to JavaBeans. The issue I'm leading up to is that of application builder tools. Think about the role beans play in application builder tools: Each bean is visually laid out and then edited to fit the application being developed. When you are finished working in the builder tool, you want the customized beans to be stored somehow so they will keep the same values you set. Without persistence, you would always have to start over each time you ran the tool. In fact, there would be no point in using beans as application building blocks because they would have no way to maintain their customized state.

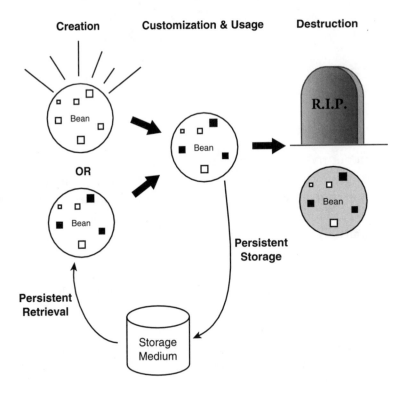

Figure 7.2.
The life cycle of a bean with persistence.

Even though application builder tools are a good example of where bean persistence is important, there are other areas as well. Consider situations in which beans serve as data objects that represent some kind of important information.

For example, you could develop a custom data bean to keep track of addresses in an address book application. The bean's role in the address book would be to provide a way to edit and maintain information about addresses for all your friends. Well, what happens after you start using your address book and you enter a bunch of addresses? Without persistence, not much. As soon as you closed the application all your data would go away. With persistence, you can easily store the addresses for future use, which is pretty much the whole point of entering them to begin with. Without persistence, your address book application is the equivalent of a physical paper address book where you replace the contents with clean paper every time you go to use it. Not very useful!

The topic I've been not so carefully dancing around is that persistence is a very important facility for JavaBeans because it provides a means of preserving the state of beans for future use. I might sound like I'm repeating myself with this definition of persistence, but it is imperative that you understand the role persistence plays in JavaBeans. It certainly sounds like a simple concept—and in fact it is—but the simplest of concepts can get messy when it comes to making them a reality. Fortunately, JavaBeans goes with a very simple and straightforward approach to persistence, which you learn about throughout the rest of this chapter.

What to Store

When you've concluded that persistence is important to JavaBeans, the next step is to determine exactly what information about a bean is worthy of being persistently stored. Like all Java objects, beans consist of data and methods that act on the data. The persistent aspects of a bean are usually some subset of the bean's data. Ultimately, the determination of what part of a bean's data needs to be persistent is up to bean developers. The simple conceptual way to look at the problem is to remember that the whole point of persistence is to enable beans to be restored to the exact same state they were in when they were last used.

Your first impulse might be to say that all of a bean's data should be stored away for persistent resurrection. However, there are a couple of thorny issues related to this brute force approach. First of all, it's not unusual for a bean to use member variables to keep track of temporary information. For example, a bean might use a member variable to keep up with whether the mouse button is down for some type of dragging operation. Clearly, this isn't something that should be stored away persistently because it is impossible to keep the value synchronized with the mouse's actual state. Besides, the state of the mouse can easily be determined when a bean is first created or loaded. Persistent state information should typically only include things that can't be assessed from the runtime environment.

A more important and much trickier issue relating to the type of information that should be persistently stored is references to other beans. It is perfectly acceptable for a bean to maintain member variables that are references to other beans. For example, container beans usually manage references to all the beans contained within them. The problem is that it isn't possible to store and retrieve references to beans via persistence because references are actually pointers to memory, which are very volatile. In other words, it is highly unlikely that a restored memory pointer will ever point to anything meaningful because memory is constantly changing.

The question is, what happens to bean references when it comes to persistence? I mean, aren't references to other beans just as important in the restoration of a bean's state as other member variables? Absolutely! But because JavaBeans can't address the reference problem through persistence, it pushes the responsibility on the application or application builder tool where beans are being used. Therefore, if you customize and connect a bunch of beans together using a builder tool and you save everything, the beans are stored via JavaBeans persistence but their relationships to each other are stored through some builder tool–specific mechanism.

OK, so you understand that most of the data for a bean should be persistently stored, excluding temporary information and references to other beans. The next issue to tackle is how JavaBeans itself determines what information about a bean to persistently store. Although this might at first seem like a fairly difficult challenge based on the discussion thus far, it turns out to be quite simple. The approach JavaBeans takes is to assume that all member variables are to be persistently stored away. There are no complicated rules or tricky algorithms for attempting to assess the usage of member variables, except for one minor exception.

Java supports the transient keyword, which identifies a member variable as not being part of an object's persistent state. JavaBeans also uses this variable for the same purpose. Therefore, if you are developing a bean and you have several member variables that reference other beans, you simply identify them as transient and all is well. Here is an example of a bean with a transient member variable:

```
public class Ratchet {
  private int length, weight;
  private transient ToolBox box;

  public Ratchet(int l, ToolBox b) {
    length = l;
    box = b;
  }

  // Methods...
}
```

In this example, the Ratchet class has a transient member variable called box that is of type ToolBox. This member variable is used to hold a reference to a ToolBox object that is passed in the Ratchet class's constructor. When it comes time to persistently store a Ratchet object, only the length and weight member variables are stored; the box member variable is left for the parent application to worry about.

Where to Store

Throughout the discussion of persistence thus far, I've left out one crucial detail: where beans are stored. It certainly is important to understand the "how" and "what" behind persistence, but at some point you have to take into consideration the "where." You've probably been assuming that I've been talking about storing beans in files, but that's not necessarily true. Indeed, the primary approach used in storing persistent beans is files, but this is not the only approach available. It is also possible to store beans in databases.

Admittedly, this route is much less common than simply storing beans in files, but it is still worth mentioning because it shows the extensibility of JavaBeans persistence. If you don't quite understand the difference between storing a bean in a file as opposed to a database, think about the differences between a raw binary file and a database. Binary files are just a big long series of bytes, where databases are well-defined data structures usually consisting of tables with rows and columns. Therefore, when a bean gets stored in a file it goes in as a series of bytes. On the other hand, when a bean gets stored in a database, it must somehow be mapped into the structure of the database. For example, each member variable being stored might correspond to a column in the database. In either case, the process of reading or writing an object to a stream of data is called *serialization*.

New Term

Serialization is the process of reading or writing an object to a stream of data.

It is worth noting that JavaBeans defaults to storing beans using automatic serialization, which means that they are stored in files. The database approach to bean persistence involves considerable effort on the part of bean developers.

A Composite Approach to Persistence

A particularly important goal for the JavaBeans architects was to somehow make persistence something that bean developers wouldn't have to worry about if they didn't want to. This is a common theme throughout the design of JavaBeans that I hope you are beginning to see. To make bean development as easy as possible, the JavaBeans architects really tried hard to make many of the standard facilities as automatic as possible, including persistence. However, the folks at JavaSoft also understand the importance of giving developers the freedom to chart their own course if they so desire. Therefore, the persistence facilities in JavaBeans allow for highly customized approaches to the storage of a bean's state as well. Database storage is an example of a customized approach to bean storage.

The customized approach to bean persistence is also referred to as an *externalization mechanism*. Support for this approach is provided so that bean developers can carefully control the way in which objects are persistently stored and retrieved. Developers who aren't concerned with this type of control are free to rely on the default persistence mechanism provided by JavaBeans. Otherwise, developers are responsible for deciding exactly how a bean is to be represented and stored for later use, which often can be a complex task.

New Term

An *externalization mechanism* is a means of storing and retrieving an object through some type of custom, externally defined format.

Serialization

Persistence in JavaBeans is tightly linked to a feature of the core Java API: object serialization. *Serialization* is the process of reading or writing an object to a stream of data. The Java object serialization facilities define a consistent format for reading and writing Java objects to a stream of bytes suitable for storage in a file. This serialization support provides a complete solution for storing and retrieving Java objects to nonvolatile locations, such as files. One of the ways in which JavaBeans uses serialization is in its automatic approach to persistence, which involves storing and retrieving a bean based on its properties.

The key to storing and retrieving an object in this manner is representing the state of the object in a serialized form sufficient to reconstruct the object. In other words, the format used to store an object must sufficiently describe the object so it can be later reconstructed to the same state. From the perspective of JavaBeans, it isn't terribly important exactly how a bean is resolved into bytes, as long as it can be completely restored. Figure 7.3 shows the process of a bean being serially stored to a file as a series of bytes.

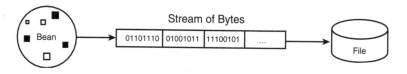

Figure 7.3.
A bean being serialized to a file as a stream of bytes.

You can see in the figure that the main premise surrounding bean serialization is the translation of a bean into a series of bytes. Because this mechanism is already handled by the core Java API, there isn't really any additional overhead required by JavaBeans to support serialization. This is a result of the fact that beans are ultimately a type of Java object, which explains why standard Java serialization is sufficient for storing and retrieving beans. JavaBeans relies on standard Java serialization by using it as an automatic approach to bean persistence.

The serialization functionality provided by the standard Java API has the following qualities, which help make it an ideal persistence solution for JavaBeans:

- Simple, yet extensible serialization mechanism
- Maintains object types and properties within the serialized format
- Is extensible enough to support remote objects
- Requires additional overhead only for customization
- Enables objects to define their own external formats through customization

At this point, you might be starting to realize that in terms of JavaBeans, persistence and serialization mean practically the same thing. This is because JavaBeans persistence is implemented entirely through the serialization facilities provided by the core Java API. Although this might seem like the JavaBeans architects were avoiding some work, the truth is that using the standard Java serialization mechanism helps JavaBeans maintain more consistency with Java itself. The end result is that developers who understand serialization in terms of Java will also be able to work with serialization in JavaBeans without having to learn anything new. This is a good example of code reuse and how important it is to Java and related technologies such as JavaBeans.

Versioning

One particularly thorny issue relating to persistence and serialization is *versioning*, which involves the evolution of object functionality. A big problem arises when an object is stored under one version and then restored under a different version. Because different versions of an object will often have different state information, the issue of versioning is a tricky one. Ultimately, the problem is in determining how to handle compatibility between different versions of an object. Versioning raises some interesting questions about object identity, including what constitutes a backwardly compatible change to an object—a compatible change being a change that does not affect the contract between the object and its parent application or application builder tool.

New Term

Versioning refers to the inevitable tendency for an object to evolve over time and gain new functionality.

To deal with versioning, the serialization facilities in Java must somehow enforce a set of rules ensuring that objects maintain compatibility across different versions. These rules dictate the evolution of objects by restricting the kinds of changes that can be made. More specifically, developers are restricted to adding only new member variables and interfaces, as opposed to being able to modify existing ones. So, if you have an object with a method called calcSum() that returns a float and you want to change it to return an int, you must add a new method instead of changing the original version. Your class would contain both of the following methods:

```
public float calcSum();   // old version
public int calcSum();     // new version
```

This might seem like an annoyance, but it guarantees that the new version will work with code that is based on the old version. If you had simply replaced the old method with the new one, all code reliant on the float version would no longer work because the int version would result in a casting problem. The point of this example is that the trick to handling versioning is to maintain consistent interfaces across all versions of an object, which includes keeping old interfaces that might not be entirely useful in newer versions.

The serialization mechanism in the Java API addresses versioning in the following ways:

- Supports communication between different versions of an object executing in different virtual machines
- Supports objects reading streams written by older versions
- Supports objects writing streams intended to be read by older versions

- Is efficient and compact in most cases
- Identifies and loads objects that match the version used to write the stream

Versioning is of even greater importance to JavaBeans because beans are often distributed to a wide audience. Furthermore, the fact that beans are highly reusable means that a great deal of code is likely to be dependent on the interfaces exposed by a bean. Consequently, it is imperative that beans evolve in such a way as to maintain compatibility across different versions. Fortunately, the automatic serialization approach used by JavaBeans encourages this type of design.

API Support

Unlike other areas of JavaBeans, persistence isn't really handled by the JavaBeans API; it is implemented entirely through the serialization facilities provided by the core Java API. JavaSoft has suggested that a future release of JavaBeans might include specific support for externalized persistence, but for now there is no additional overhead in the JavaBeans API. Because the standard Java API is a little beyond the scope of this book, please feel free to refer to it on your own if you are curious about how it supports serialization. JavaSoft provides a guide to serialization as part of its standard documentation for Java, which is available separately from the JDK; just look in the JavaSoft Web site at www.javasoft.com for more information.

> **Note:** Support for serialization was added in Java 1.1, so make sure you have this version of the JDK (or higher) if you are interested in learning more about serialization. You can download the latest version of the JDK directly from JavaSoft; just visit its Web site at http://www.javasoft.com.

Summary

This chapter explained persistence and how it relates to JavaBeans. You learned that persistence is the mechanism that enables beans to be stored and used later.

Without persistence, a lot of the other features in JavaBeans would be ineffective. For example, what good would the builder tool customization facilities be if you couldn't save the customized beans for later use? Not much!

Even though it is very simple in concept, persistence is yet another area of JavaBeans that could have been implemented through layers of complex protocols, but instead relies on a mechanism inherent to Java itself: object serialization. Although this chapter didn't overburden you with specifics about how persistence is implemented under the hood of Java, it hopefully gave you an idea of the importance of persistence and how it applies to JavaBeans. The beauty of the persistence approach taken by JavaBeans (serialization) is that it enables you to build beans with implicit support for persistence. You don't have to perform any additional coding unless you want to customize how a bean is stored at a low level.

Your next stop on this five-chapter tour of the JavaBeans API is JavaBeans' support for application builder tools. After the next chapter, you'll have all you need to know to begin creating and using your own custom beans.

CHAPTER 8

Customization: Bean Support for Application Builders

The last section of the JavaBeans API covered in this part of the book deals with JavaBeans' support for application builder tools, which is also known as bean customization. One of the most touted features of JavaBeans is its direct support for the visual editing of beans within the context of a builder tool. Although JavaBeans pulls off implementing this functionality in an elegant fashion, it's important to realize that builder support is not a minor part of JavaBeans. In fact, it is this very part of JavaBeans that encourages widespread reuse of beans. These facilities fulfill a major design goal of the JavaBeans API in that they offer a means for beans to be reused constructively with little or no programming effort.

In this chapter, you learn all about the application builder support provided by JavaBeans. You find out about property editors and property sheets, which make it possible to visually edit beans at design time. You also learn about the default property editors provided by JavaBeans, which enable you to visually edit built-in Java types with no additional overhead. Toward the end of the chapter you move on to customizers, which take a more advanced approach to the visual editing of a bean's properties by enabling bean developers to create elaborate visual editing interfaces. You finish up the chapter by taking a look at the specific support for application builder tools provided by the JavaBeans API.

You learn about the following topics in this chapter:

- Customization basics
- Property editors
- Property sheets
- Customizers
- API support for customization

Customization Basics

Customization involves the editing and manipulation of bean properties in a design-time environment. Customization plays a critical role in JavaBeans development because it provides the means by which beans can be integrated and used within a visual design tool. This might not seem like all that big of a deal because visual design tools have become commonplace these days. However, consider the fact that there is no global object model that supports the use of cross-platform objects across a variety of different tools. The customization support in JavaBeans really is groundbreaking in some ways because it establishes a generic standard for the design-time manipulation of beans.

You might be familiar with other object models such as VBX, OCX, and ActiveX objects, which can be visually edited using application builder tools such as Visual Basic and Visual C++. Even though component models such as these offer a solution similar to the customization features in JavaBeans, they fall short in many ways because of the overhead and complexity involved in supporting such visual interfaces. JavaBeans offers a much simpler and more automatic solution that enables developers to put minimal effort into constructing the visual side of bean customization. This not only helps speed bean development, but it also helps bring bean development to a wider crowd because of its simplicity.

Development with Beans Versus Java Classes

The real motive behind bean customization is that of making application development easier and smoother through the use of reusable beans with visual application builder tools. If you don't quite see the significance of customization in this light, contrast how a bean is used as opposed to a traditional Java class. A traditional Java class is always used in a programmatic fashion, meaning that Java code must be written to create and interact with it. Furthermore, programmers must study a traditional class's API to figure out how to use the class. This is assuming the class ships with a well-documented API, which isn't always the case. The point is that Java classes are always used at the code level, which limits their usability to developers with a fair degree of programming knowledge.

Now consider the case of a bean. Beans can be used in all the same ways as Java classes, and they also can be used as visual building blocks in application builder tools. When used in an application builder tool, beans are selected and laid out graphically by the user, with their properties and events exposed for editing entirely through visual interfaces. The ability to build applications visually lessens the technical expertise necessary to partake in application development. In other words, JavaBeans customization helps bring application development to a less technical crowd because of its support for visual bean editing.

If you're feeling left out because I've made it sound like bean customization only benefits beginner developers, let me clarify that there's also a big benefit to gearheads like you and me who are just as comfortable working with straight source code. Customization benefits highly skilled Java programmers by enabling them to focus more on the task at hand rather than worrying about building a visual interface by hand in code. As much as I don't mind hacking out Java code, I'm not going to pass up an opportunity to do something easier and faster, which is exactly what visual bean editing affords. The fact of the matter is that building a visual interface using textual programming code just doesn't make sense; visual applications should be designed using visual design tools. By using beans in a visual design tool, it is possible to graphically design the appearance of an application and write Java source code only where necessary.

Runtime and Design-Time Distribution

One interesting issue the JavaBeans architects had to tackle was the problem of keeping beans as compact as possible in the midst of supporting advanced features like customization. In working through this problem, the JavaBeans architects reasoned that the overhead required for the customization of a bean is only required at design time, when a bean is used in a visual editing environment. At runtime there is no need to carry the dead weight of the customization support. After coming to this realization, the decision was made to separate the customization support for a bean and require it to be physically stored apart from the bean. In other words, the customization support for a bean must not be included directly in a bean; it must somehow be stored in a separate helper class. Figure 8.1 shows the difference between how a bean is shipped for use in runtime and design-time environments.

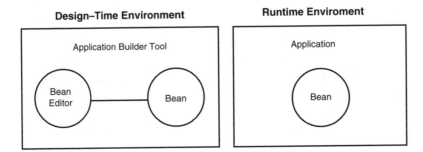

Figure 8.1.
The difference between shipping a bean for use in runtime and design-time environments.

The nice thing about this arrangement is that it enables beans to be shipped in different forms, depending on how they are being used. For development environments that enable the visual customization of beans, a bean can be shipped with its related customization support. On the other hand, in a runtime environment such as a commercial application, a bean can be shipped on its own without the extra customization overhead. This approach not only makes more sense from a design perspective, but it also results in more compact beans, which is a major goal of JavaBeans.

Property Editors

The application builder tool support in JavaBeans begins with property editors, which are visual interfaces for editing a particular type of property. Property editors form the basis of bean customization because they are implemented at the property level, which facilitates reusing them in more comprehensive scenarios such as property sheets and customizers. Don't worry, you learn about property sheets and customizers a little later in this chapter in the "Property Sheets" and "Customizers" sections.

The aim of property editors is to enable you to add visual editing capabilities to every conceivable bean property type. With each property type having a corresponding editor, it then becomes possible to edit entire beans simply as a group of properties. JavaBeans provides property editors for built-in Java data types such as integers, booleans, and strings. Figure 8.2 shows how a string property editor looks. Incidentally, for custom properties it is expected that developers provide a suitable editor if they want their property to be available for bean development. Developers do this by designing a class that implements the `PropertyEditor` interface, which is defined in the JavaBeans API.

Figure 8.2.
The property editor for a string property.

In this example, the string property is the label for a button. You can see how this property editor provides a straightforward visual approach to modifying the string property through a text edit box. Contrast this visual approach with traditional Java programming, where you would have to call a method on the button class and pass the name of the property as a `String` object. Granted, it's not all that hard to call a method, but it's tough to argue with the increased level of intuitiveness offered by the visual approach.

If a string property editor doesn't sound all that amazing, consider another type of property editor that makes a little more of an impact in terms of its interface being more effective. Figure 8.3 shows the property editor for a font property, which is a little more involved than the string property editor.

Figure 8.3.
The property editor for a font property.

As you can see, the font property editor is actually implemented as a dialog box rather than as a simple component. It contains three different drop-down lists that enable you to tweak the specific aspects of a font with ease. Now contrast this approach with that of programming with straight Java classes. Each selection made in the drop-down lists corresponds to an initialization parameter for a Java Font object. The programming approach has the additional inconvenience of providing no type of guidance. You have to be very careful to enter the correct information for the font and make sure not to misspell the name of the typeface. The property editor approach guarantees that you don't make any mistakes because it forces you to pick from a predefined list of options. This is a very nice usage of property editors in that you can try out different font settings and see the results immediately.

Because you're having so much fun learning about property editors, I'm going to show you one more that really highlights the visual aspect of property editing. Figure 8.4 contains the property editor for a color property, which enables you to set the red, green, and blue values for a color and see the results before accepting the final color.

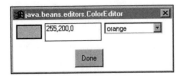

Figure 8.4.
The property editor for a color property.

As you can see, this property really makes the visual aspect of property editing come to life. I don't know about you, but I don't have a very good imagination when it comes to guessing at what colors the different combinations of red, green, and blue make. The color property editor enables you to see exactly the color you are getting as you change the values of each color component. Unlike the other two property editors you've seen, the color property editor is also interesting in that it provides two options to editing a color. You can either type in the red, green, and blue (RGB) color components or you can select a standard color from a drop-down list. Being able to choose a standard color without having to worry about RGB values is a very nice touch, especially when you consider that most of the time you are probably going to use a standard color anyway. The ability to select standard colors is also valuable because it enables you to see what the RGB values for different colors are. With this knowledge, you can slightly alter the standard colors to get different shades. In short, this is a very cool property editor!

Property Sheets

Although property editors are very useful at the property level, the editing of properties always takes place within the context of a complete bean. In other words, editing a bean usually involves interacting with a group of property editors because beans usually contain multiple properties. To facilitate the editing of complete beans, JavaBeans provides property sheets, which are visual interfaces that consist of all the property editors necessary to edit the public properties of a bean. Property sheets are usually implemented as dialog boxes that contain a variety of different individual property editors, depending on the specific properties within a bean.

Property sheets are the interfaces you will most often think of when it comes to editing a bean because they group all of a bean's properties into one convenient location. Figure 8.5 shows how the property sheet for a simple button bean looks.

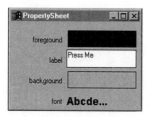

Figure 8.5.
The property sheet for a button bean.

The property sheet shown in the figure exposes property editors for four different properties: foreground, label, background, and font. The foreground and background properties are both color properties, the label property is a string property, and the font property is a font property. Editing these properties involves the three property editors you saw in the last section. However, only one of them, the string property editor, looks familiar in Figure 8.5. Why?

Well, the color and font editors are both implemented as dialog boxes, which means they can't be placed directly within a property sheet. Instead, some representation of the property is displayed in the property sheet and the associated editor is automatically presented to the user when the property is clicked in the property sheet. For example, the foreground property is displayed in the property sheet as a colored area (in this case black). When the user clicks this colored area, the color property editor shown in Figure 8.4 is displayed. This approach of providing a preview of a property value that links to the property's editor is very powerful and helps make the whole property editing process much more intuitive.

One other issue relating to property sheets is how they are used within a visual design tool. Because users interact with property sheets on an individual bean basis, it makes sense that a property sheet should appear whenever an individual bean is being edited. Most visual design tools enable you to graphically lay out beans in some kind of container such as a window or dialog box. Users are free to drag beans around and resize them however they choose. When it comes to editing a bean, most tools require the user to double-click the bean in question. It is at this point that a property sheet for the bean is displayed, enabling you to edit the bean's properties.

Figure 8.6 shows the layout of a few beans in the BeanBox test container that ships with the Bean Developer's Kit by JavaSoft. You learn much more about the Bean Developer's Kit in Chapter 9, "Bean Construction Basics."

In this example, a few beans are shown in the BeanBox test container, which provides a test environment similar in function to what most visual design tools offer. There are three beans shown in this figure: a button bean, a juggling animation bean, and a molecule bean. The bean of interest to this discussion is the button bean, because you've already seen what the property sheet looks like for this bean (Figure 8.5). In fact, the property sheet shown in Figure 8.5 displays the properties with the exact settings for the bean that is displayed in Figure 8.6. This is evident by the "Press Me" label of the button and the font to which it is set.

Figure 8.6.
Some beans laid out in the BeanBox test container.

I don't want to get into any details here about the BeanBox program because you learn all about it in the next chapter. I mainly just want you to see the relationship between a bean in a visual editor and its associated property sheet that is displayed when the bean is double-clicked.

Customizers

For those cases in which a property sheet doesn't quite do a bean justice, JavaBeans provides another option: customizers. Bean customizers are more elaborate visual interfaces that enable you to edit beans in a hopefully more intuitive fashion. Customizers are similar to property sheets in that they enable you to edit a complete bean, but they differ in that they take on a totally different approach to presenting the individual property editors. Most customizers act like wizards, which are visual editors that gather property information in a multiple-step process. The purpose of offering this route to bean editing is to give bean developers the freedom to implement more intuitive visual interfaces.

Customizers often attempt to provide editing facilities within the context of a series of questions. By presenting property information in the form of questions, the task of customizing a bean is made much simpler. Of course, for simple beans customizers are probably overkill; they are primarily useful for beans that would be complex to edit using normal property sheets. Keep in mind that customizers are designed and implemented entirely by bean developers. JavaBeans supports the use of customizers, but it doesn't go much further than that. All JavaBeans really provides is an interface, Customizer, that must be implemented by customizers. In other words, building a customizer for a bean can involve a significant amount of work on the developer's part. On the other hand, a powerful customizer interface can make a bean infinitely more useful to the end user, so it's often worth the extra development effort.

API Support

None of the customization features you've learned about in this chapter would mean much without the underlying classes and interfaces that make it all happen. You wrap up the chapter with a quick look at the classes and interfaces that make the customization facilities provided by the JavaBeans API a reality. Here are the classes and interfaces that make up the customization portion of the JavaBeans API:

- PropertyEditorManager
- PropertyEditorSupport
- Customizer
- PropertyEditor

> Note: All of these classes and interfaces are covered in much greater detail in Appendix B, "JavaBeans API Quick Reference."

PropertyEditorManager

The PropertyEditorManager class is used to locate the property editor for a property of a given type. Property editors capable of being located by the PropertyEditorManager class must implement the PropertyEditor interface. The PropertyEditorManager class provides a means of registering property types so that their editors can be easily found. For property types that haven't been registered, the PropertyEditorManager class looks for property editors using the name of the property with Editor appended to the end.

PropertyEditorSupport

The PropertyEditorSupport class is a helper class implementing the PropertyEditor interface that is used to make the construction of custom property editors a little easier.

Customizer

The Customizer interface defines the overhead required to provide a complete visual editor for a bean. Classes implementing the Customizer interface are typically derived from the Component class so that they can be used within the context of a dialog box or panel.

PropertyEditor

The PropertyEditor interface defines a means of visually editing a single bean property of a given type. Because JavaBeans provides standard property editors for built-in data types, you are only required to develop property editors for custom data types. The PropertyEditor interface provides a couple of different options in regard to editing a property. It is up to bean developers which specific type of editing they want to provide via the PropertyEditor interface.

Summary

This chapter took you on a tour through the exciting world of bean customization. OK, maybe it wasn't all that exciting, but it was at least informative. You learned in this chapter the reasoning behind JavaBeans providing support for visual bean customization, which is based on the fact that visual application construction is much more straightforward and efficient than brute force programming. From there, you moved on to learn about property editors and property sheets, which provide the core capabilities for beans to be visually customizable. You also learned about a more elaborate approach to visual bean editing that involves customizers. You finished up the chapter by peering into the specific classes and interfaces that make the customization support in JavaBeans tick.

This chapter rounds out this tour of the JavaBeans API. I trust you now have a pretty good understanding of the major features and services offered by the JavaBeans API. With those services in mind, you're ready to press on to more exciting things such as building your own beans!

PART III

Creating Your Own Beans

Bean Construction Basics

This chapter begins a very hands-on part of the book in which you eventually learn how to develop your own beans. Even though you don't actually create any beans in this chapter, you learn all about the tools and techniques necessary to do so. By the end of this chapter, you will have all the information you need to begin constructing and using your own beans. So, if you are anxious to get started developing your own beans, just bear with me through this chapter and I promise you won't be let down throughout the rest of the book.

This chapter recaps the major parts of a bean and what types of decisions you need to make in terms of these parts when you are developing a new bean. With these design concepts out of the way, you move on and learn how to install and configure the Beans Development Kit (BDK). You then move on to possibly the most interesting topic of the chapter: the BeanBox. The BeanBox is a test container in which you can try out beans while you are developing them. You can use the BeanBox to easily test out all aspects of your beans, including visual property editing, event wiring, and bound property management. The chapter finishes off with a look at Java ARchive (JAR) files and how you use them to compress and group beans together for distribution.

You learn about the following major issues in this chapter:

- Bean design basics
- Installing the Beans Development Kit (BDK)
- Testing beans
- Packaging beans for distribution

Designing a Bean

Although beans typically are small development projects in terms of the sheer amount of code involved, the fact that they are reusable makes their initial design very critical. It's important for you to fully evaluate the functional requirements of a bean before you jump into writing code. Of course, this is good wisdom to apply to any programming situation, but it is especially important in JavaBeans because of the nature of bean components and how they are used. For example, the very fact that a bean must be backwardly compatible as it evolves is reason enough to make sure that the interfaces you define are extensible enough to provide room for future functionality.

The planning process you go through when you initially design a bean will pay off in many ways when it comes down to first developing the bean as well as maintaining the bean in the future. Too many programmers fall victim to the urge to get an object working in a hurry without thinking of the larger picture in which it will be used. Even though this narrow-minded approach can work in some limited environments with a certain degree of success, it must be strictly avoided when it comes to JavaBeans. Trying to hack together a bean in a hurry when the overall aim is to make beans widely reusable in a variety of different ways simply isn't smart.

Stepping down from my soap box, let me now soften the tone and add that the initial design phase for a typical bean isn't very involved. Beans usually are such small pieces of software that they just don't warrant a large or complex design. Furthermore, because beans are geared toward being simple and minimal at the very core, it only makes sense that bean developers should carry on with this tradition in the design of beans at a higher level. All I'm really suggesting is that you spend a little time pondering what exactly your bean is going to accomplish, along with how it will be practically used and in what ways it might evolve in the future. Just so you get the idea, let me break these three ideas down as questions to ask yourself while you are designing a bean.

1. What does the bean do?
2. How is the bean used?
3. How might the bean change in the future?

The first question might be the easiest to answer because it is probably the question that drove you to design a bean in the first place. Even so, it's important to clearly identify what the bean is going to accomplish as a piece of reusable software. The second question also is fairly straightforward because you probably already have an application in mind that could use your bean. You might even be developing a bean as a specific part of an application, in which case you decided on making it a bean so that you would have the option of reusing it in other projects. Regardless of the motives that drove you to develop your bean, make sure you have a good idea of how the bean is going to be used by an end user, whether that user is yourself or thousands of developers who are going to buy your bean for use in their own projects.

The third and final question is the one you probably haven't given much thought to because most people tend to think in terms of the present and what problems need to be addressed immediately. However, a little insight on the front end of a bean development effort can make things infinitely easier for you later when the inevitable time comes that you want to add a new feature or alter an old one. Try to assess any potential features or changes you might see as being possible in the future, along with how they impact the bean in its current state. You might see that a small concession in an initial design might leave the door open for future enhancements. On the other hand, you might decide that you are content that your bean is fine for your purposes and that it will never need to evolve. That's a perfectly acceptable attitude to have as long as you understand that it limits your options in the future. How far you want to go in trying to assess the future direction of a bean is ultimately up to you. All I can do is encourage you to at least entertain the thought of making a bean more open for future modification.

Note: I personally know that I'm sometimes fickle and short-sighted enough that I feel better with a design that is very extensible. I like the idea of knowing that decisions I make today are open for change in the future just in case I manage to figure out a better way of doing things. This attitude is actually useful far beyond the realm of programming and JavaBeans, but that's another book!

Now that I've grilled you a little about approaching bean development with at least a minimal amount of planning, it's time to move on to some specifics. The design of a bean ultimately should culminate in a detailed description of the various parts of a bean. The rest of this section is devoted to the design issues surrounding the three primary parts of a bean, which follow:

- Properties
- Methods
- Events

Laying Out the Properties

The heart of a bean is its internal state. Similar to normal Java classes, the internal state of a bean is reflected by the bean's member variables. Properties are public member variables that are accessible externally. Even though all member variables are important to a bean's functionality, properties take on a more critical importance because they enable you to query a bean for information or modify a bean's state from outside the bean. Of course, you are never allowed to directly read or write properties externally; you must always do so through accessor methods.

Even if you aren't sure about all the data your bean will need to function properly, you should make a solid attempt to define all of the bean's properties during the initial design. Trust me, this isn't asking too much. Properties are usually fairly easy to determine because they often directly relate to a piece of functionality. For example, it's pretty obvious that a button bean would need a property representing the label that is drawn on the button. Furthermore, you could define properties for the background and foreground colors of the button.

When you lay out the properties for your bean, be sure to decide whether the property is read-only, write-only, or read/write, because it will impact the accessor methods you have to implement later. Again, this should be a very simple and straightforward task because you've no doubt already thought about the characteristics of the bean that map to properties. You should also decide at this point if any of the properties are bound or constrained, because this will also impact methods you must implement later.

Although defining properties is an important step in the design of a bean, it is by no means something that you can't go back and change later. It might turn out that you will think of some more properties for the bean later based on some new functionality you want to add. By all means, feel free to add or modify the properties of your bean while you are coding. I'm mainly just trying to encourage you to think about a core set of properties to begin with, because they will become the first member variables you define when you begin to code.

Defining Public Methods

After you've determined a set of suitable bean properties, you are ready to decide on some methods that interact with them. Similar to properties, at this point you should focus on the public methods that are going to be accessible outside of the bean. If you happen to already have an idea about non-public methods, feel free to go ahead and make note of them, just don't feel like you have to worry about them just yet. The primary goal is to define the public interface that will be used to access your bean, which is determined by the public methods implemented by the bean.

The first place to start when you are defining public methods is with accessor methods, which enable you to read and write the values of properties. Because you've already defined the properties for the bean, defining accessor methods is a simple task of listing getter and setter methods for each property based on its read/write capabilities. Keep in mind that these methods form the only direct link between a user and your bean's properties.

After you've established your bean's accessor methods, you need to check and see whether any of the bean's properties are bound or constrained. If so, you need to add methods for registering and removing appropriate bound and constrained listeners. This is very straightforward because these methods come in pairs and conform to a strict design pattern.

After the property-related methods are squared away, you need to assess other public methods needed by your bean. These methods are entirely bean dependent, so deciding what other public methods are required of your bean is totally up to you. Typically, public non-accessor methods are used to perform some type of more involved function, as opposed to the simple getting and setting of properties performed by accessor methods. For example, you might have a bean that performs some type of complex calculation that impacts a variety of properties. You obviously would want this functionality available externally, so you would place it in a public method.

Keep in mind that the constructors for your bean should also be defined at this stage. You are free to provide as many or as few constructors as you want; just remember that it's often nice to give users a variety of constructors that use default values for some properties and require less explicit information.

Communicating with Events

The last major design area you need to assess is events. In terms of bean design there are two different ways that events come into play. The first has to do with the events that a bean is capable of firing. The functionality of a bean determines the types of events it is capable of firing. Your bean can fire standard events defined in the Java API, or you can choose to define your own custom events and go from there. In the latter case, remember that you will need to implement a class for each type of custom event you are going to use. Regardless of whether you decide on standard events, custom events, or a mixture of the two, the next step is to define the registration methods for listeners of each type. These methods are very similar to the methods defined for bound and constrained property listeners because they conform to similar design patterns.

The second way in which events come into play when you are designing beans relates to events that a bean handles for itself. For example, a button bean would need to catch and respond to mouse clicks, focus changes, and some key presses. These are the types of things you should decide up front how to handle so you will have less surprises when you start coding. The events processed by a bean basically result in overriding methods that handle different groups of events. Because most of your beans will be derived from an AWT class such as Canvas, these event processor methods will simply be overridden in your bean class. Even so, go ahead and try to determine which ones you plan on overriding and why.

Now What?

After you have carefully designed the three major parts of your bean, you are ready to start actually building the bean. Although the initial design work isn't always the most thrilling part of bean development, it will pay huge dividends when you begin coding. For example, you should be able to put together a pretty solid skeletal bean based on the properties and methods just covered. In other words, by merely defining properties and creating empty methods for the methods you listed in the design of the bean, you will have a pretty good start on your bean class.

With a skeletal bean class in hand, you are ready to push on to the meat of JavaBeans development. Unfortunately, you'll have to wait until the next chapter to get into the details. However, the rest of this chapter covers some critical tool-related issues that are necessities for practical bean development.

Installing the BDK

Turning a bean design into reality wouldn't be possible without the Beans Development Kit (BDK), which is freely available from JavaSoft. You can download the latest version of the BDK from JavaSoft's Web site at `http://www.javasoft.com`. The BDK comes complete with all the classes and documentation necessary to create and test your own beans. Please note that the BDK requires the Java Developer's Kit (JDK) version 1.1 or later, which provides all the core Java functionality used by JavaBeans.

> **Note:** The BDK for Windows 95/NT and Solaris 2.4 and 2.5 and JDK for Windows, Solaris, and Macintosh are included on the CD-ROM accompanying this book. Even so, you might want to check JavaSoft's Web site to ensure that you have the very latest version. Development kits like these tend to evolve very rapidly, so new versions are released periodically.

The custom beans about which you learn in this book were developed using a beta version of the BDK, which has a few caveats in regard to how it must be installed. Because of these subtle installation details, I felt compelled to at least describe how I installed the JDK and BDK so that they work together seamlessly for bean development. Again, you can download both of these development kits for free directly from JavaSoft's Web site.

First, it's important that you install the JDK before the BDK because it has all the core support required of the BDK. Although you are free to install the JDK however you choose, I recommend creating a `jdk` directory just below your root directory. Copy the JDK installation executable to this directory and execute it to install the JDK. The JDK will expand into a `java` directory beneath the `jdk` directory you created.

After you install the JDK, you are ready to install the BDK. Copy the BDK installation executable to the top-level `jdk` directory just as you did with the JDK, and then execute it to install the BDK. Similar to the JDK installation, the BDK will expand into a `beans` directory beneath the `jdk` directory.

Note: When you are finished installing the JDK and BDK, be sure to delete the setup files used for the installation of each. These files are not cleaned up automatically and must be manually deleted.

After you install the JDK and BDK, you should have a directory structure just like the one shown in Figure 9.1.

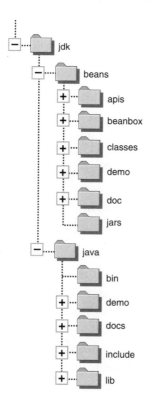

Figure 9.1.

The directory structure for the JDK and BDK installations.

This directory structure is by no means a strict requirement for JavaBeans development, but it is consistent and has worked well for me. The consistency comes from the fact that the JDK and BDK are separate development kits for Java, which implies that they should reside at a similar level hierarchically. By creating a common jdk directory and installing different development kits below this directory, you have a very clear picture of how the development kits relate to each other.

Testing Beans with the BeanBox Test Container

As you've learned throughout the book thus far, one of the key benefits of JavaBeans is the capability for beans to be used in visual application builder tools. You've learned a great deal about the inner workings of JavaBeans that make this type of functionality possible, and now it's time to see it all in action and learn how to work with JavaBeans in a visual environment. The BDK ships with a test container called the BeanBox that enables you to lay out, edit, and interconnect beans visually. The BeanBox isn't intended to be a fully functional development tool for creating applications with beans, but instead is intended to provide a simple example of how beans can be manipulated visually. Even so, the BeanBox is an indispensable tool for bean development because it provides a simple test bed for trying out beans.

The BeanBox is a stand-alone application that is executed using the JDK interpreter. Rather than running it directly using the interpreter, however, the BeanBox comes with a batch file, run.bat, which is in the BDK's beanbox directory and is responsible for setting the CLASSPATH environment variable before executing. You should use this batch file to run the BeanBox because it sets CLASSPATH to values that are specific to using the BeanBox. Following are the contents of the run.bat batch file used to execute the BeanBox:

```
set CLASSPATH=../classes;classes;unjar
java sun.beanbox.BeanBoxFrame
```

As you can see, the batch file first sets CLASSPATH to a few different paths, and then it executes the BeanBox within the JDK interpreter. Don't worry too much about the CLASSPATH settings, because they are based on the internal workings of the BeanBox. To run the BeanBox, just execute the run batch file. When you run the batch file, the BeanBox will execute and display three different windows. Each of these windows performs a different function within the scope of the BeanBox. The first window is the ToolBox, which lists all the beans registered for use with the BeanBox. Figure 9.2 shows the BeanBox's ToolBox window.

Figure 9.2.
The BeanBox's ToolBox window.

As you can see, the ToolBox lists a variety of different available beans. These beans are all demo beans provided with the BDK to demonstrate the development and use of beans. Notice that some of the beans have graphical icons associated with them. These beans use a bean information class to specify the icon to be displayed in visual development environments. Other beans are listed in the ToolBox by name only.

The second window associated with the BeanBox is the main container window, which is shown in Figure 9.3.

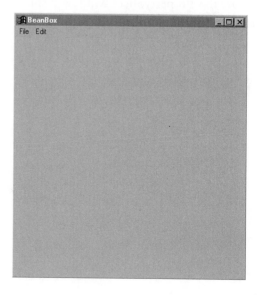

Figure 9.3.
The BeanBox's main container window.

The main container window is the central BeanBox window because it is where you actually lay out beans. The main container window is very similar in function to form windows in other types of visual development environments such as Visual Basic. This window has two menu items, File and Edit, which enable you to load and save BeanBox files and connect beans together.

The last window in the BeanBox is the PropertySheet window, which lists the properties associated with the currently selected bean. Figure 9.4 shows how the PropertySheet window looks.

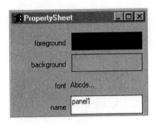

Figure 9.4.
The BeanBox's PropertySheet window.

This window is responsible for providing the visual editing capabilities of the BeanBox because it displays a property editor for each property defined in a bean. When you first run the BeanBox, the PropertySheet window displays the properties for the BeanBox container itself. You can try to edit these properties by clicking one of them with the mouse. For example, try clicking the background property to change the background color for the container. Figure 9.5 shows the property editor dialog box displayed for changing the background color.

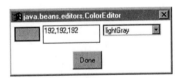

Figure 9.5.
The property editor dialog box for the background color property.

This property editor dialog box enables you to easily change the background color for the container by either entering RGB (Red, Green, Blue) colors or by selecting a standard color from a drop-down list. Try selecting a different color and clicking Done to see how it affects the container.

Note: For beans that have an associated customizer, the Edit menu in the BeanBox provides a Customize command that runs the customizer on the bean.

Working with Beans in the BeanBox

Working with beans in the BeanBox is very simple and demonstrates the real benefit of visual editing with beans. The first thing you do is select a bean from the ToolBox and add it to the main container window. You do this by clicking a bean's name or icon in the ToolBox window, which turns the mouse pointer into a cross. You then click the container window in the location where you want the bean to be placed. A new bean will appear in the location with a default size and set of properties.

Try laying out one of the demo beans that comes with the BDK. Click the OurButton bean in the ToolBox window, and then click somewhere in the container window to place the bean. After you do this, the container window should look similar to Figure 9.6.

Figure 9.6.
The main container window after adding an OurButton bean to the BeanBox.

Notice that the new bean is drawn with a hashed boundary. This indicates that the bean is the currently selected bean, which means that the PropertySheet window reflects the properties for this bean. Beans are selected by default when you add them to the container window. To select a bean that isn't selected, just click outside of the bean in the area where the hashed boundary is to appear. Some beans enable you to click anywhere on them to select them, but in the beta version of the BDK this behavior is somewhat inconsistent. The version of the BeanBox in the final release of the BDK will no doubt be more robust.

You're going to be using the OurButton bean you just laid out to control an animation bean in a moment, but first you need to change its label property. You accomplish this through the PropertySheet window, where you must change the bean's label property to Start Animation. Now you need to add one more OurButton bean, so follow the same steps you just went through by clicking the bean in the ToolBox and positioning it in the container. Then edit its label property and set the value to Stop Animation. After you've done this, the container window should look similar to Figure 9.7.

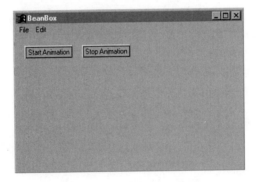

Figure 9.7.
The main container window after adding both OurButton beans to the BeanBox.

Now it's time to throw in a little excitement by adding a bean that displays an animation. Select the Juggler bean from the ToolBox and add it to the container just below the OurButton beans. After you've done this, the container window should look similar to Figure 9.8.

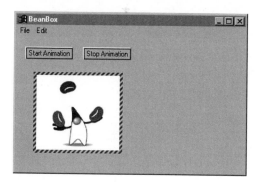

Figure 9.8.
The main container window after adding a Juggler bean to the BeanBox.

If your beans aren't quite lined up the way they are in the figure, feel free to move them around. You can do this by selecting one of the beans, clicking the hashed border, and holding down the button while you drag the mouse. This enables you to move the bean around in the container. You also can resize beans that support resizing by clicking in one of the corners on the hashed border and dragging the mouse. There is no need to resize any of the beans in this example because they automatically size themselves to fit their content.

Wiring Beans Together with Events

A particularly useful function of the BeanBox is wiring beans together using events. For example, you can easily connect a bean's event to a public method defined in another bean, which effectively ties the two beans together functionally. The BeanBox enables you to do this visually, which makes the task very simple. As you might guess, the two buttons you've laid out thus far are perfectly situated to control the Juggler animation bean. So, let's go ahead and wire them up to see what happens.

Select the first OurButton bean and click the Edit menu in the BeanBox. You'll see an Events menu item that has a group of event types beneath it. Select the action event menu item and then the `actionPerformed` command beneath it. You'll see a line originating from the button that moves as you move the mouse around. Move the mouse over the Juggler bean and click to connect the button bean's action event to the Juggler bean. You'll be presented with a dialog box that shows the available target methods defined in the Juggler bean. Figure 9.9 shows this dialog box.

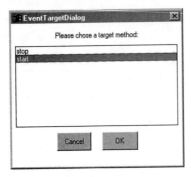

Figure 9.9.
The EventTargetDialog box for the Juggler bean.

Select the start() method from the dialog box to signify it as the receiver of the event action. When you do this, the start() method is called on the Juggler bean any time the first OurButton bean is pressed. Repeat this procedure to connect the second OurButton bean to the stop() method of the Juggler bean. After you do this, you can test the buttons by clicking them to start and stop the animating Juggler bean. It's as simple as that!

> Note: It's worth noting that the version of the BeanBox available as of this writing (beta 3) is a little tricky to use at times. The selection of beans tends to be inconsistent at times, occasionally resulting in the addition of a new bean when you really wanted to select an existing bean. I think it's safe to assume that the final version of the BeanBox will be much more robust.

Saving Your Work

You can easily save the contents of the BeanBox using the Save command in the File menu. When you save the contents of the BeanBox, the persistence features of JavaBeans are used to store the state of each bean. You then can reload the beans later using the Load command, in which case the persistence features are used to reconstruct the beans just as you left them.

Packaging Beans with JAR Files

After you have developed and tested your bean, you have to consider packaging it so others can use it. Things aren't so simple as the good old days of Java 1.0 where you could just provide executable class files and everyone would be happy. The standard method of distributing beans involves packaging them into compressed archives called JAR (Java ARchive) files. JAR files are similar to other types of compressed files such as ZIP files or TAR files, except they are specifically tailored around packaging Java classes and resources.

> Note: JAR files use a compression scheme based on the one used in ZIP files. Check out the java.util.zip package in the JDK 1.1 documentation for more information.

JAR files basically enable you to group the classes and resources for beans into one compressed unit to organize them and conserve space. Bean resources can include anything from images and sounds to custom resources such as data files. Being able to group resources with the classes for a bean cleans up the delivery of beans considerably because it eliminates the chore of keeping up with a bunch of different support files. Additionally, having a single file for beans being delivered over an Internet connection results in only one HTTP transaction, which is much faster than transferring multiple individual files.

Just in case you are thinking maybe you don't need to worry about bundling your bean in a JAR file, understand that most visual development tools expect beans to be included in JAR files. The BeanBox is an example of such a tool because it strictly looks for JAR files when it assembles the beans in its ToolBox. You might be wondering how a tool such as the BeanBox knows what beans are included in a JAR file, because JAR files ultimately are just a bunch of classes and associated resources. The answer to this question is found in manifest files, which are text files that describe the beans contained in a JAR file, along with encryption information if so desired. The encryption information is used for code signing purposes, which is another whole topic beyond the scope of this chapter. You learn more about bean security and code signing in Chapter 15, "Advanced JavaBeans." You learn more about manifest files in the next chapter when you build your first custom bean.

> Note: JAR files are capable of storing multiple beans. Just as with individual beans, the manifest file is responsible for formally listing all the beans contained in a JAR file.

Version 1.1 of the JDK ships with a tool called jar that enables you to create and modify JAR files. It works similar to PKZip or tar in that it enables you to combine and compress multiple files into a single archive. The jar utility also enables you to sign individual files in a JAR file for security purposes. The syntax for jar follows:

```
jar Options Files
```

The Files argument specifies the files to be used when working with a JAR file and varies according to the options. The Options argument specifies options related to how the jar utility manipulates a JAR file. Following is a list of the jar utility options:

- c—Specifies that a new archive is to be created.
- m—Specifies that the manifest file for the archive is to be created based on an external manifest file. The external manifest file is provided as the second file in the list of files following the options.
- t—Used to list the contents of an archive.
- x *File*—Extracts all the files in an archive, or just the named files if additional files are provided.
- f—Used to specify the name of the archive in question, where the name is provided as the first file in the file list. The f option is used in conjunction with all the other options.
- v—Causes the jar utility to provide verbose output, which results in greater information about what actions are being performed on a JAR file.

> Caution: Unlike most command-line utilities, the jar utility doesn't require the use of a / or - when specifying options.

So you can see how the jar utility works in a practical scenario, following is a jar command that compresses and adds all the Java classes in the current directory into a JAR file called BigStuff:

```
jar cf BigStuff.jar *.class
```

In this example, the c and f options are used to specify that a new archive is to be created with the name BigStuff.jar. The files to be added to the archive are specified by the wildcard *.class. As you can see, there's nothing complicated about JAR files. Granted, it gets a little messier when you start dealing with code signing, but you don't have to worry with any of that at this point.

Summary

This chapter took a sharp turn from the first two parts of the book by tackling some practical issues concerning bean development. You first learned about initial design issues relating to beans, including the importance of carefully defining the different parts of a bean before you write any code. You then moved on to the installation of the Beans Development Kit (BDK), which has a few caveats that must be dealt with in order for things to work smoothly. From there, you dove straight into visual bean manipulation with the BeanBox test container. The BeanBox is perhaps the most significant tool provided by the BDK because it enables you to test the capabilities of your beans in a minimal environment. Finally, you ended the chapter with a look at JAR (Java ARchive) files, which enable you to compress the classes and resources for a bean into a single file for distribution.

This chapter covered a variety of different topics to prepare you for developing your own beans from scratch. You now are ready to get into the specifics of building your own beans and testing them, which is ultimately the most fun part of this book if you like to see things in action. Sure, concepts and theories are great, but at some point you want to see something real. The next chapter takes you through the design and development of a complete bean, which will put much of your newfound knowledge to the test and enable you to have some fun along the way.

CHAPTER 10

A Fancy Button Bean

This chapter marks your first foray into practical bean development, which is the focus of this part of the book. Throughout this chapter you learn to develop a bean that is somewhat similar in function to the standard AWT button provided in Java 1.1, but a little fancier. You develop this bean entirely from scratch, while observing the design suggestions covered in Chapter 9, "Bean Construction Basics," along the way. The bean you create in this chapter serves as a great starting point for developing other beans because it tackles many of the common issues related to building practical beans. By the end of the chapter, you will have both the know-how and source code necessary to start building beans of your own.

Along with developing the code for a custom bean in this chapter, you will see how to test the bean in the BeanBox test container, which is a vital part of the development process. You'll find that the BeanBox is a fun way to try out your beans as you develop them. You finish the chapter by brainstorming some areas in which you can improve and extend the bean on your own.

You learn the following major topics in this chapter:

- Designing the fancy button bean
- Developing the code for the fancy button bean
- Testing the fancy button bean
- Ideas for enhancing the fancy button bean

Designing the Fancy Button Bean

As you learned in Chapter 9, the first step in building any bean is to come up with a preliminary design. This design should be carried out to some degree of detail before embarking on the actual coding of the bean. The bean you develop in this chapter is a *fancy button bean*, meaning that it functions similarly to the standard Java AWT button but adds some functionality to make it a little fancier. So that you can see how the design for the fancy button bean comes together, it doesn't derive from the AWT Button class but instead implements all of its own button functionality from scratch.

There are a few things about the fancy button bean that set it apart from the standard AWT button. Similar to the AWT button, the fancy button bean enables you to set the label for the button to any text you choose. However, it also enables you to set the font for the label, which can be one of a variety of typefaces in virtually any size. The fancy button bean knows how to automatically resize itself to accommodate the varying sizes of the label based on the font selection. Another neat feature of the fancy button bean is that you can change the background and foreground colors. The background color corresponds to the face of the button, and the foreground color determines the color of the label text.

The fancy button bean also supports a feature in which it can be used to represent an on/off state, much like a checkbox. In this mode, instead of automatically raising after you click it, the button remains down. Another mouse click restores it to its normal position. This feature is useful in toolbars, where some buttons reflect a two-state option. A good example is the bold button in some popular word processor toolbars, which remains down when clicked to indicate that the bold option is turned on.

Now that you have an idea of what the fancy button does, let's move on to designing some specifics about it. Recall from the previous chapter that the design of a bean can be broken down into three major parts: properties, methods, and events. The rest of this section focuses on the fancy button bean and the design of these major functional parts.

Properties

The properties for the fancy button bean must somehow represent the information required to support the functionality you just learned about. Fortunately, you don't have to specifically define all these properties yourself because you are going to derive the bean from an existing AWT class, which provides a great deal of overhead, including some very useful properties. The AWT class I'm referring to is Canvas, which represents a rectangular area onto which you can draw or trap input events from the user. The Canvas class provides the base functionality typically required of graphical beans, including background color, foreground color, name, and font properties. Actually, most of this functionality is provided by the Component class, which is the parent of Canvas.

Even though the Canvas and Component parent classes help out, you still must provide some properties of your own. You know the fancy button bean will have a label, so you can start off with a string label property. You also know the bean must support a sticky mode, which can easily be represented by a boolean property. Because the bean supports a sticky mode, you also need a property to keep track of whether the bean is up or down. Another boolean property serves this purpose just fine. These three properties are pretty well sufficient for modeling the high-level functionality required of the bean. In fact, combined with the properties provided by the Canvas class, these properties form the full set of properties for the fancy button bean. Keep in mind that although these are the only three properties you must define yourself, there could be other member variables in the fancy button bean that aren't exposed as properties. You'll learn about these member variables when you start writing the actual code in the "Developing the Fancy Button Bean" section.

Following are the properties required of the fancy button bean:

- Label
- Sticky mode (on/off)
- Button state (up/down)

Methods

Now that you've defined the properties, it's time to move on to determine the public methods required of the fancy button bean. The easiest place to start is with the accessor methods for the bean. You already know the properties for the bean, so determining the accessor methods you need is pretty easy. Both the label and sticky mode properties for the bean are readable and writable, so you will need a pair of accessor methods for each of them. The property representing the bean's up/down state is a little different, because the state is determined by the user clicking the button. In other words, this property shouldn't be directly writable like the other two properties; instead, it should always be set indirectly by interacting with the button visually. So, for this property you only need one accessor method: a getter method.

Recall that the fancy button bean is supposed to resize itself based on the typeface and size of the font for the label text. This is necessary because selecting a larger font requires more physical space on the bean's surface to display the label text. Knowing that the bean must resize itself whenever the font property's value changes, what do you think this means in terms of accessor methods? If you're thinking that you must override the setter method for the font property, you are exactly right. It turns out that the setter method for the font property is defined in the Component class, along with the font property itself. By overriding it in the fancy button bean, you can easily resize the bean after setting the new font value.

Beyond accessor methods, you have to consider the other public methods that the bean must provide. It turns out that the fancy button bean needs only two other public methods. The first of these, paint(), is overridden from the parent Canvas class to enable the bean to paint itself. The paint() method is pretty much required of all graphical beans because it provides a central location for placing all of a bean's drawing code. The other public method required of the bean isn't quite as obvious: It is the getPreferredSize() method, which calculates and returns the preferred size of the bean based on its current state. This method is necessary only because the fancy button bean has a preferred size based on the label text and font.

Following are the public methods required of the fancy button bean:

- Label property getter/setter methods
- Sticky mode property getter/setter methods

- Button state property getter method
- Overridden font property setter method
- Overridden `paint()` method
- Overridden `getPreferredSize()` method

Events

The last part of the fancy button bean you must focus on at this stage is events. Because the bean is a button, it's necessary for it to fire an action event when the user clicks it. This is what enables the bean to be wired to other beans or applications in order to trigger them with a button click. Because the event fired in this case is an action event, part of supporting it is providing event listener registration methods. A pair of these methods is all you need to support the addition and removal of action event listeners.

The actual firing of the action event is another issue altogether. The bean is required to support some type of mechanism by which an action event is passed on to all the listeners registered. This mechanism must be handled by a single event-processing method that iterates through the listeners and dispatches the event to each one appropriately.

The final area of interest relating to events is how the bean processes events for itself. It's one thing to be able to broadcast events to others, but the fancy button bean must also manage events that occur within itself. For example, when the user clicks the bean it must change its appearance to show the button pressing down. The events that the bean must respond to consist of focus changes, mouse clicks, mouse drags, and key presses. The focus change events are necessary to process because the button draws a focus rectangle on its surface whenever it has focus. The mouse click-and-drag events must be processed in order for the bean to change its state appropriately and act like a button. Finally, the key press events must be processed to provide a keyboard interface for the bean and simulate a mouse button click for keys like the Enter key. These events are processed in individual event processor methods that are overridden from the bean's parent class.

Following are the event-related methods required of the fancy button bean:

- Action event listener registration methods
- Action event-processing method for firing events

- Focus event-processing method
- Mouse click event-processing method
- Mouse drag event-processing method
- Key press event-processing method

Developing the Fancy Button Bean

Now that you have a pretty solid design to go by, you're ready to jump right into the code for the fancy button bean. You will probably be pleasantly surprised by how little difference there is between the code for beans and the code for normal Java classes. Beans are, in fact, normal Java classes with support for a few extra facilities such as introspection and serialization. In many cases these extra facilities are handled automatically, so the bean code really does look just like a normal Java class.

In this section you learn about different parts of the code for the fancy button bean. The discussion here tackles small parts of the code, so you might not immediately see how everything fits into the overall bean class structure purely from a code perspective. If you are having trouble with this approach, check out the complete source code for the bean, which is included on the accompanying CD-ROM. The main code for the fancy button bean is in the `FancyButton` class, which appears on the CD-ROM in the file `FancyButton.java`.

Properties and Member Variables

The first place to start in developing the fancy button bean is laying out the properties. Following are the member variable properties for the bean based on the initial design:

```
private String   label;
private boolean  sticky;
private boolean  down;
```

As you can see, these member variables directly correspond to the properties mentioned earlier in the initial design. Notice that they are all built-in Java types, which means that property editors are already provided by JavaBeans for each of them. This means you don't have to do any extra work to provide visual editing support for the fancy button bean's properties. Along with these properties, the bean also requires a few other member variables for internal use:

```
private transient ActionListener   actionListener = null;
private transient boolean          hasFocus;
```

The `actionListener` member is an `ActionListener` interface used to manage the list of action event listeners. This list is used by the action event processing method to fire events to each listener. You learn more about the `actionListener` member later in the chapter when you get into the specifics of how the fancy button bean processes events. The `hasFocus` member is used to keep track of the focus state of the bean. The focus is important to keep up with because it affects the visual appearance of the bean.

You might be a little curious as to why both of these member variables are declared as being transient. If you recall from Chapter 7, "Persistence: Saving Beans for a Rainy Day," transient member variables are those that aren't saved and restored through bean persistence. The `actionListener` and `hasFocus` member variables represent information that is specific to a particular session, meaning that it isn't necessary to save them persistently as part of the bean's state. That sums up all the member variables for the bean. Let's move on to the constructors!

Constructors

The fancy button bean provides two constructors: a default constructor and a detailed constructor that takes all three properties as arguments. Following is the code for both of these constructors:

```
public FancyButton() {
  this("Push Me", false, false);
}

public FancyButton(String l, boolean s, boolean d) {
  // Allow the superclass constructor to do its thing
  super();

  // Set properties
  label = l;
  sticky = s;
  down = d;
  setFont(new Font("Dialog", Font.PLAIN, 12));
  setBackground(Color.lightGray);

  // Enable event processing
  enableEvents(AWTEvent.FOCUS_EVENT_MASK |
  ➡AWTEvent.MOUSE_EVENT_MASK |
    AWTEvent.MOUSE_MOTION_EVENT_MASK | AWTEvent.KEY_EVENT_MASK);
}
```

The first constructor simply calls the second constructor with default property values. The second constructor is responsible for actually doing all the work. This constructor begins by calling the superclass constructor and then moves on to set all the properties. Notice that the two inherited properties, font and background color, are set by calling their setter methods instead of directly setting the member variables. This is a result of the fact that properties are always declared as private, which means that you are required to use a setter method to access them. In this case, it works out well because the fancy button bean provides its own setter method for the font property.

With the properties set, the constructor moves on to enabling a group of events for the bean to process by calling the enableEvents() method. If it didn't call this method, the bean would be incapable of directly trapping any events. The purpose of selectively enabling certain events is to optimize the event-handling procedure by only looking for events in which you are specifically interested. In this case, the fancy button bean is interested in focus, mouse click, mouse move, and key press events.

Accessor Methods

Moving right along, the next piece of the bean puzzle is accessor methods, which provide access to bean properties. Following is the code for the label property's accessor methods:

```
public String getLabel() {
  return label;
}

public void setLabel(String l) {
  label = l;
  sizeToFit();
}
```

The getLabel() getter method is pretty self-explanatory in that it simply returns the value of the label member variable. The setLabel() setter method is slightly more involved in that it calls the sizeToFit() method after setting the label member variable. The sizeToFit() method, about which you learn in detail in the "Support Methods" section, is responsible for determining the optimal button size based on the label and font.

The accessor methods for the sticky property, isSticky() and setSticky(), are very minimal in that they simply get and set the value for the sticky member variable, with no additional functionality. Likewise, the getter method for the button state, isDown(), simply returns the value of the down member variable. Things get a little more interesting when you get to the overridden setter method for the font property, setFont(), which follows:

```
public void setFont(Font f) {
  super.setFont(f);
  sizeToFit();
}
```

The whole point of overriding this method is to make sure the bean is resized when any change occurs in the value of the font property. Notice that the superclass setFont() method is called to perform the actual setting of the property before the bean is resized with a call to sizeToFit().

Public Methods

There are two important public methods in the bean to look at now: paint() and getPreferredSize().The paint() method is used to paint the visual appearance of the bean; its source code follows:

```
public synchronized void paint(Graphics g) {
  int width = size().width;
  int height = size().height;

  // Paint the background with 3D effects
  g.setColor(getBackground());
  g.fillRect(1, 1, width - 2, height - 2);
  g.draw3DRect(0, 0, width - 1, height - 1, !down);
  g.setColor(Color.darkGray);
  if (down) {
    g.drawLine(1, height - 3, 1, 1);
    g.drawLine(1, 1, width - 3, 1);
  }
  else {
    g.drawLine(2, height - 2, width - 2, height - 2);
    g.drawLine(width - 2, height - 2, width - 2, 1);
  }

  // Paint the foreground text
  g.setColor(getForeground());
  g.setFont(getFont());
  FontMetrics fm = g.getFontMetrics();
  if (down)
    g.drawString(label, ((width - fm.stringWidth(label)) / 2) + 2,
      ((height + fm.getMaxAscent() - fm.getMaxDescent()) / 2) + 1);
  else
    g.drawString(label, (width - fm.stringWidth(label)) / 2,
      (height + fm.getMaxAscent() - fm.getMaxDescent()) / 2);
```

```
  // Paint the focus rect
  if (hasFocus) {
    g.setColor(Color.gray);
    g.drawRect(4, 4, width - 8, height - 8);
  }
}
```

The paint() method starts off by getting the width and height of the bean, filling the background, and painting a 3D effect around the edges. Notice that the 3D effect is painted differently depending on the value of the down member variable. The foreground label text is painted next by selecting the appropriate font and calculating the coordinates so that the text is centered within the bean. Finally, if the hasFocus member variable is set to true, a focus rectangle is drawn on the bean to indicate that it has the input focus.

The getPreferredSize() method is used to return the favored size of the bean to any interested party, including itself. When I say "favored size" I mean the ideal visual size of the bean so that the label text is positioned in the bean with a proper spacing from the edges. The calculation of this size takes into account the selected font along with the label text. Following is the code for the getPreferredSize() method:

```
public Dimension getPreferredSize() {
  // Calculate the preferred size based on the label text
  FontMetrics fm = getFontMetrics(getFont());
  return new Dimension(fm.stringWidth(label) + TEXT_XPAD,
    fm.getMaxAscent() + fm.getMaxDescent() + TEXT_YPAD);
}
```

Event Registration Methods

The event registration methods in the fancy button bean are used to enable the addition and removal of listeners for the bean's action events. The code for these methods follows:

```
public synchronized void addActionListener(ActionListener l) {
  actionListener = AWTEventMulticaster.add(actionListener, l);
}

public synchronized void removeActionListener(ActionListener l) {
  actionListener = AWTEventMulticaster.remove(actionListener, l);
}
```

These methods simply add and remove action listeners from the actionListener vector, which is the ActionListener interface used to keep up with what receives action events. The listeners themselves are managed by the underlying AWTEventMulticaster class, which is a helper class in the Java API designed to keep track of event listeners.

Event-Processing Methods

The fancy button bean provides a variety of event-processing methods, primarily because the bean must listen for a few different types of input events to function properly. The first of these methods, processActionEvent(), isn't related to processing an input event, however; instead, it is used to dispatch action events to all the registered action event listeners. Following is the code for this method:

```
protected void processActionEvent(ActionEvent e) {
  // Deliver the event to all registered action event listeners
  if (actionListener != null)
    actionListener.actionPerformed(e);
}
```

The processActionEvent() method is responsible for firing actionPerformed events to all registered event listeners. It does this by calling the actionPerformed() method on the actionListener member, which represents a chain of event listeners. The actionPerformed() method is the only method defined in the ActionListener interface, and is typically called any time an action occurs in an event source such as a bean. In the case of the fancy button bean, an action is defined as a button push, but an action can mean other things in other beans.

There are four other event-processing methods used by the fancy button bean, although they act a little differently than processActionEvent(). Following is the code for the first of these methods, processFocusEvent():

```
protected void processFocusEvent(FocusEvent e) {
  // Get the new focus state and repaint
  switch(e.getId()) {
    case FocusEvent.FOCUS_GAINED:
      hasFocus = true;
      repaint();
      break;

    case FocusEvent.FOCUS_LOST:
      hasFocus = false;
      repaint();
      break;
  }

  // Let the superclass continue delivery
  super.processFocusEvent(e);
}
```

This method is called whenever the focus for the bean changes. Its only function is to monitor changes in the bean's focus and update the appearance of the bean accordingly. The processMouseEvent() method is a little more interesting in that it responds to mouse button presses and releases. Following is the code for this method:

```
protected void processMouseEvent(MouseEvent e) {
  // Track mouse presses/releases
  switch(e.getId()) {
    case MouseEvent.MOUSE_PRESSED:
      down = !down;
      repaint();
      break;

    case MouseEvent.MOUSE_RELEASED:
      if (down && !sticky) {
        fireActionEvent();
        down = false;
        repaint();
      }
      break;
  }

  // Let the superclass continue delivery
  super.processMouseEvent(e);
}
```

The processMouseEvent() method is responsible for trapping mouse button presses and releases and making sure the bean behaves appropriately. When the mouse button is pressed, the down member variable is toggled and the bean is repainted. However, when the mouse button is released, the down and sticky member variables are first checked to determine the state of the button. If the bean isn't in sticky mode and is down, an action event is fired by the fireActionEvent() method, which you learn about in the "Support Methods" section. The down member variable is then set to false and the bean is repainted.

The processMouseMotionEvent() method is used to respond to events related to the movement of the mouse. Following is the code for this method:

```
protected void processMouseMotionEvent(MouseEvent e) {
  // Track mouse drags
  if (e.getId() == MouseEvent.MOUSE_DRAGGED && !sticky) {
    Point pt = e.getPoint();
    if ((pt.x < 0) || (pt.x > size().width) ||
        (pt.y < 0) || (pt.y > size().height)) {
      if (down) {
```

```
        down = false;
        repaint();
      }
    }
    else if (!down) {
      down = true;
      repaint();
    }
  }

  // Let the superclass continue delivery
  super.processMouseMotionEvent(e);
}
```

The processMouseMotionEvent() method is responsible for detecting mouse drags and making sure the bean behaves properly. The only purpose of responding to mouse drags is so the bean button raises up when the mouse is dragged off it, providing it's not in sticky mode. (In sticky mode, drags have no meaning because the bean changes state as soon as the mouse button is pressed.) If the bean isn't in sticky mode, the coordinates of the mouse are checked by the processMouseMotionEvent() method to see if they fall within the bean's bounding rectangle. If not, processMouseMotionEvent() restores the bean button to its raised position by setting the down member to false. If the mouse is within the bounding rectangle for the bean and the bean is raised, the down member is set to true.

The last of the event-processing methods is the processKeyEventMethod(), which is used to respond to key presses. Following is the code for this method:

```
protected void processKeyEvent(KeyEvent e) {
  // Simulate a mouse click for certain keys
  if (e.getKeyCode() == KeyEvent.VK_ENTER ||
    e.getKeyChar() == KeyEvent.VK_SPACE) {
    if (sticky) {
      down = !down;
      repaint();
    }
    else {
      down = true;
      repaint();
      fireActionEvent();
      down = false;
      repaint();
    }
  }

  // Let the superclass continue delivery
  super.processKeyEvent(e);
}
```

The processKeyEventMethod() is used to provide a keyboard interface for the bean. If the bean has focus and the Return or Spacebar key is pressed, it is treated just like clicking the mouse on the bean. The mouse click is simulated by setting the down member to true, firing an action event by calling fireActionEvent(), and then setting the down member to false. This is kind of a tricky way to get extra functionality without doing much work, which is something I'm always in favor of!

> **Note:** You might be a little confused at this point about the processXXXEvent() methods, because one of them is being used to dispatch events whereas the others are used to respond to events. The reason for this apparent inconsistency is that the event-processing methods that respond to events are overridden versions of superclass methods. The original superclass versions are responsible for dispatching the events to listeners, whereas your versions are free to just add response code.
>
> Notice that all four of these methods call their respective superclass versions, which is a sure sign that the superclass methods are doing some additional work. In the case of the processActionEvent() method, there is no superclass version, so it must take on the responsibility of dispatching events to registered listeners.

Support Methods

The fancy button bean uses two private support methods that you haven't learned about yet: sizeToFit() and fireActionEvent(). These two methods provide functionality that the bean needs only internally, which is why they are declared as private. Nevertheless, they play a vital role in the inner workings of the bean. The code for the sizeToFit() method follows:

```
private void sizeToFit() {
  // Resize to the preferred size
  Dimension d = getPreferredSize();
  resize(d.width, d.height);
  Component p = getParent();
  if (p != null) {
    p.invalidate();
    p.layout();
  }
}
```

The `sizeToFit()` method is responsible for sizing the bean to fit the label text with just enough space between the text and the border so that the button looks visually appealing. The `getPreferredSize()` method is used to get the optimal button size, which is then used to resize the bean. Note that calling the `resize()` method alone isn't sufficient to resize the bean; you must also notify the bean's parent to lay out the bean again by calling the `invalidate()` and `layout()` methods on the parent.

The `fireActionEvent()` method is also important to the internal functioning of the bean. Following is its code:

```
private void fireActionEvent() {
  processActionEvent(new ActionEvent(this,
    ➥ActionEvent.ACTION_PERFORMED,null));
}
```

`fireActionEvent()` is a simple method in that it consists of only a single call to the `processActionEvent()` method. The purpose of providing the `fireActionEvent()` method is to clean up the task of firing an action event by hiding the creation of the `ActionEvent` object passed into `processActionEvent()`. This isn't a big deal, but it does make the code calling `fireActionEvent()` in other methods a little cleaner.

Additional Overhead

You've now covered all the source code for the fancy button bean itself. Although the `FancyButton` class is all you really need to have a fully functioning bean, there is actually one other class worth mentioning: `FancyButtonBeanInfo`. If you recall from Chapter 5, "Introspection: Getting to Know a Bean," it is possible to provide explicit information about a bean in an associated bean information class. Part of this explicit information is the graphical icons used to display a bean for selection purposes in application builder tools. It is easy to provide selection icons for a bean through a bean information class. Following is the complete source code for the `FancyButtonBeanInfo` class, which is a bean information class that defines selection icons for the fancy button bean:

```
// FancyButtonBeanInfo Class
// FancyButtonBeanInfo.java

package PJB.Source.Chap10.FancyButton;

// Imports
import java.beans.*;
```

```
public class FancyButtonBeanInfo extends SimpleBeanInfo {
  // Get the appropriate icon
  public java.awt.Image getIcon(int iconKind) {
    if (iconKind == BeanInfo.ICON_COLOR_16x16) {
      java.awt.Image img = loadImage("FancyButtonIcon16.gif");
      return img;
    }
    if (iconKind == BeanInfo.ICON_COLOR_32x32) {
      java.awt.Image img = loadImage("FancyButtonIcon32.gif");
      return img;
    }
    return null;
  }
}
```

The only method defined in the FancyButtonBeanInfo class is getIcon(), which is typically called by application builder tools to retrieve an icon representing the bean. Notice that two icons are actually provided by the bean information class using different resolutions. The first icon is 16×16 pixels in size, and the second is 32×32 pixels. This enables application builder tools some degree of flexibility as to how they represent beans graphically for selection. The BeanBox tool that comes with the BDK specifically uses the 16×16 size icons. Both of the bean icons are provided as GIF 89A images, which is pretty standard for Java. Figure 10.1 shows how the icons for the fancy button bean look.

Figure 10.1.
The bean information icons for the fancy button bean.

There is one final part of the fancy button bean required before the bean can be used in an application builder tool. I'm referring to the manifestation file required of the JAR file in which the bean is placed. If you recall from Chapter 9, beans must be distributed in a JAR file along with an appropriate manifestation file describing the contents of the JAR file.

I'm not going to go into the details of manifest files because you really need to know very little about them in most scenarios. In the simple case of packaging up a bean for distribution, all you have to do is provide a few pieces of information. Signing a file for security purposes is a little more involved, but you don't need to worry about that for now. The code for the fancy button bean's manifestation file, FancyButton.mf, follows:

```
Manifest-Version: 1.0

Name: PJB/Source/Chap10/FancyButton/FancyButton.class
Java-Bean: True
```

As you can see, the manifest file is very simple; you basically just provide the name of your bean class and specify that it is in fact a bean. It is important to note that the package of the bean is specified as the bean's path in the manifest file. This is the only additional overhead you have to place in the JAR file for application builder tools to be able to extract information about your bean.

Of course, before you build the JAR file you still need to compile all of the bean's Java source code files into classes using the JDK compiler (javac). Before doing this, you need to make sure you have the CLASSPATH environment variable set so the compiler can find the bean's classes. This is necessary because the fancy button bean is defined as being part of a package (PJB.Source.Chap10.FancyButton). You basically just need to add the root path above the bean package hierarchy to the listing of paths in CLASSPATH. This directory is the parent directory of the PJB directory. So, if you installed the source code off the CD-ROM into a directory called Stuff, you would end up with a directory structure like this:

```
\Stuff\PJB\Source\Chap10\FancyButton
```

In this case, you would add the path \Stuff to CLASSPATH so that the compiler can locate support classes for the fancy button bean. This setting will also impact beans you develop in later chapters, so even if you don't plan on compiling the fancy button bean right now, you might want to go ahead and set the CLASSPATH variable accordingly. After setting CLASSPATH, you should be able to compile the fancy button bean by executing the following two commands:

```
javac FancyButton.java
javac FancyButtonBeanInfo.java
```

With the bean successfully compiled, you are ready to create the JAR file for it. Unfortunately, creating the JAR file for a bean isn't quite as straightforward as you might think. As you know, the fancy button bean is part of a package, which means that the classes and related resource files for the bean are found within a hierarchical directory structure dictated by the package name. This directory structure has implications that affect how the bean is placed in a JAR file, because classes are always loaded with respect to a package hierarchy. In other words, classes that reside in a package are always referenced from a directory structure that matches the package name, even when the classes are part of a JAR file. So, the classes and resource files for a bean must preserve their directory structure when they are placed in a JAR file.

The package hierarchy of a bean is enforced in a JAR file by way of the manifest file. As you saw a little earlier in this chapter, the fancy button bean's manifest file includes path information based on the package name of the bean. Although the manifest file handles the problem of enforcing a package hierarchy on a bean in a JAR file, it doesn't address a subtle problem in creating the JAR file in the first place. The problem I'm referring to has to do with the fact that the jar utility specifically looks for a bean class file that matches the package directory structure whenever it is used to create a JAR file for a bean. The problem is made more apparent by the fact that the jar utility won't even find a bean class file if the utility is run in the same directory where the file is located. The reason for this is that the jar utility tries to traverse a package directory structure to find the class. The solution is to execute the jar utility from a directory above the package directory structure where the bean files are located. In this case, you need to run the jar utility from the directory just above the PJB directory.

Even though the jar utility expects the bean class to be located within a directory structure, it doesn't automatically know to look for the class files and resources in this structure. This means you must specify explicit paths when you execute the jar utility from the directory above the package hierarchy. So, to build a JAR file that contains the fancy button bean and its resources, execute the following command in the directory above the bean package hierarchy:

```
jar cfm PJB\Source\Chap10\FancyButton\FancyButton.jar
  PJB\Source\Chap10\FancyButton\FancyButton.mf
  PJB\Source\Chap10\FancyButton\*.class
  PJB\Source\Chap10\FancyButton\*.gif
```

Notice in this command that the paths to all the files used by the jar utility are explicitly declared. This is necessary because the utility is being executed from the top of the bean package hierarchy. If you're thinking this seems like a roundabout way of doing things, you're exactly right. However, as of the beta 3 release of the JDK/BDK, this was the only way to build JAR files that contain beans that are part of a package. Hopefully, JavaSoft is working out a better approach for the final release, which might be available by the time you read this, so check the JavaSoft Web site (www.javasoft.com) for the latest information.

There is one other small problem that needs to be addressed in regard to the jar command just described. Many operating system shells don't provide a big enough command-line buffer to enter commands that long. Fortunately, there is an easy solution to this problem. I created a simple batch file that could be used to add any bean and its associated resources to a JAR file, without concerns about the length of the command line. The following is this batch file, which I named beanjar.bat:

```
@echo off
echo Rejar'ing %2...
jar cfm %1\%2.jar %1\%2.mf %1\*.class %1\*.gif %1\*.au
echo Rejar'ing finished.
```

This batch file takes two arguments: a path and a bean name. The path argument describes the relative path of the bean's class files and resources, while the bean name is the name of the main bean class file without the .class extension.

> Note: The beanjar.bat batch file is intended to be an all-purpose utility for creating JAR files for beans. For this reason, it attempts to add all of the classes, images, and sounds for a bean to the JAR file, even if a bean doesn't necessarily use images or sounds. For beans that don't use images or sounds, an error message will appear stating that no files could be found matching the *.gif and *.au wildcards. You can just ignore this error message if your bean doesn't rely on image or sound resources.

Following is an example of creating a JAR file that contains the fancy button bean using the beanjar.bat batch file:

```
beanjar PJB\Source\Chap10\FancyButton FancyButton
```

Keep in mind that this command still needs to be executed from the top of the package directory hierarchy for the bean. After you execute this command, you should have a JAR file that contains the fancy button bean that is ready to be distributed and used.

> Note: Keep in mind that the complete source code and related resources for the fancy button bean are located on the accompanying CD-ROM.

Testing the Fancy Button Bean

I mentioned in the previous section that most application builder tools, including the BeanBox test container, require beans to be packaged as JAR files. You just created a JAR file that contains the fancy button bean, which you will now test in the BeanBox. To add the bean to the BeanBox, you must first copy the JAR file to the `jars` directory beneath your BDK installation. If you installed the BDK according to the instructions in Chapter 9, then the appropriate directory is `\jdk\beans\jars`. The reason for copying the JAR file to this directory is that the BeanBox looks in this directory for all the beans to add to its ToolBox.

> **Note:** As of this writing, the JavaBeans architects were in the process of working out a better way to integrate new beans into the BeanBox. One of the possible solutions was a new menu command under the Edit menu that would let you add beans through a file selection dialog box. You might want to check your version of the BeanBox and see if it supports this functionality.

You launch the BeanBox by executing the `run.bat` batch file, which you learned about in Chapter 9. The BeanBox should appear at this point with your fancy button bean added to the ToolBox. Figure 10.2 shows what the ToolBox looks like with the bean added.

> **Note:** Keep in mind that the `run.bat` batch file alters the CLASSPATH environment variable in order for the BeanBox to run properly. You'll need to manually set CLASSPATH back to its original value before compiling any beans again.

Notice in the figure that the last bean in the ToolBox is the fancy button bean, complete with the 16×16 icon you specified in the bean information class. Add a fancy button bean to the BeanBox by clicking it in the ToolBox and then clicking the main container window. Figure 10.3 shows the newly added fancy button bean.

Figure 10.2.
The BeanBox ToolBox window with the fancy button bean added.

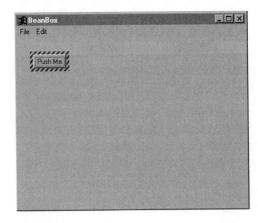

Figure 10.3.
The BeanBox main container window with a fancy button bean added.

Now that the bean has been added to the container window, the real fun begins. Check out Figure 10.4, which shows the PropertySheet window for the fancy button bean.

Figure 10.4.
The BeanBox PropertySheet window for the fancy button bean.

The PropertySheet window shows all the properties for the bean, including the inherited foreground color, background color, font, and name properties, along with your own sticky and label properties. All of these properties are fully editable using the PropertySheet window. Try editing the label and font for the bean, because they impact the appearance the most. Figure 10.5 shows the bean with the label and font properties modified.

Figure 10.5.
The BeanBox main container with a modified fancy button bean.

You should also try out the sticky mode for the bean just to make sure it works · like you expected it to. Also keep in mind that the bean is designed to fire action events whenever it is clicked, so you can easily wire it to other beans just as you did with the OurButton bean in Chapter 9. You already know how to wire buttons to other beans, so I'll let you explore that use of the fancy button bean on your own.

Enhancing the Fancy Button Bean

The last topic of this chapter deals with some areas in which the fancy button bean could be improved. I did all the work for you in developing the guts of the bean, so I want to give you some ideas about some modifications you could make yourself. No matter how good a bean is, there is always room for improvement in one way or another, and this bean is no different. So, following are a few suggestions for ways to add more features to the bean.

- Add support for images
- Add button down/up events for the sticky mode

The first suggestion involves adding support for images, which means that the button would display an image along with the label text. As you are no doubt aware, image buttons are popular in most graphical environments. This addition could be as simple as adding a string property that holds the filename for an image drawn in the paint() method.

The second suggestion is related to the sticky mode of the button. In some situations it would be useful for the button to fire events based on the state changing while it is in the sticky mode. In other words, it would be nice to know when the button is being pushed and raised. This basically consists of adding a new event interface and providing event types for the button being pushed and raised in the sticky mode.

You might not feel up to the challenge of implementing these suggestions just yet, because this was your first bean. However, at least try to think about the conceptual aspects of modifying the bean to support these features, because it will help you a great deal to gain bean design experience.

Summary

This chapter introduced you to the fine art of JavaBeans programming at a practical level; you built your very first bean! Although the theory you've learned throughout the book thus far is important in its own right, this chapter finally shows you how to do something real with JavaBeans. You started the chapter with an idea for a fancy button bean and carried it through a preliminary design and on to a complete implementation. You then took the bean for a spin and finished off by brainstorming some ways to improve it on your own. How empowering!

One of the most important things you learned in this chapter is how little JavaBeans programming differs from traditional Java programming. This chapter should have solidified the fact that beans are just Java classes with some extra features thrown in. This is no accident, seeing how the folks at JavaSoft wanted to make it easy for Java programmers to shift into JavaBeans programming. You should have been able to follow along in this chapter without too much trouble, because the bean you developed is so similar to normal AWT Java classes.

If you liked the practicality and hands-on aspect of this chapter, then you're in luck, because you are facing three more that are similar. Chapter 11, "A Meter Bar Bean," focuses on a meter bar bean that can be used to represent the status of time-consuming operations.

A Meter Bar Bean

Chapter 10, "A Fancy Button Bean," takes you step by step through the design and development of your first complete bean, the fancy button bean. This chapter continues along the same lines by stepping you through the design and development of a meter bar bean. *Meter bars* are often used to represent the status of time-consuming operations such as copying a large file. A meter bar basically consists of a graphical bar that increases in size, depending on the status of an operation. This chapter takes you through the complete design of the meter bar bean and presents you with the complete source code and related resources required to implement the bean.

Although the process of designing and developing a bean is roughly the same for all beans, you'll notice throughout this chapter some differences between the meter bar bean and the fancy button bean you developed in Chapter 10. These differences primarily involve the fact that the meter bar bean performs an entirely different function than the fancy button bean. The design and development of every bean is different in some way; this means that the more beans you create, the easier bean construction gets. That is the main reason Part III, "Creating Your Own Beans," focuses on the creation of four different beans. But enough about other beans, let's get started with the meter bar bean.

This chapter covers the following major topics:

- Designing the meter bar bean
- Developing the code for the meter bar bean
- Testing the meter bar bean
- Ideas for enhancing the meter bar bean

Designing the Meter Bar Bean

You learned a great deal about bean design in Chapters 9, "Bean Construction Basics," and 10, which should make the design of the meter bar bean a little easier to work through. Fortunately, the design of the meter bar bean is straightforward, as you'll soon see. To start, let's go over exactly how a meter bar works, so you'll better understand the requirements of the bean. A meter bar is basically a rectangular area that reflects a measurement of some process or changing value. You can think of a meter bar as being visually similar to a mercury thermometer, in which the mercury line increases with increasing temperature and decreases with decreasing temperature. A meter bar can also increase and decrease, usually to reflect the state of some process or changing value within the context of an application.

The range of values represented by the meter bar bean can be changed easily. Regardless of the range, the meter bar is always drawn in terms of a fractional relationship in which you have a total number of parts and a current number of parts. So, if you wanted to model a thermometer using the meter bar, for example, you would set the total number of parts to 100 degrees Celsius, and then the current number of parts would always be between 0 and 100 degrees. The meter bar would be empty when the current temperature is 0 degrees and full when the current temperature is 100 degrees. At values between 0 and 100 degrees, the bar would be of varying lengths.

Like the fancy button bean, the meter bar bean supports the capability to change the background and foreground colors. The background color corresponds to the area immediately surrounding the meter bar, and the foreground color determines the color of the bar itself. The meter bar doesn't support any type of user interface interaction such as mouse clicks or key presses. This is a reflection of the fact that the meter bar bean is purely an output bean.

Now that you have an idea of what the meter bar does, let's move on to designing some specifics about it. As you might recall from Chapters 9 and 10, the design of a bean can be broken down into three major parts: properties, methods, and events. The rest of this section focuses on the meter bar bean and the design of these major functional parts.

Properties

The properties for the meter bar bean must somehow represent the information required to support the functionality mentioned in the previous section. Similar to the fancy button bean, you don't have to specifically define all these properties yourself. The reason for this is that you are going to derive the meter bar bean from the AWT Canvas class, which represents a rectangular area onto which you can draw or trap input events from the user. In this case, you are only deriving from Canvas, so you can draw the bean. The Canvas class is derived from the Component class, which provides the base functionality typically required of graphical beans, including background and foreground colors, name, and font properties. This brings up a subtle point in regard to the meter bar: The meter bar draws no text, so the font property doesn't make any sense. Therefore, it would be preferable not to see the font property when editing the bean in a visual environment. You'll deal with this situation in the "Additional Overhead" section later in this chapter, when you develop a bean information class for the meter bar bean.

The first property to address in the bean's design is probably the least obvious in terms of its functionality. I'm referring to the orientation property, which specifies whether the meter bar is filled horizontally or vertically. This property is actually quite useful, because it provides some flexibility as to how the meter bar bean appears. Unfortunately, there is no built-in property type for representing the bean's orientation, which means that you will have to develop your own. In addition to developing a class that represents the orientation property type, you must also develop a property editor class so that the property can be edited in an application builder tool. Don't get too worried just yet, because it turns out to be easy to develop custom properties and property editors. You'll find out firsthand in "The HVOrientation Property Class."

Another meter bar bean property that isn't entirely obvious is the raised property, which determines how the 3D border of the bean is drawn. If the raised property is true, then the border is drawn to look raised from the screen. If not, the border is drawn to look inset. This is a simple boolean property, but it adds a certain degree of flair to the meter bar bean.

The last two properties the meter bar bean needs are the most obvious ones, because they are necessitated by the basic functionality of the bean: the current number of parts and total number of parts properties. These two properties form a fractional pair that is used to determine how much of the meter bar is drawn. Keep in mind that the total number of parts property should always be greater than or equal to the current number of parts.

These properties are sufficient for modeling all the functionality requirements of the meter bar bean. Combined with those provided by the parent `Canvas` class, these properties form the full set of properties for the bean. To recap, following are the properties required of the meter bar bean:

- Orientation
- Raised 3D border (`true`/`false`)
- Current number of parts
- Total number of parts

Methods

Now that we've defined the properties, it's time to press onward and determine the public methods required of the meter bar bean. The easiest place to start is with the accessor methods for the bean, because you already have a good idea about the properties for the bean. All the properties in the bean are readable and writable, so you know they will all require a pair of accessor methods. Therefore, the accessor methods for the bean consist of method pairs for each property.

Beyond accessor methods, you also have to consider the other public methods that the bean must provide. It turns out that the meter bar bean needs only a few additional public methods. The first of these, `paint()`, is overridden from the parent `Canvas` class to enable the bean to paint itself. The other public methods required of the bean are provided to add a little more flexibility as to how the bean can be used. These methods are called `incParts()` and `decParts()` and are used to increment and decrement the current number of parts property. This gives bean users an alternative way to change the meter bar state beyond the setter method for the current number of parts property.

Following are the public methods required of the meter bar bean:

- Orientation property getter/setter methods
- Raised property getter/setter methods
- Current number of parts property getter/setter methods
- Total number of parts property getter/setter methods
- Overridden `paint()` method
- Increment/decrement parts methods

Events

Because the meter bar bean is primarily used for output purposes, there really is no need for it to process events in any way. You technically could have the bean fire an event whenever the number of parts reaches the total number of parts, but it doesn't seem like a very important feature at this point. So, the design of the meter bar bean includes no provision for events.

Developing the Meter Bar Bean

With the design for the meter bar bean behind you, it's time to move on to writing the actual code. You'll find that some aspects of the meter bar code are similar to the code for the fancy button bean covered in Chapter 10. This is because all beans share a certain amount of common functionality, such as properties, accessor methods, and so on. Even so, there is plenty of new code in the meter bar bean for you to have fun with!

Check out the complete source code for the meter bar bean, which is included on the accompanying CD-ROM, as you read through this section. The main code for the meter bar bean is in the `MeterBar` class, which appears on the CD-ROM in the file `MeterBar.java`.

Properties and Member Variables

The first area to address in terms of the code for the meter bar bean is the properties. Following are the member variable properties for the bean based on the initial design:

```
private HVOrientation orientation;
private boolean       raised;
private float         numParts;
private float         totalParts;
```

These member variables are the only ones defined in the meter bar bean and directly correspond to the properties mentioned earlier in the "Designing the Meter Bar Bean" section. Unlike the fancy button bean, one of these member variables, `orientation`, is not of a built-in Java type but rather of type `HVOrientation`, which is a custom property class. (You learn more about the `HVOrientation` property type in the following section.) For now, turn your attention toward the other properties defined in the meter bar bean. The rest of the properties in the bean are built-in Java types, which means that JavaBeans has already provided property editors for them. Therefore, you don't have to add any overhead to provide visual editing support for these properties. However, the orientation property is a different story, as you learn next.

The `HVOrientation` Property Class

The orientation property uses the `HVOrientation` property class to specify its property type. This class represents a horizontal or vertical orientation that can be applied to a graphical interface element such as the meter bar bean. The reason for having this class is so that the orientation for the meter bar can be appropriately represented. The different orientations could have been represented by static integers, but this wouldn't be nearly as intuitive for users of the bean. Listing 11.1 contains the complete source code for the `HVOrientation` property class.

Listing 11.1. The complete source code for the `HVOrientation` property class (`HVOrientation.java`).

```
// HVOrientation Property Class
// HVOrientation.java

package PJB.Source.Chap11.MeterBar;

// Imports
import java.io.Serializable;

public class HVOrientation implements Serializable {
  public static final HVOrientation HORIZONTAL =
  ➥ new HVOrientation(0);
  public static final HVOrientation VERTICAL =
  ➥ new HVOrientation(1);
  private int                        orientation;

  // Constructors
  public HVOrientation() {
    this(0);
  }
```

```
  public HVOrientation(String s) {
    this(toInt(s));
  }

  private HVOrientation(int o) {
    orientation = o;
  }

  // Public methods
  public String toString() {
    if (orientation == 0)
      return "Horizontal";
    else
      return "Vertical";
  }

  public boolean equals(Object o) {
    if (o == null || !(o instanceof HVOrientation))
      return false;
    if (orientation != ((HVOrientation)o).orientation)
      return false;
    return true;
  }

  public static HVOrientation valueOf(String s) {
    return new HVOrientation(toInt(s));
  }

  // Private support methods
  private static int toInt(String s) {
    if (s == null || s.toLowerCase().equals("vertical"))
      return 1;
    return 0;
  }
}
```

This might seem like a lot of code for simply representing the type of the orientation property. However, most of the code in this class is used to provide information about the property for use in a variety of situations. I think you'll find this code to be pretty straightforward when you understand its significance.

The whole point of providing a property class is to encapsulate the information about a custom property in one place while providing a well-defined interface. The HVOrientation class accomplishes this by wrapping the horizontal and vertical orientation values in a self-contained unit. Notice in the code that these values are represented by public static final member variables. These standard values can be used anywhere as orientation settings, which is the whole purpose of this class. Also notice that an integer is used to store the internal representation of the orientation property. However, this internal representation is hidden from the outside world, forcing users of the class to always work in terms of the HORIZONTAL and VERTICAL standard values.

The rest of the code in the HVOrientation class is devoted to manipulating the property information in a variety of ways for external access. For example, the toString() method returns a string representation of the property's value. The equals() method compares the property's value with another HVOrientation object to see if they are equal. The last of the public methods in HVOrientation is valueOf(), which returns an HVOrientation object based on a string representation of the property.

There is a private method defined in HVOrientation in addition to the public methods just covered: toInt(). The toInt() method returns the integer representation of an orientation based on a string representation. This method is useful internally for converting string orientations to integer orientations.

The HVOrientationEditor Class

Even though you've successfully created a custom property class to represent the orientation property for the meter bar bean, your job isn't quite done in terms of the orientation property. All editable properties should have a property editor that can be used by application builder tools to provide visual editing capabilities. The property editor for the HVOrientation property class comes in the form of the HVOrientationEditor class. Listing 11.2 contains the complete source code for the HVOrientationEditor property editor class.

Listing 11.2. The complete source code for the HVOrientationEditor property editor class (HVOrientationEditor.java).

```
// HVOrientationEditor Class
// HVOrientationEditor.java

package PJB.Source.Chap11.MeterBar;

// Imports
import java.beans.*;

public class HVOrientationEditor extends PropertyEditorSupport {
  public String getJavaInitializationString() {
    if (((HVOrientation)getValue()).equals(HVOrientation.
    ➥HORIZONTAL))
      return "HVOrientation.HORIZONTAL";
    return "HVOrientation.VERTICAL";
  }
```

```
public String getAsText() {
  if (((HVOrientation)getValue()).equals(HVOrientation.
  ➡HORIZONTAL))
    return "Horizontal";
  return "Vertical";
}

public void setAsText(String text) throws
  java.lang.IllegalArgumentException {
  if (text.toLowerCase().equals("horizontal"))
    setValue(HVOrientation.HORIZONTAL);
  else if (text.toLowerCase().equals("vertical"))
    setValue(HVOrientation.VERTICAL);
  else
    throw new java.lang.IllegalArgumentException(text);
}

public String[] getTags() {
  String result[] = { "Horizontal", "Vertical" };
  return result;
}
}
```

First, note that the naming of the HVOrientationEditor class is not mere convenience; you are required to name property editors the name of the property class, with the text Editor appended to the end. This consistent naming is how JavaBeans can automatically detect property editors and enable them to be used without a bunch of registration overhead.

To understand how the HVOrientationEditor class works, it is important to understand first what it is supposed to do. The role of a property editor class is to provide a means of visually editing a property. You might be thinking that this sounds like a daunting task involving lots of user interface management code. Fortunately, JavaBeans goes a long way in providing built-in functionality to help build property editors, so you often can create a custom property editor with very little work. The HVOrientation property editor is an example of a property editor that requires little additional overhead.

Most of the code you see in the HVOrientationEditor class is devoted to manipulating the HVOrientation property nonvisually. The visual functionality is provided automatically by built-in JavaBeans support classes. The first method in HVOrientationEditor, getJavaInitializationString(), is required to return a string representation of the property value suitable for inclusion in Java code that is setting the value of a property. This method is called by application builder tools to generate the appropriate Java code. In other words, the return value must be a string in a form suitable for an assignment in Java code.

The getAsText() and setAsText() methods provide a means of converting the property to text and back, which is important because many visual tools rely on textual presentation of properties. Possibly the most important method in HVOrientationEditor is the getTags() method, which returns a list of string tags for the property. The getTags() method specifies that the property value is one of a fixed set of tagged values, which in this case is a list of strings. This simple method is responsible for giving the property editor the capability to present the property values as a drop-down list.

Constructors

With the properties squared away, let's move on to the constructors for the meter bar bean. The meter bar bean provides two constructors: a default constructor and a detailed constructor that takes all four properties as arguments. Following is the code for both of these constructors:

```
public MeterBar() {
  this(HVOrientation.HORIZONTAL, false, 50, 100);
}

public MeterBar(HVOrientation o, boolean r, float n, float t) {
  // Allow the superclass constructor to do its thing
  super();

  // Set properties
  orientation = o;
  raised = r;
  numParts = n;
  totalParts = t;
  setBackground(Color.lightGray);

  // Set a default size
  if (orientation.equals(HVOrientation.HORIZONTAL))
    resize(60, 15);
  else
    resize(15, 60);
}
```

The first constructor simply calls the second constructor with default property values. The second constructor is responsible for actually initializing the bean. This constructor begins by calling the superclass constructor, which is pretty standard in AWT-derived classes. The constructor then moves on and sets all the properties, including the inherited background color property.

With the properties set, the constructor then sets the default size for the bean. The bean is sized based on its orientation, which is logical because most horizontal meter bars are wider than they are tall—vice versa for vertical meter bars.

The initial size of the bean in either case is arbitrary, based only on a guess as to the average size of a meter bar in common scenarios.

Accessor Methods

The next part of the meter bar bean to tackle is its accessor methods, which provide access to bean properties. Following is the code for the orientation property's accessor methods:

```
public HVOrientation getOrientation() {
  return orientation;
}

public void setOrientation(HVOrientation o) {
  if (orientation != o) {
    orientation = o;

    // Swap the width and height to reorient the meter bar
    resize(size().height, size().width);
    Component p = getParent();
    if (p != null) {
      p.invalidate();
      p.layout();
    }
  }
}
```

The getOrientation() getter method is self-explanatory, because it simply returns the value of the orientation member variable. The setOrientation() setter method is more involved, because it resizes the bean after setting the orientation member variable. The reason for resizing the bean is so the meter bar will keep the same look, regardless of its orientation. In other words, a horizontal meter bar that is wider than it is tall would look more natural in a vertical orientation that is taller than it is wide. You determine the new size of the bean simply by swapping the existing width and height.

The accessor methods for the raised property, isRaised() and setRaised(), are straightforward in that they simply get and set the value for the raised member variable. The only additional code is the call to repaint() in setRaised(), which forces the bean to repaint itself to reflect the change in its appearance. Following is the code for these accessor methods:

```
public boolean isRaised() {
  return raised;
}
```

```
public void setRaised(boolean r) {
  raised = r;
  repaint();
}
```

The accessor methods for the number of parts property are minimal as well.
Following is the code for them:

```
public float getNumParts() {
  return numParts;
}

public void setNumParts(float n) {
  numParts = Math.max(0.0f, Math.min(totalParts, n));
  repaint();
}
```

The getter method, getNumParts(), simply returns the value of the numParts
member variable. The setter method, setNumParts(), sets the value of the
numParts member variable while making sure the new value isn't greater than
the total number of parts. This method then repaints the bean to reflect the
change in the meter bar position caused by modifying the number of parts.

The last set of accessor methods belongs to the total number of parts property.
Following is the code for these methods:

```
public float getTotalParts() {
  return totalParts;
}

public void setTotalParts(float t) {
  totalParts = Math.max(0.0f, t);
  if (numParts > totalParts)
    numParts = totalParts;
  repaint();
}
```

The getter method, getTotalParts(), not surprisingly just returns the value
of the totalParts member variable. The setter method, setTotalParts(), sets
the value of the totalParts member variable while making sure it is greater
than or equal to zero. This method then checks the value of the numParts member variable and constrains it to the value of totalParts if it is greater. The
method finishes by repainting the bean to reflect the change in the meter bar
position caused by modifying the total number of parts.

Public Methods

There are a few public methods in the bean: paint(), incParts(), and
decParts(). Let's take a look at the paint() method first, because it is the most

involved. Following is the source code for the `paint()` method:

```java
public synchronized void paint(Graphics g) {
  int width = size().width;
  int height = size().height;

  // Paint the background with 3D effects
  g.setColor(getBackground());
  g.fillRect(1, 1, width - 2, height - 2);
  g.draw3DRect(0, 0, width - 1, height - 1, raised);

  // Paint the foreground meter bar
  g.setColor(getForeground());
  if (orientation.equals(HVOrientation.HORIZONTAL))
    g.fillRect(3, 3,
      (int)((numParts * (width - 6)) / totalParts), height - 6);
  else
    g.fillRect(3, height - 3 - (int)((numParts * (height - 6)) /
    ↪totalParts),
      width - 6, (int)((numParts * (height - 6)) / totalParts));
}
```

The `paint()` method starts off by getting the width and height of the bean, filling in the background, and painting a 3D effect around the edges. This code should look somewhat familiar to you, because it is similar to the code used to paint the fancy button bean. The `paint()` method paints the meter bar itself next by selecting the foreground color and filling a rectangle according to the values of the `numParts` and `totalParts` member variables.

The other public methods implemented in the meter bar bean, `incParts()` and `decParts()`, provide a means of incrementing and decrementing the number of parts by a certain amount. These methods each come in two versions: one for incrementing and decrementing by a specific value, and one for incrementing and decrementing by one. The code for these methods follows:

```java
public void incParts(float i) {
  numParts = Math.max(0.0f, Math.min(totalParts, numParts + i));
  repaint();
}

public void decParts(float i) {
  numParts = Math.max(0.0f, Math.min(totalParts, numParts - i));
  repaint();
}

public void incParts() {
  incParts(1.0f);
}

public void decParts() {
  decParts(1.0f);
}
```

The first `incParts()` method increments the number of parts by an amount passed as an argument. It is careful to constrain the newly incremented number of parts against 0 and the total number of parts. You might not immediately see why it is important to constrain the value against 0, because it is being incremented rather than decremented. Well, it is possible to pass a negative number as the amount to increment, in which case the value would really be decremented. This attention to detail and potential misuses of public bean methods is critical in developing robust beans. This `incParts()` method finishes by repainting the bean to reflect the incremented number of parts.

The first `decParts()` method is practically identical to `incParts()`, except it decrements the number of parts. `decParts()` performs the same constraints for the same reasons and finishes by repainting the bean. The second version of each of these methods simply calls the first version, with a value of 1.

Additional Overhead

You've now covered all the source code for the meter bar bean itself. Although the `MeterBar`, `HVOrientation`, and `HVOrientationEditor` classes are all you need to have a fully functioning bean, there is actually one other class that makes the meter bar bean complete: `MeterBarBeanInfo`. Recall from Chapter 10 that the fancy button bean uses a bean information class to specify icons that graphically represent the bean in application builder tools. The `MeterBarBeanInfo` class performs this function, as well as another one that the fancy button bean didn't have to worry about: hiding an inherited property. Listing 11.3 contains the complete source code for the `MeterBarBeanInfo` class.

Listing 11.3. The complete source code for the `MeterBarBeanInfo` bean information class (`MeterBarBeanInfo.java`).

```
// MeterBarBeanInfo Class
// MeterBarBeanInfo.java

package PJB.Source.Chap11.MeterBar;

// Imports
import java.beans.*;

public class MeterBarBeanInfo extends SimpleBeanInfo {
  // Get the appropriate icon
  public java.awt.Image getIcon(int iconKind) {
    if (iconKind == BeanInfo.ICON_COLOR_16x16) {
```

```
      java.awt.Image img = loadImage("MeterBarIcon16.gif");
      return img;
    }
    if (iconKind == BeanInfo.ICON_COLOR_32x32) {
      java.awt.Image img = loadImage("MeterBarIcon32.gif");
      return img;
    }
    return null;
  }

  // Explicit declare the properties
  public PropertyDescriptor[] getPropertyDescriptors() {
    try {
      PropertyDescriptor
        // Inherited properties
        foreground = new PropertyDescriptor("foreground",
        ➥MeterBar.class),
        background = new PropertyDescriptor("background",
        ➥MeterBar.class),
        font = new PropertyDescriptor("font", MeterBar.class),
        name = new PropertyDescriptor("name", MeterBar.class),
        // New properties
        orientation = new PropertyDescriptor("orientation",
        ➥MeterBar.class),
        raised = new PropertyDescriptor("raised", MeterBar.class),
        numParts = new PropertyDescriptor("numParts",
        ➥MeterBar.class),
        totalParts = new PropertyDescriptor("totalParts",
        ➥MeterBar.class);

      // Hide the font property
      font.setHidden(true);

    PropertyDescriptor[] pd = { foreground, background, font,
    ➥name, orientation,
        raised, numParts, totalParts };
      return pd;
    }
    catch (IntrospectionException e) {
      throw new Error(e.toString());
    }
  }
}
```

The first method in the MeterBarBeanInfo class, getIcon(), is almost identical to the same method in the fancy button bean's information class. The only difference is the specification of the GIF files for the icons themselves. These icons are provided as GIF 89a images and are shown in Figure 11.1.

Figure 11.1.
The bean information icons for the meter bar bean.

The second method used in the `MeterBarBeanInfo` class is `getProperty-Descriptors()`, which is used to explicitly specify the properties exposed by the bean. The purpose of implementing this method is to exclude the font property from being exposed by the bean. This is necessary because the inherited font property has no significance to the meter bar bean. The `getPropertyDescriptors()` method requires you to declare every property that is to be exposed by the bean. So, excluding the font property is a simple matter of calling the `setHidden()` method on the property before it is returned by `getPropertyDescriptors()`. Notice that the other inherited properties (foreground, background, and name) are still exposed normally.

Like the fancy button bean, the meter bar bean also requires a manifestation file to be included in the JAR file that contains the bean. The code for the meter bar bean's manifestation file, `MeterBar.mf`, follows:

```
Manifest-Version: 1.0

Name: PJB/Source/Chap11/MeterBar/MeterBar.class
Java-Bean: True
```

No surprises here! The only difference between this manifest file and the one used for the fancy button bean is the name of the bean class and its package association.

Caution: Before you compile the meter bar bean, make sure you have the CLASSPATH environment variable properly set so that the compiler can locate its support classes. In other words, make sure the root path above the bean package hierarchy is included in CLASSPATH. This directory is the parent directory of the PJB directory.

Note: The complete source code and related resources for the meter bar bean are located on the accompanying CD-ROM.

Testing the Meter Bar Bean

As with all custom beans, you must follow a few steps to add the meter bar bean to the BeanBox before you can test it. Once the bean is compiled, you need to create a JAR file containing the bean and its resources. You then copy this JAR file to the jars directory beneath your BDK installation. The BeanBox looks in this directory for all the beans to add to its ToolBox. Following are the steps necessary to get the meter bar bean up and running in the BeanBox:

1. Create a JAR file that contains the bean and its resources, using the jar utility (via the beanjar.bat batch file you learned about in Chapter 10).

2. Copy the JAR file that contains the bean to the jars directory beneath your BDK installation.

3. Execute the run.bat batch file to launch the BeanBox with the new bean added to the ToolBox.

To build a JAR file that contains the meter bar bean, execute the following command from the directory above the meter bar package hierarchy:

```
beanjar PJB\Source\Chap10\FancyButton FancyButton
```

To launch the BeanBox, simply execute the run.bat batch file, like this:

```
run
```

After you execute this command, the BeanBox should appear with your meter bar bean added to the ToolBox. Figure 11.2 shows how the ToolBox looks with the bean added.

Figure 11.2.
The BeanBox ToolBox window with the meter bar bean added.

Notice in the figure that the last bean in the ToolBox is the meter bar bean, complete with the 16×16 icon you specified in the bean information class. Try using the bean by adding it to the BeanBox; just click it in the ToolBox and then click the main container window. Figure 11.3 shows the newly added meter bar bean.

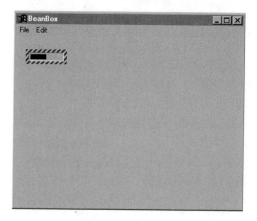

Figure 11.3.
The BeanBox main container window with a meter bar bean added.

After the bean has been added to the container window, you are ready to check the PropertySheet window and see how the properties look. Figure 11.4 shows the PropertySheet window for the meter bar bean.

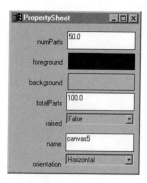

Figure 11.4.
The BeanBox PropertySheet window for the meter bar bean.

The PropertySheet window shows all the properties for the bean, including the inherited foreground and background colors, name properties, and your properties. Notice first that the font property is missing, thanks to the method you overrode in the bean information class. Also take a close look at the orientation property, which is using the custom property editor you implemented. The orientation property is displayed as a drop-down list from which you choose a value. Pretty slick, huh?

Try editing the foreground color, orientation, number of parts, and total parts for the bean. Figure 11.5 shows the bean with these properties modified.

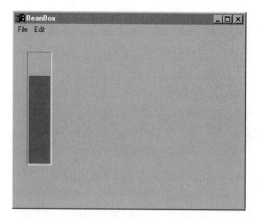

Figure 11.5.
The BeanBox main container with a modified meter bar bean.

As you can see, the meter bar bean provides some pretty neat functionality without all that much work. Most important is the fine control you exercised over the property editing support in the meter bar bean, which clearly pays off at this stage, when it comes to actually using the bean.

Enhancing the Meter Bar Bean

The last topic of this chapter deals with how the meter bar bean can be improved. I thought you might be feeling a little cheated because I did all the work for you, so I've come up with some ideas for how you can improve the meter bar bean on your own. You're gaining enough experience with bean development that you should be able to try out some of these suggestions if you have the desire. Following is a list of possible improvements that you could make to the meter bar bean:

- Draw percentage text on top of the meter bar
- Add support for firing an event when the meter reaches full capacity
- Add an input mode in which the user can click and set the value of the meter bar

The first suggestion involves adding code to the paint() method so that it also draws text that indicates the percentage of the meter bar that is filled. For example, if the current number of parts property is set to 25 and the total number of parts property is set to 50, then the string 50% would be drawn on top of the meter bar. The only trick to adding this feature is dealing with the fact that the text would be drawn on top of different colors in some cases. Consider the situation in which the meter bar is oriented horizontally and set to 50 percent. In this situation, the left side of the bean is painted in the foreground color, and the right side is painted in the background color. If you paint the percentage text in the center, you have to deal with this issue and make sure the text is visible over both colors.

The second suggestion is related to situations in which it might be nice to know when the meter bar has reached its full capacity. In other words, whenever the number of parts property is incremented to equal the total number of parts property, you could fire an event to notify any interested listeners. This enhancement is straightforward in that it involves adding an event type, as well as event listener registration and processing methods.

The final suggestion involves adding an input mode for the meter bar bean. This would effectively enable the bean to function somewhat like a slider input control, which means you can click the meter bar to set its value.

Summary

This chapter continues with the theme of Part III by guiding you through the development of another complete bean. You developed a complete meter bar bean, which can be used in a variety of different scenarios involving the presentation of the status of a process or of some changing value. You first went through a preliminary design of the meter bar bean, just as you did in Chapter 10 with the fancy button bean. You then moved quickly into developing the actual code for the bean, after which you put the bean through its paces in the

BeanBox. You finished the chapter by looking at a few ways in which the meter bar bean can be improved.

The meter bar bean you designed and developed in this chapter is useful as an output bean, which means that it handles no user interaction and is merely a means of displaying information in a more interesting format. This is a popular use of beans, because graphical environments encourage the graphical presentation of information. Chapter 12, "An LED Display," follows up on this approach by presenting another interesting output-oriented bean, an LED display bean. The LED display bean displays numeric output in a graphical format similar to a calculator's LED display.

CHAPTER 12

An LED Display Bean

This chapter carries you through the design and development of your third complete bean. At this point you should be starting to get more comfortable with custom bean development as you are no doubt gaining experience quickly. In this chapter you design and build an LED display bean, which is similar to the meter bar bean from Chapter 11, "A Meter Bar Bean," in that it is an output bean. The LED display bean is used to display numeric values in a form similar to the output of a calculator with an LED display. This bean admittedly has limited usefulness, but it can be used to jazz up the output of an application with ease. I have to admit that I'm a sucker for cool forms of output, even when they aren't totally necessary.

You'll find that the design and implementation of the LED display bean are very similar to those of the meter bar bean. For this reason, the discussion of the LED display bean is geared more toward the unique details of the bean, as opposed to rehashing all the same issues you dealt with in Chapters 10, "A Fancy Button Bean," and 11. You no doubt will notice throughout this chapter that the LED display bean is pretty simple in function. I deliberately wanted to lighten things up with this bean because this part of the book is difficult enough just based on the sheer amount of code.

You learn about the following issues in this chapter:

- Designing the LED display bean
- Developing the code for the LED display bean
- Testing the LED display bean
- Ideas for enhancing the LED display bean

Designing the LED Display Bean

The LED display bean is a visual representation of the output of a calculator with an LED display. The bean isn't a calculator, but it does imitate the output style of calculators with LED displays. The LED display bean can be used in any situation in which you want to present a number with a little more impact than simply drawing it as text. For example, the bean would be perfect in games as a scoreboard, because it draws attention to the number being displayed.

The LED display bean enables you to adjust the number of digits that can be displayed but imposes a limit on them. Unlike the beans you created in Chapters 10 and 11, the LED display bean doesn't support the capability to change the background and foreground colors. This is because the bean always has a black background with green foreground digits; the digits are represented by images. Similar to the meter bar bean, the LED display bean doesn't support any type of user interface interaction such as mouse clicks or key presses, because the LED display bean is purely an output bean.

Now that you have an idea of what the LED display does, let's move on to some specifics by designing its properties, methods, and events. The rest of this section focuses on the design of these major functional parts of the LED display bean.

Properties

Like the other beans you've developed, the LED display bean derives from the AWT Canvas class. Recall that the Canvas class is derived from the Component class, which provides the base functionality typically required of graphical beans, including background and foreground colors, name, and font properties. Based on the description of the LED display bean, you might already be thinking that something is amiss with these inherited properties. If you're thinking some of them aren't necessary in this bean, then you are right on track! Because the LED display bean has a fixed background color (black), it has no use for the background color property. The bean also has no use for the foreground color or font properties because it draws its state purely by using GIF images representing each numeric digit. You'll use a technique similar to what you used with the meter bar bean to hide these unnecessary properties from the user.

The first property to address in the bean's design is the raised property, which determines how the 3D border of the bean is drawn. Remember this property from the meter bar bean? If raised is true, then the border is drawn to look raised from the screen. If not, the border is drawn to look inset. The raised property is a simple boolean property that gives the user a little more control over the appearance of the LED display bean.

I mentioned already that the bean provides a way to adjust the number of digits being displayed, along with limiting them. This sounds like an ideal place for a property. The number of digits property does the trick by specifying how many digits the bean is to display. Understand that these digits are drawn regardless of the numeric value being displayed. The number of digits property is functionally equivalent to the number of digits capable of being displayed on a calculator's LED display, because it determines the physical size of the bean.

The last property required of the bean is the actual numeric value being displayed. There are no surprises here, except to keep in mind that this property must be checked against the number of digits property to make sure it can be sufficiently displayed.

These properties are sufficient for modeling all the functionality requirements of the LED display bean. To recap, following are the properties required of the LED display bean:

- Raised 3D border (true/false)
- Number of digits displayed
- Numeric value displayed

Methods

Now that we've defined the properties, it's time to move on to the public methods required of the LED display bean. The best place to start is with the accessor methods for the bean, because you now know the bean's properties. All the properties in the bean are readable and writeable, so you know they all will require a pair of accessor methods.

Beyond accessor methods, you also have to consider the other public methods that the bean must provide. It turns out that the LED display bean needs only two additional public methods. The first of these, paint(), should be familiar to you, because it has played a critical role in both of the beans you created in Chapters 10 and 11. The other public method required of the bean is the getPreferredSize()method, which calculates and returns the preferred size of the bean based on its current state. This method is necessary because the LED display must be carefully sized around the digits being displayed. Recall that the fancy button bean from Chapter 10 uses this method to return the preferred size of the button, based on the label text and font. The LED display bean is performing a similar function, except that it calculates the preferred size based on the number of digits being displayed.

Following are the public methods required of the LED display bean:

- Raised property getter/setter methods
- Number of digits property getter/setter methods
- Numeric value property getter/setter methods
- Overridden paint() method
- Overridden getPreferredSize() method

Events

The LED display bean is used solely for output purposes, so there is no need for it to process events in any way. For this reason, the design of the LED display bean includes no provision for events.

Developing the LED Display Bean

With the design for the LED display bean behind you, it's time to jump into writing the actual code. You'll find that many aspects of the LED display code are similar to the code for the meter bar bean covered in Chapter 11. This is because both are output beans and therefore require a similar type of overhead. Regardless of the similarities, however, you still encounter some new challenges in the code for the LED display bean.

At some point you should check out the complete source code for the LED display bean, which is included on the accompanying CD-ROM. The main code for the LED display bean is in the LEDDisplay class, which appears on the CD-ROM in the file LEDDisplay.java.

Properties and Member Variables

The first place to start in developing the LED display bean is laying out the properties. Following are the member variable properties for the bean, based on the initial design:

```
private boolean raised;
private int     numDigits;
private int     value;
```

Not surprisingly, these member variables directly correspond to the properties mentioned in the previous section. Notice that they are all built-in Java types, which means that property editors are already provided by JavaBeans for each of them. As a result, you do not have to do any extra work to provide visual editing support for the bean's properties. Along with these properties, the bean also requires another member variable for internal use:

```
private transient Image[] digits;
```

The digits member variable is an array of images that represent the digits used in painting the bean. Each image in the array corresponds to a digit. For convenience and consistency, the digits are stored in the array according to their numeric representation. In other words, the array element at index four of the array is the image for the number four. This makes the code that paints the digits a little easier to follow. Figure 12.1 shows how the digit images look.

Figure 12.1.
The digit images used in the LED display bean.

That wraps up the member variables for the LED display bean. The constructors are next!

Constructors

With the properties wrapped up, it's time to turn your attention toward the constructors for the LED display bean. The LED display bean provides two constructors: a default constructor and a detailed constructor that takes all three properties as arguments. Following is the code for both of these constructors:

```
public LEDDisplay() {
  this(false, 5, 0);
}

public LEDDisplay(boolean r, int n, int v) {
  // Allow the superclass constructor to do its thing
  super();

  // Load the digit images
  digits = new Image[10];
  for (int i = 0; i < 10; i++) {
    String name = "LED" + i + ".gif";
    digits[i] = loadImage(name);
    if (digits[i] == null)
      System.err.println("Couldn't load image " + name + ".");
  }

  // Set properties
  setNumDigits(n);
  raised = r;
  value = v;
  setBackground(Color.black);
}
```

The first constructor simply calls the second constructor with default property values. The second constructor is responsible for actually initializing the bean. This constructor begins by calling the superclass constructor, which is standard fare in AWT derived classes. The constructor then moves on to loading the digit images into the digits image array. The loading of the images is handled by the loadImage() method, which you learn about in the "Support Methods" section a little later in this chapter. With the images loaded, the constructor then sets all the properties, including the inherited background color property.

You might be wondering why the setNumDigits()setter method was called instead of just setting the numDigits member variable manually. As you learn in the next section, the setNumDigits() method does a little more than just set the underlying member variable. It also resizes the bean to fit the number of digits being displayed.

Accessor Methods

The next part of the LED display bean is its accessor methods, which provide access to bean properties. You've already seen the accessor methods for the raised property in the meter bar bean, so let's just skip it. The next property is the number of digits property, whose accessor methods follow:

```
public int getNumDigits() {
  return numDigits;
}

public void setNumDigits(int n) {
  numDigits = Math.max(0, Math.min(8, n));   // maximum of 8 digits
  sizeToFit();
}
```

The getNumDigits() getter method is self-explanatory in that it simply returns the value of the numDigits member variable. The setNumDigits() setter method is a little more interesting, because it resizes the bean after setting the numDigits member. You resize the bean so the size of the LED display will closely fit the digits being displayed. The actual resizing is handled by the sizeToFit() method, about which you learn in the "Support Methods" section, later in this chapter.

The other set of accessor methods in the LED display bean belongs to the numeric value property. Following is the code for these methods:

```
public int getValue() {
  return value;
}

public void setValue(int v) {
  // Constrain to a maximum value of (10 ^ numDigits) - 1
  if (v <= (int)Math.pow(10.0, (double)numDigits) - 1)
    value = Math.max(0, v);
  repaint();
}
```

The getter method, getValue(), simply returns the value of the value member variable. The setter method, setValue(), sets the value of the value member, while ensuring that it doesn't overflow the LED display. This is important because you don't want to be able to set a value that can't sufficiently be displayed in the bean's display area. The method finishes up by repainting the bean to reflect the change in the LED display value.

Public Methods

There are a few public methods in the bean: `paint()` and `getPreferredSize()`. The source code for the `paint()` method follows:

```
public synchronized void paint(Graphics g) {
  int width = size().width;
  int height = size().height;

  // Paint the background with 3D effects
  g.setColor(getBackground());
  g.fillRect(1, 1, width - 2, height - 2);
  g.setColor(Color.lightGray);
  g.draw3DRect(0, 0, width - 1, height - 1, raised);

  // Paint the LED digits exp
  for (int i = 0; i < numDigits; i++) {
    int div = (int)Math.pow(10.0, (double)(numDigits - i - 1));
    g.drawImage(digits[(value / div) % 10],
      3 + i * (2 + DIGIT_WIDTH), 3, this);
  }
}
```

The `paint()` method starts by getting the width and height of the bean, filling the background, and painting a 3D effect around the edges. This code should look familiar to you by now, because it is based on the code used to paint both of the beans you developed in Chapters 10 and 11. The LED display itself is painted next by drawing each digit in the numeric value being displayed. This is accomplished by looping through the number of digits being displayed and drawing the appropriate digit image for each one. If this digit image drawing code appears to be a little confusing at first, take a look at the following equation:

```
digit = (num / (10 ^ place)) % 10;
```

This equation describes how to determine a digit at any particular place in a number, which is what is required of the `paint()` method. As an example, if the number in question is 453 and you want to know what the middle digit is, you would use the following equation:

```
digit = (453 / (10 ^ 1)) % 10;
```

In this example, `10 ^ 1` results in 10, which simplifies the equation to this:

```
digit = (453 / 10) % 10;
```

The equation is further simplified by the result of `453 / 10`, which is 45:

```
digit = 45 % 10;
```

Finally, 45 % 10 leaves a result of 5, which is the middle digit of the original number 453. Is it magic? Not quite. This is just an equation that looks messier in Java code than it really is. Nevertheless, it gets the job done.

The getPreferredSize() method is used to return the preferred size of the bean. You saw a version of this method in action in the fancy button bean. The version of getPreferredSize() in the LED display bean is internally different from the one in the fancy button bean, but it ultimately serves the same purpose. Following is the code for the getPreferredSize() method:

```
public Dimension getPreferredSize() {
  // Calculate the preferred size based on the label text
  return new Dimension(((2 + DIGIT_WIDTH) * numDigits) + 4,
    DIGIT_HEIGHT + 6);
}
```

The getPreferredSize() method calculates the size of the LED display, based on the number of digits being displayed and the size of the digit images. Notice that the calculation also includes some padding so that the images are spaced out and more visually appealing.

Support Methods

The LED display bean uses two private support methods that you haven't learned about yet: sizeToFit() and loadImage(). These two methods provide functionality that the bean needs only internally, which is why they are declared as private. You've actually used the sizeToFit() method before, in the fancy button bean. Even so, check out the code again just to make sure you remember how it works:

```
private void sizeToFit() {
  // Resize to the preferred size
  Dimension d = getPreferredSize();
  resize(d.width, d.height);
  Component p = getParent();
  if (p != null) {
    p.invalidate();
    p.layout();
  }
}
```

The sizeToFit() method is responsible for sizing the bean to closely fit the displayed digits. The getPreferredSize() method is called by sizeToFit() to get the optimal LED display size, which is then used to resize the bean.

The `loadImage()` method is also important to the internal functioning of the LED display bean. Following is its code:

```
public Image loadImage(String name) {
  try {
    URL url = getClass().getResource(name);
    return (Image)url.getContent();
  }
  catch (Exception e) {
    return null;
  }
}
```

This method returns an `Image` object corresponding to the string name of an image. This is accomplished by first constructing a URL (Uniform Resource Locator) based on the name of the image. This URL is then used to load the image using the `getContent()` method.

Additional Overhead

You've now covered all the source code for the LED display bean itself. Based on your newly gained bean development experience, however, you probably suspect that the development of this bean isn't quite finished. The LED display bean still requires a bean information class to specify icons that graphically represent the bean in application builder tools. The bean information class is also required to hide some of the bean's inherited properties that aren't applicable to the bean. Listing 12.1 contains the complete source code for the `LEDDisplayBeanInfo` class.

Listing 12.1. The complete source code for the `LEDDisplayBeanInfo` bean information class (`LEDDisplayBeanInfo.java`).

```
// LEDDisplayBeanInfo Class
// LEDDisplayBeanInfo.java

package PJB.Source.Chap12.LEDDisplay;

// Imports
import java.beans.*;

public class LEDDisplayBeanInfo extends SimpleBeanInfo {
  // Get the appropriate icon
  public java.awt.Image getIcon(int iconKind) {
    if (iconKind == BeanInfo.ICON_COLOR_16x16) {
      java.awt.Image img = loadImage("LEDDisplayIcon16.gif");
      return img;
```

```
    }
    if (iconKind == BeanInfo.ICON_COLOR_32x32) {
      java.awt.Image img = loadImage("LEDDisplayIcon32.gif");
      return img;
    }
    return null;
  }

  // Explicit declare the properties
  public PropertyDescriptor[] getPropertyDescriptors() {
    try {
      PropertyDescriptor
        // Inherited properties
        foreground = new PropertyDescriptor("foreground",
        ➥LEDDisplay.class),
        background = new PropertyDescriptor("background",
        ➥LEDDisplay.class),
        font = new PropertyDescriptor("font", LEDDisplay.class),
        name = new PropertyDescriptor("name", LEDDisplay.class),
        // New properties
        raised = new PropertyDescriptor("raised",
        ➥LEDDisplay.class),
        numDigits = new PropertyDescriptor("numDigits",
        ➥LEDDisplay.class),
        value = new PropertyDescriptor("value", LEDDisplay.class);

      // Hide the foreground, background, and font properties
      foreground.setHidden(true);
      background.setHidden(true);
      font.setHidden(true);

      PropertyDescriptor[] pd = { foreground, background, font,
      ➥name, raised,
        numDigits, value };
      return pd;
    }
    catch (IntrospectionException e) {
      throw new Error(e.toString());
    }
  }
}
```

The first method in the LEDDisplayBeanInfo class, getIcon(), is almost identical to the versions of the method you provided in the beans you developed in Chapters 10 and 11. The only difference is the specification of the GIF files for the icons themselves. These icons are provided as GIF 89a images and are shown in Figure 12.2.

Figure 12.2.
The bean information icons for the LED display bean.

The second method used in the `LEDDisplayBeanInfo` class is `getPropertyDescriptors()`, which is used to explicitly specify the properties exposed by the bean. The purpose of implementing this method is to exclude the foreground, background, and font properties from being exposed by the bean. This is necessary because these inherited properties have no significance to the LED display bean. The `getPropertyDescriptors()` method requires you to declare every property that is to be exposed by the bean. Excluding these properties is simply a process of calling the `setHidden()` method on the `PropertyDescriptor` objects corresponding to each of them.

Like the other beans you've developed, the LED display bean also requires a manifestation file to be included in the JAR file that contains the bean. The code for the LED display bean's manifestation file, `LEDDisplay.mf`, follows:

```
Manifest-Version: 1.0

Name: PJB/Source/Chap12/LEDDisplay/LEDDisplay.class
Java-Bean: True
```

The only difference between this manifest file and the others you've seen is the name of the bean class and its package association.

Caution: Before you compile the LED display bean, make sure you have the `CLASSPATH` environment variable properly set so that the compiler can locate its support classes. In other words, make sure the root path above the bean package hierarchy is included in `CLASSPATH`. This directory is the parent directory of the `PJB` directory.

Note: The complete source code and related resources for the LED display bean are located on the accompanying CD-ROM.

Testing the LED Display Bean

As in all custom beans, the LED display bean must be compressed into a JAR file and added to the BeanBox through a few steps before it can be tested. Just to recap, these steps follow:

1. Create a JAR file that contains the bean and its resources, using the jar utility (via the beanjar.bat batch file you learned about in Chapter 10).

2. Copy the JAR file containing the bean to the jars directory beneath your BDK installation.

3. Execute the run.bat batch file to launch the BeanBox with the new bean added to the ToolBox.

When you perform these steps, the BeanBox should appear with your LED display bean added to the ToolBox. Figure 12.3 shows how the ToolBox looks with the bean added.

Figure 12.3.
The BeanBox ToolBox window with the LED display bean added.

Notice in the figure that the LED display bean has been added to the end of the ToolBox, complete with the 16×16 icon you specified in the bean information class. Try out the bean by adding it to the BeanBox; just click it in the ToolBox and then click the main container window. Figure 12.4 shows the newly added LED display bean.

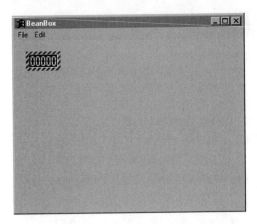

Figure 12.4.
The BeanBox main container window with an LED display bean added.

Now turn your attention to the PropertySheet window and see how the properties look for the bean. Figure 12.5 shows the PropertySheet window for the LED display bean.

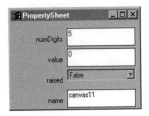

Figure 12.5.
The BeanBox PropertySheet window for the LED display bean.

The PropertySheet window shows all the properties for the bean, including the inherited name property and the properties you defined. Notice that the background, foreground, and font properties are all missing, thanks to the method you overrode in the bean information class. Try using the PropertySheet window to modify the number of digits and value properties to see how the LED display changes. Figure 12.6 shows the bean with these properties modified.

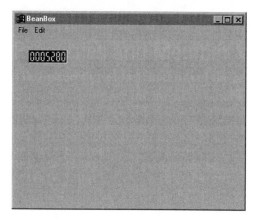

Figure 12.6.
The BeanBox main container with a modified LED display bean.

As you can see, the LED display bean provides an interesting way to present numeric values without too much effort. I hope you are beginning to see how powerful beans can be, especially considering the ease with which they can be designed and built.

Enhancing the LED Display Bean

The last topic of this chapter covers some ways in which you can improve the LED display bean. No bean is ever really perfect; I think there's always room for improvement in some form. Following is a list of possible improvements that you could make to the LED display bean:

- Change the display so that leading zeros aren't drawn.
- Provide digit images in other colors.
- Support special characters, such as a decimal point for displaying decimal places and a colon for displaying time.

The first suggestion involves modifying the code in the paint() method so that it doesn't draw leading zeros. In other words, only the digits specifically required to display a number are drawn. As an example, if the number 242 is being displayed with the number of display digits set to 5, it would be drawn as 242 instead of 00242. In this case, the two leftmost digits would be left blank.

This improvement actually makes the bean behave more like a calculator's LED display.

The second suggestion is to provide other sets of images in different colors. This change would require a new property to represent the color of the digits. As an alternative, you could change the entire drawing mechanism for the bean so that it doesn't rely on images at all. With this approach, you could enable the inherited foreground property and allow the LED digits to be drawn in any color.

The final suggestion involves supporting more than just numbers in the display. Most LED displays in the real world support decimal places, and some (usually in clocks) support colons for separating hours and minutes when displaying time. You could make this enhancement through a few different approaches. One of them is to provide a mode property that places the bean in either time mode or numeric mode. In time mode, it would automatically insert colons in the display between pairs of digits. Of course, you would need to create a new image for the colon.

To support decimal places, you would probably need to change the value property from an integer to a float. You then would need to alter the drawing code for the bean to check for the decimal point within the floating point value and draw it accordingly. Again, you would need to create an image for the decimal point.

Summary

This chapter adds to your bean development skills by presenting you with another complete bean construction project. In this chapter you tackled an LED display bean that imitates the visual output of a calculator with an LED display. You began the chapter with the initial design of the bean, just as you did in Chapters 10 and 11 with other beans. You then moved on to develop the actual code for the bean, after which you put the bean to the test in the BeanBox. You wrapped up the chapter by covering some ways you could improve the LED display bean.

If you're starting to get weary from all this bean development, don't give up just yet. Chapter 13, "An Audio Player Bean," finishes this hands-on part of the book by leading you through the development of an audio player bean, which provides an easy approach to playing audio clips.

An Audio Player Bean

This chapter marks the final chapter of your foray into building your own JavaBeans components. So far, you've developed a fancy button bean (Chapter 10, "A Fancy Button Bean), a meter bar bean (Chapter 11, "A Meter Bar Bean"), and an LED display bean (Chapter 12, "An LED Display Bean"). All of these beans are primarily graphically oriented, which means that their goal is to either accept visual input provided by the user or display graphical output for the user to see. The bean you develop in this chapter is a little different because it doesn't serve much of a purpose in terms of graphics. It is an audio player bean capable of playing audio clips. Its only graphical output is a simple icon that can be clicked to play the audio clip.

You begin this chapter by designing the audio player bean in conceptual terms just as you have done for all the other beans throughout Part III, "Creating Your Own Beans." You then move right into coding the bean, after which you test it out in the BeanBox test container. You finish the chapter with a look at some possible enhancements to the audio player bean you can make yourself. Keep in mind throughout this chapter that the audio player bean has a unique use in practically any environment; it is just as useful in a Java application as it is by itself in a Web page. This actually is true for practically any bean, but it is worth pointing out for this bean because of its interesting functionality.

You learn the following major topics in this chapter:

■ Designing the audio player bean

■ Developing the code for the audio player bean

■ Testing the audio player bean

■ Ideas for enhancing the audio player bean

Designing the Audio Player Bean

The audio player bean is strikingly different from the other beans you've developed thus far in that its functionality doesn't rely on graphical input or output. The bean primarily serves as a means of playing audio clips, and ultimately has only a graphical appearance so that a user can click it to hear an audio clip. It is possible to play an audio clip through the audio player bean purely by calling its public methods, so the bean really doesn't even need a graphical representation at all. However, it makes the bean a little more fun to give it an appearance and enable the user to click it to play (or replay) the associated audio clip.

> Note: Beans that don't have a graphical representation are known as invisible beans and are used primarily for performing background tasks or as functional components in a nongraphical server application. You learn more about invisible beans in Chapter 15, "Advanced JavaBeans."

The audio player bean acts somewhat like a wrapper for a Java AudioClip interface, in that it provides all the overhead for loading and accessing an audio clip. If you aren't familiar with the AudioClip interface, it is provided in the java.applet package and defines a minimal interface for working with audio clips. Unfortunately, the AudioClip interface doesn't provide a means of loading an audio clip as a resource. Before Java 1.1, the only way you could even use the AudioClip interface was to load an audio clip using the getAudioClip() method provided in the Applet class. Although this is how JavaSoft intended the AudioClip interface to be used initially, it obviously doesn't cut it in the long run.

In the case of JavaBeans, you clearly don't want to be reliant on a parent applet as a means of loading an audio clip. In other words, the bean must be capable of loading and playing audio clips by itself without depending on functionality provided by a parent applet or application. So, to successfully implement a bean that can play audio clips, you must take another route altogether. Fortunately, Java 1.1 helped open the door for wider audio clip use by adding the getResourceAsName() method to the Class class. This method enables you to find and load a resource based on a URL, which in this case is a path to the audio clip file. Following is the definition of the getResourceAsName() method in the Java 1.1 API:

```
public String getResourceAsName(String name)
```

As you can see, getResourceAsName() takes a string as its only argument and also returns a string. The string argument is the name of the audio clip you want to load, and the returned string is the name of the URL corresponding to the audio clip. When you know the URL, you can load the audio clip using the URL class's getContent() method. If you are a little confused at this point about the importance of all this stuff, keep in mind that one of the main functions of the audio player bean is wrapping the overhead required to load a bean. The getResourceAsName() and getContent() methods are a big part of making this all possible. Without these two methods, there wouldn't be much of a point to designing the audio player bean because it wouldn't work.

Note: You might be thinking that this discussion of loading audio clips sounds vaguely familiar. You actually used this same technique to load images in Chapter 12's LED display bean. In that chapter, you wrote a method called loadImage() that uses both getResourceAsName() and getContent() to load images. The approach used for loading audio clips is no different, except the end result is an audio clip instead of an image.

With the big issue of loading audio clips behind you, let's move on to some more functional aspects of the audio player bean. The main function of the bean is to load and play audio clips. Knowing this, there are a few fairly obvious features that the bean must include. The first two of these are the simple capability to play and stop the audio clip. The next feature on the list is the capability to play audio clips in a loop, which means that the clip is played continuously until it is explicitly stopped. Normal nonlooped clips automatically stop after they have played through once. In the AudioClip interface, looping is handled by a completely different method than the one used to play clips normally. In the case of the bean, however, it makes more sense to use a single consistent method to play the clip, and then have the looping feature controlled by a separate boolean property. I'm getting a little ahead by talking about properties at this point; they are covered in the next section, "Properties."

You can also incorporate an autostart feature into the audio player bean, which means a serialized bean will immediately start playing its associated audio clip upon the bean's creation. The reason I say this feature applies only to serialized beans is because any other bean wouldn't know what audio clip to play. Serialized beans have typically already been set to a particular audio clip and therefore, when they are created, are capable of automatically playing the clip.

That pretty much sums up the functionality required of the audio player bean. As you can see, it's a simple bean because of its design, and fortunately it turns out to be straightforward on the coding side, too, as you learn in the "Developing the Audio Player Bean" section. For now, let's move on to covering some of the fundamental parts of the bean's design so the coding will go even more smoothly.

Properties

Like all the other beans you've developed throughout the book, the audio player bean derives from the Canvas class so that it can render itself graphically. You should recall from the development of the other beans that the Canvas class brings with it a group of properties: background and foreground colors, name, and font. Because the audio player bean needs to draw only an icon as its graphical representation, none of these inherited properties except the name apply. To keep users of the audio player bean from seeing these properties and getting confused, you'll use a familiar technique to hide them.

The first audio player bean property to cover is the raised property, which by now you should remember by heart from implementing it in the other beans you've developed. Just in case you are as forgetful as I am, I'll give you a quick recap of how to use this property. The raised property is used to determine the look of a 3D border drawn around the bean. In the audio bean, this border appears around the icon image for the bean. If raised is set to true, then the border is drawn to look raised from the screen. If not, the border is drawn to look inset. The raised property is a boolean property that adds a little flair to the look of the bean with very little additional overhead.

The next property to address is the audio clip filename property, which represents the name of the file for the audio clip. This property is necessary so that the user can change the audio clip being played. The audio clip filename property is a string property that the bean uses to load the appropriate audio clip resource.

An important property mentioned in the previous section, "Designing the Audio Player Bean," is the looping property, which determines whether the audio clip is to be played looped. The looping property is a boolean property whose value determines whether the audio clip is looped whenever it is played. This means that setting the looping property alone doesn't play the clip looped, it just states that the clip will be played looped whenever the appropriate play method is called.

The last property for the audio player bean is the autostart property, which determines whether a serialized bean automatically starts playing a clip when the bean is created. This is a boolean property that applies only to beans that are going to be loaded and re-created by serialization, because an existing bean has already passed its creation stage.

These properties are sufficient for modeling the functionality of the audio player bean. As a quick recap, following are the properties required of the audio player bean:

- Raised 3D border (true/false)
- Audio clip filename
- Looping (true/false)
- Autostart (true/false)

Methods

After you have fixed the properties, you can move on to the public methods required of the audio player bean. The best place to start is with the accessor methods for the bean. All the properties in the bean are readable and writable, so you know they will all require a pair of accessor methods.

Beyond accessor methods, you also must address the other public methods that the bean needs. The audio player bean needs four additional public methods: `paint()`, `getPreferredSize()`, `play()`, and `stop()`. The first of these, `paint()`, should be familiar to you because it plays a critical role in every bean you've created. The `getPreferredSize()` method is necessary because the audio player must be carefully sized around the icon image being displayed. Recall that both the fancy button and LED display beans from Chapters 10 and 12 use this method to return their own preferred sizes. The audio player bean requires similar functionality, except it calculates its preferred size based on the size of the icon image.

The other two public methods required of the bean, `play()` and `stop()`, are used to play and stop the audio clip. These two methods are essentially interfaces to the underlying audio clip represented by the audio player bean. The `play()` method is responsible for playing the associated audio clip based on the value of the looping property. If the looping property is set to `true`, the clip is repeated; otherwise, it is played only once. The `stop()` method stops the playing of the clip regardless of whether it is looping. If the clip isn't playing, the `stop()` method has no effect.

Following are the public methods required of the audio player bean:

- Raised property getter/setter methods
- Audio clip filename property getter/setter methods
- Looping property getter/setter methods
- Autostart property getter/setter methods
- Overridden `paint()` method
- Overridden `getPreferredSize()` method
- `play()` method
- `stop()` method

Events

The audio player bean is used primarily for audio output purposes, so its event processing overhead is minimal. Even so, there is one area the bean must address in terms of events. I'm referring to how the bean processes mouse-click events, which is an issue because you want the user to be able to click the bean to play an audio clip. As you learned in Chapter 10 with the fancy button bean, mouse-click events are processed in an individual event processor method that is overridden from the bean's parent class.

Developing the Audio Player Bean

Now that the initial bean design is finished, let's move on to the actual implementation. To reference the complete source code as you work through the implementation of the bean, look on the accompanying CD-ROM. The main code for the audio player bean is in the `AudioPlayer` class, which appears on the CD-ROM in the file `AudioPlayer.java`.

Properties and Member Variables

The starting point in developing the audio player bean is laying out the properties. The following are the member variable properties for the bean based on the initial design:

```
private boolean        raised;
private String         audioFilename;
private boolean        looping;
private boolean        autoStarting;
```

These member variables directly correspond to the properties mentioned in the "Properties" section, which by now is just as you expected. Because they are all based on built-in Java types, property editors are already provided by JavaBeans for each of them. This saves you the trouble of having to implement your own property editors like you did with the meter bar bean in Chapter 11. Along with these properties, the bean also requires the following other member variables for internal use:

```
private transient AudioClip audio;
private transient Image     image;
```

The audio member variable is an AudioClip object used to represent the audio clip being played. This member variable holds the audio clip after it has been loaded. The image member variable is an Image object that represents the icon image used to paint the bean. The image member variable is loaded similarly to the audio member variable. The image stored in the image member variable is the 32×32 icon image for the bean, which you see next in the "Constructors" section.

That wraps up the member variables for the audio player bean. Let's move on to the constructors.

Constructors

The audio player bean provides two constructors: a default constructor and a detailed constructor that takes all four properties as arguments. Following is the code for both of these constructors:

```
public AudioPlayer() {
  this(false, "Audio.au", false, false);
}

public AudioPlayer(boolean r, String afn, boolean l, boolean as) {
  // Allow the superclass constructor to do its thing
  super();

  // Load the icon image
  image = (Image)loadResource("AudioPlayerIcon32.gif");
  if (image == null)
    System.err.println("Couldn't load the AudioPlayerIcon32.gif
    ➥image.");

  // Set properties
  raised = r;
  setAudioFilename(afn);
  looping = l;
  autoStarting = as;
  setBackground(Color.lightGray);
  sizeToFit();

  // Autostart the audio clip if necessary
  if (autoStarting)
    play();

  // Enable mouse event processing
  enableEvents(AWTEvent.MOUSE_EVENT_MASK);
}
```

The first constructor simply calls the second constructor with default property values. The second constructor is responsible for handling the bean initialization. This constructor begins by calling the superclass constructor, which is standard in AWT derived classes. The constructor then loads the icon image into the `image` member variable. The loading of the image is handled by the `loadResource()` method, about which you learn in the "Support Methods" section. With the image loaded, the constructor then sets all the properties. Notice that the audio clip filename is set using the `setAudioFilename()` setter method instead of setting the property directly. This is necessary because the audio clip is loaded from within the `setAudioFilename()` method.

You might also have noticed that the `sizeToFit()` method is called immediately after setting the properties. This call ensures that the bean is sized to appropriately fit the icon image and 3D border. Because the constructor is executed whenever the bean is created, it only makes sense that the constructor contain the code for autostarting the bean if the autostart property is set. If the property is set, the audio clip is played with a call to the `play()` method, about which you learn in the "Accessor Methods" section.

The last order of business for the constructor is enabling the group of events related to the mouse by calling the `enableEvents()` method. Without calling this method, the bean would be incapable of directly trapping any mouse events.

Accessor Methods

The next part of the audio player bean to check out is its accessor methods, which provide access to the bean's properties. You've already seen the accessor methods for the raised property in earlier beans, so I'll save you the trouble of seeing them again by not covering them here. The first new property to address is the audio clip filename property, whose accessor methods follow:

```
public String getAudioFilename() {
  return audioFilename;
}

public void setAudioFilename(String af) {
  audioFilename = af;

  // Load the audio clip
  audio = (AudioClip)loadResource(audioFilename);
  if (audio == null)
    System.err.println("Couldn't load the " + audioFilename +
      " audio clip.");
}
```

The getAudioFilename() getter method is self-explanatory in that it simply returns the value of the audioFilename member variable. The setAudioFilename() setter method takes on the responsibility of loading the audio clip after setting the property member variable. The loading is accomplished by the loadResource() method, about which you learn in the "Support Methods" section.

The next set of accessor methods in the audio player bean belong to the looping property. The code for these methods follows:

```
public boolean isLooping() {
  return looping;
}

public void setLooping(boolean l) {
  looping = l;
}
```

The getter method, isLooping(), simply returns the value of the looping member variable. Likewise, the setter method, setValue(), is simple in that it just sets the value of the looping property.

The final set of accessor methods in the audio player bean belong to the autostart property. The code for these methods follows:

```
public boolean isAutoStarting() {
  return autoStarting;
}

public void setAutoStarting(boolean as) {
  autoStarting = as;
}
```

Like the accessor methods for the looping property, these accessor methods get and set the autostart property without any additional responsibilities.

Public Methods

There are a few public methods in the bean that you need to tackle now: paint(), getPreferredSize(), play(), and stop(). The source code for the first of these methods, paint(), follows:

```
public synchronized void paint(Graphics g) {
  int width = size().width;
  int height = size().height;
```

```
    // Paint the background with 3D effects
    g.setColor(getBackground());
    g.fillRect(1, 1, width - 2, height - 2);
    g.draw3DRect(0, 0, width - 1, height - 1, raised);

    // Paint the icon image
    g.drawImage(image, 3, 3, this);
}
```

The paint() method starts off by getting the width and height of the bean, filling the background, and painting a 3D effect around the edges. This code should look familiar to you because it is borrowed directly from the other beans you've developed in Chapters 10–12. The icon image for the audio player is painted last with a call to drawImage().

The getPreferredSize() method is used to return the preferred size of the bean. You've seen other versions of this method in beans you developed in Chapters 10–12. The version of getPreferredSize() in the audio player bean is a little different from the other versions you've seen, but it ultimately serves the same purpose. Following is the code for the getPreferredSize() method:

```
public Dimension getPreferredSize() {
    // Calculate the preferred size based on the label text
    return new Dimension(IMAGE_SIZE + 6, IMAGE_SIZE + 6);
}
```

The getPreferredSize() method calculates the size of the audio player based on the size of the icon image, which is 32×32. Notice that the calculation also includes some padding so the image fits nicely inside the 3D border.

The last two all-purpose public methods defined in the audio player bean are play() and stop(), which provide a clear and concise means of playing and stopping the audio clip. Following is the code for the play() method:

```
public void play() {
    if (audio != null) {
        if (looping)
            audio.loop();
        else
            audio.play();
    }
    else
        System.err.println("Error playing audio clip.");
}
```

The play() method is responsible for playing the audio clip either looped or normally, depending on the value of the looping property. This functionality is easy to see in the source code by examining the inner if statement that tests the looping property. Based on the value of the looping property, the `play()` method calls the appropriate method on the underlying `AudioClip` object. Notice that the transient audio clip member variable, `audio`, is checked for a null value before it is played. This is to make sure there are no problems in case the `play()` method is called on an invalid audio clip. An audio clip could be invalid because of some type of initialization error such as a load error.

The `stop()`method forms the second half of the audio clip control interface. Following is its source code:

```
public void stop() {
  if (audio != null)
    audio.stop();
  else
    System.err.println("Error playing audio clip.");
}
```

This method is similar to the `play()` method in that it first checks the `audio` member variable to make sure it isn't `null`. If this member variable checks out, then the `stop()` method is called on the underlying `AudioClip` object to actually stop the playing of the audio clip. That's it for the public methods!

Event Processing Methods

As you learned in the "Designing the Audio Player Bean" section, the audio player bean requires an event processing method for responding to mouse clicks. The source code for this method, `processMouseEvent()`, follows:

```
protected void processMouseEvent(MouseEvent e) {
  // Track mouse presses
  if (e.getId() == MouseEvent.MOUSE_PRESSED)
    play();
}
```

The `processMouseEvent()` method is responsible for trapping mouse button presses, which are used to trigger and play the audio clip. When the user presses the mouse button, the `play()` method is called to play the audio clip. There isn't a whole lot more to say about `processMouseEvent()`, so let's move on to the support methods for the audio player bean.

Support Methods

The audio player bean uses a few private support methods that haven't been covered yet: `sizeToFit()` and `loadResource()`. These two methods provide functionality that the bean needs only internally, which is why they are declared as private. You've seen the sizeToFit() method a few times before in earlier beans, so there's no sense in rehashing it here.

The loadResource() method is much more important to the internal functioning of the audio player bean. The source code for it follows:

```
private Object loadResource(String name) {
  try {
    URL url = getClass().getResource(name);
    return url.getContent();
  }
  catch (Exception e) {
    return null;
  }
}
```

The loadResource() method returns an Object object corresponding to the string name of a resource such as an image or audio clip. This is accomplished by first constructing a URL (Uniform Resource Locator) based on the name of the image, and then using the URL to load the resource by the getContent() method. You used this same approach to load images in the LED display bean from Chapter 12. The audio player bean must load both images and audio clips, so the loadImage() method was generalized to loadResource(), which works for both. The difference is that the Object object returned from loadResource() must be cast to the specific resource type (Image or AudioClip).

Additional Overhead

That wraps up the source code for the audio player bean itself. As you well know by now, that isn't quite all there is to the story. The audio player bean still requires a bean information class to specify icons that graphically represent the bean in application builder tools, as well as to hide the bean's inherited properties that aren't applicable. Listing 13.1 contains the complete source code for the AudioPlayerBeanInfo class.

Listing 13.1. The complete source code for the AudioPlayerBeanInfo bean information class (AudioPlayerBeanInfo.java).

```
// AudioPlayerBeanInfo Class
// AudioPlayerBeanInfo.java

package PJB.Source.Chap13.AudioPlayer;

// Imports
```

continues

Listing 13.1. continued

```java
import java.beans.*;

public class AudioPlayerBeanInfo extends SimpleBeanInfo {
  // Get the appropriate icon
  public java.awt.Image getIcon(int iconKind) {
    if (iconKind == BeanInfo.ICON_COLOR_16x16) {
      java.awt.Image img = loadImage("AudioPlayerIcon16.gif");
      return img;
    }
    if (iconKind == BeanInfo.ICON_COLOR_32x32) {
      java.awt.Image img = loadImage("AudioPlayerIcon32.gif");
      return img;
    }
    return null;
  }

  // Explicit declare the properties
  public PropertyDescriptor[] getPropertyDescriptors() {
    try {
      PropertyDescriptor
        // Inherited properties
        foreground = new PropertyDescriptor("foreground",
        ➡AudioPlayer.class),
        background = new PropertyDescriptor("background",
        ➡AudioPlayer.class),
        font = new PropertyDescriptor("font", AudioPlayer.class),
        name = new PropertyDescriptor("name", AudioPlayer.class),
        // New properties
        raised = new PropertyDescriptor("raised",
        ➡AudioPlayer.class),
        audioFilename = new PropertyDescriptor("audioFilename",
          AudioPlayer.class),
        looping = new PropertyDescriptor("looping",
        ➡AudioPlayer.class),
        autoStarting = new PropertyDescriptor("autoStarting",
          AudioPlayer.class);

      // Hide the foreground, background, and font properties
      foreground.setHidden(true);
      background.setHidden(true);
      font.setHidden(true);

      PropertyDescriptor[] pd = { foreground, background, font,
      ➡name, raised,
        audioFilename, looping, autoStarting };
      return pd;
    }
    catch (IntrospectionException e) {
      throw new Error(e.toString());
    }
  }
}
```

The first method in the `AudioPlayerBeanInfo` class, `getIcon()`, is practically identical to the versions of the method you provided in the other beans you've developed in Chapters 10–12. The only difference is the specification of the GIF files for the icons themselves. These icons are provided as GIF 89A images and are shown in Figure 13.1.

Figure 13.1.
The bean information icons for the audio player bean.

The second method used in the `AudioPlayerBeanInfo` class is `getPropertyDescriptors()`, which is used to explicitly specify the properties exposed by the bean. The purpose of implementing this method is to keep the inherited foreground, background, and font properties from being exposed by the bean.

As in all the other beans you've developed, the audio player bean requires a manifestation file to be included in the JAR file that contains the bean. The code for the audio player bean's manifestation file, `AudioPlayer.mf`, follows:

```
Manifest-Version: 1.0

Name: PJB/Source/Chap13/AudioPlayer/AudioPlayer.class
Java-Bean: True
```

The only difference between this manifest file and the others you've seen is the name of the bean class and its package association.

Caution: Before you compile the audio player bean, make sure you have the `CLASSPATH` environment variable properly set so that the compiler can locate its support classes. In other words, make sure the root path above the bean package hierarchy is included in `CLASSPATH`. This directory is the parent directory of the `PJB` directory.

Note: The complete source code and related resources for the audio player bean are located on the accompanying CD-ROM.

Testing the Audio Player Bean

Before the audio player bean can be used in the BeanBox, you need to add it to the BeanBox by following these steps:

1. Copy the JAR file that contains the bean and its resources to the `jars` directory beneath your BDK installation.

2. Run a `make` utility on the make file (`MakeFile`) that ships with the BeanBox to reconstruct the ToolBox.

After you perform these steps, which should be old hat to you by now, the BeanBox will appear with your audio player bean added to the ToolBox. Figure 13.2 shows how the ToolBox looks with the bean added.

Figure 13.2.
The BeanBox ToolBox window with the audio player bean added.

The figure shows that the audio player bean has been added to the end of the ToolBox, complete with the 16×16 icon you specified in the bean information class. Try out the bean by adding it to the BeanBox; just click it in the ToolBox and then click the main container window. Figure 13.3 shows the newly added audio player bean.

Look at the PropertySheet window and assess the properties exposed by the bean. Figure 13.4 shows the PropertySheet window for the audio player bean.

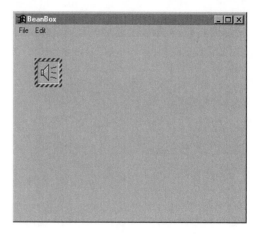

Figure 13.3.
The BeanBox main container window with an audio player bean added.

Figure 13.4.
The BeanBox PropertySheet window for the audio player bean.

The PropertySheet window shows all the properties for the bean, including the inherited name property and the properties you defined. Notice that the background, foreground, and font properties are all missing due to the bean information class. At this point, you can use the PropertySheet window to modify the audio filename, looping, and autostart properties for the bean. Before you do, try clicking the bean to make sure you hear an audio clip being played. The default audio clip the bean plays is called Audio.au, which is provided with the bean. You could enter the name of your own audio clip if you had one with the bean.

> Note: It's worth noting that the bean will look for audio clips in the location in which the bean is stored. In this case, it means that the bean will look in the JAR file that contains the bean. This might seem like a nuisance until you realize that the JAR utility makes adding and removing files to and from an archive very easy. In addition, if you are using the audio player on the Web, you will want to benefit from the compression and packaging provided by JAR files.

Test the looping property by setting it to true and then clicking the bean. You should hear the musical audio clip repeat over and over. Unfortunately, you can't stop it because the BeanBox doesn't give you a direct means of calling methods. However, you can wire a button to the stop() AWT response method, which has the same effect as calling the public stop() method directly. Try this by adding a fancy button bean to the container window with its label set to Stop. Figure 13.5 shows how the main container window looks with both of these beans added.

Figure 13.5.
The BeanBox main container window with an audio player bean and a fancy button bean.

You begin wiring the button to the audio player by clicking the Edit menu with the button bean selected. From the Edit menu, select Events | Action. You'll then have only one menu item available: the actionPerformed event. Figure 13.6 shows how to select this event item from the menu.

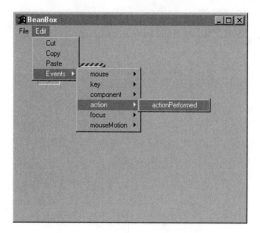

Figure 13.6.
The Edit menu with the `actionPerformed` *event selected.*

After you select this event, you'll be presented with a moving line that is controlled by the mouse. The line originates from the fancy button bean and is meant to be guided to the bean with which you want to connect the `actionPerformed` event. Click the audio player bean and you will be presented with the EventTargetDialog dialog box in Figure 13.7.

Figure 13.7.
The EventTargetDialog dialog box for the audio player bean.

This dialog box shows the two AWT event response methods you defined in the audio player bean. To connect the button to the `stop()` method, just click the `stop()` method in the list and then click OK. At this point, you can click the fancy button bean and it will stop the playing of the audio player. Pretty slick! You can also add a button that connects to the `play()` method to finish the visual interface.

You can try out the autostart property by setting it to `true` and then cutting the audio player bean by selecting Cut from the Edit menu. Then select Paste from the Edit menu to add the bean back to the container. The cut and paste functions in the BeanBox use JavaBeans persistence services to save and restore beans, so the audio player bean is re-created and automatically played based on the autostart property.

> **Note:** Note that the bean connection and cut and paste features in the BeanBox were all tested on an early beta version of the BeanBox, which was somewhat unstable. It is expected that the version of the BeanBox that ships with the final BDK will be much more robust.

Enhancing the Audio Player Bean

Just like all the other beans covered throughout the book, the audio player could benefit from a few enhancements here and there. Following is a list of possible improvements that would make the audio player bean a little more interesting and useful:

- Provide play and stop button controls
- Display an animation while the audio is being played
- Redesign the audio player as an invisible bean

The first enhancement involves adding play and stop buttons as part of the bean itself. These buttons would be very useful because they would enable you to play and stop the audio clip without any additional manipulation of the bean, such as wiring other buttons to it. This modification requires the bean to be derived from `Container` instead of `Canvas` so that it can hold the buttons. Even though this is a little trickier than just adding another property or tweaking a method, you should now have enough Java skills to tackle it.

The second suggestion is to provide a set of animation images that are cycled while the audio clip is being played. This change would require a new transient member variable to hold the array of images. The only problem with this approach is that there isn't currently a way to detect when an audio clip has finished playing, so you would just have to tie the animation to the play() and stop() methods. Admittedly, this approach doesn't quite get the desired effect, but it works well enough to make the bean a little more fun.

The final suggestion involves redesigning the bean so that it is invisible. Recall from the "Designing the Audio Player Bean" section that an invisible bean has no graphical representation. The audio player bean's graphical output is mostly for show, so it could easily work as an invisible bean. To do this, you would derive the bean from Object instead of Canvas, which removes the bean's graphical underpinnings. You would still provide the bean information icons so that the bean could be viewed and manipulated at design time.

Summary

In this chapter you learned about the audio player bean, which is used to play audio clips. You began the chapter as you have Chapters 10–12 by working through a preliminary design of the bean. You then actually coded the bean, which should be familiar to you based on the experience you gained in building other beans. After working through the code for the audio player bean, you gave it a test spin in the BeanBox and even connected it with the fancy button bean developed in Chapter 10. You also tried out the default persistence support in JavaBeans by cutting and pasting an audio player bean in the BeanBox. From there, you learned a few ways in which the bean could be enhanced.

This chapter caps off what you probably will agree is the most difficult part of the book so far. Although the code listings might have been taxing at times, you learned a great deal in working through the hands-on examples in Chapters 10–13. Just think, you now have four complete beans under your belt, which puts you in a position to hit the ground running in terms of building your own beans. Just in case this part of the book has left you too tired to do any running, you'll be glad to know that the next part of the book lightens up on the coding just a little.

PART IV

Advanced Issues and the Future of JavaBeans

Hand Coding Applications with JavaBeans

In the previous four chapters, you saw how beans are used and manipulated in the BeanBox test container, which imitates the visual design approach used by application builder tools. Although this is the ideal approach in using beans to their fullest, there is no reason why you can't use beans in straight Java code just as you use traditional Java classes. This chapter begins the final part of the book by taking a look at how JavaBeans components are used in a hand-coded application. You probably will be pleasantly surprised to learn that integrating beans into applets and applications at the code level is extremely similar to traditional Java programming with classes.

The chapter begins with a general discussion about the issues surrounding the use of beans in a non-visual environment. Although you lose all the application builder tool support with this approach, beans are just as functionally full-featured when they are used directly in source code. After learning about the main issues surrounding the hand coding of beans, you spend the rest of the chapter coding by hand a complete application that uses all of the beans you built in the previous part of the book. This application is very interesting because it shows how beans work together at the code level. Even if you fully plan to use beans in visual application builder tools, you still gain a lot of insight into how beans work by manipulating them at the code level.

You learn about the following topics in this chapter:

- Hand coding with JavaBeans
- Designing the bean tester application
- Developing the bean tester application
- Testing the bean tester application

JavaBeans By Hand

One of the biggest benefits of the JavaBeans technology is its built-in support for visual layout and editing using application builder tools. You've learned a great deal about this support throughout the book, including how your own beans operate in a visual environment. Even though laying out and editing beans visually is the design approach promoted by JavaBeans for a variety of reasons, it isn't the only approach available to developers. You also can use beans directly in source code very much like traditional Java classes. This source code approach doesn't really provide any higher degree of flexibility, but it might still be favored by some developers who are more comfortable working directly with code. For this reason, it is important for you to understand how to use beans directly in Java source code.

The first thing to understand about using beans directly in Java code is that beans are not very different from any other Java classes. In fact, the only real difference is that beans include additional overhead for component-related features such as exported properties, introspection, and application builder tool support. Beans also support persistence and event processing, but these two services are useful for all Java classes, not just beans. The point I'm getting at here is that a bean can be treated like a normal Java class with some extra over-head that can be largely ignored when working directly with code.

The process of building applets or applications out of beans at the code level is conceptually similar to using application builder tools for the same purpose. The primary difference, obviously, is that you have to do everything in code that the builder tools enable you to do visually. More specifically, the following steps are required to build applets or applications out of beans in a non-visual environment:

- Create the beans
- Customize the beans
- Connect the beans

> **Note:** This discussion focuses on using beans directly in Java code to build stand-alone applications. Developing applets with beans is a very similar process, so the discussion applies to it as well.

Creating the Beans

In a visual application builder tool, creating an instance of a bean is as simple as selecting the bean from a toolbox and clicking in the editing window for the application you are developing. Creating instances of a bean directly in source code isn't much more difficult, but it definitely isn't as elegant as pointing and clicking with the mouse. To create a bean directly in code, you basically create an instance of the bean class just as if it were any other Java class. In applications, the best place to perform this creation is within the constructor for the application class. The following line of code creates a meter bar bean with default settings:

```
MeterBar meter = new MeterBar();
```

If you want to use settings that are different than the default, you can use the second constructor for the bean and pass in all the settings as arguments. The following line of code does this:

```
MeterBar meter = new MeterBar(HVOrientation.VERTICAL, true, 0.0f,
➥100.0f);
```

After you have created the meter bar bean, you still need to add it to the application's window in order for it to be associated with the application. This is due to the fact that an application class is a container class, which means that it is capable of holding graphical AWT elements such as beans. To add a bean to an application, you just call the add() method, which is inherited from the Container class. The following is an example of adding the meter bar bean to an application using the add() method:

```
add(meter);
```

As you can see, adding a bean to an application is a very simple process. Keep in mind that this code is placed in the application class's constructor along with the bean creation code. You typically will create all your beans and then add them to an application in the application class's constructor.

Customizing the Beans

After you create and add all of your beans to an application, you must then customize them to fit the needs of the application. Bean customization is just as important as bean creation because it determines how the beans will function and appear in the application. If you used detail constructors to create some of the beans, you might not even need to customize them. However, you typically will need to customize at least a few beans before you can use them. Customizing a bean is simply a matter of calling one or more of its public methods with the desired settings. Usually, you will use a bean's accessor methods to customize the bean by setting its properties to different values.

The initial bean customization should occur just after you create and add beans to an application. Within the application class's constructor is also a good place to handle this chore. You can use the following piece of code to customize the meter bar bean after you create it and add it to an application:

```
MeterBar meter = new MeterBar();
add(meter);
meter.setRaised(true);
meter.setNumParts(75.0f);
```

This code creates and adds a meter bar bean and then customizes it by setting two of its properties. The raised property is first set to true, which results in the meter having a raised 3D border. The number of parts property is also set, which determines how much of the meter bar is filled in. You're probably thinking that you could have just as easily set these properties by using the detail constructor for the meter bar bean, like this:

```
MeterBar meter = new MeterBar(HVOrientation.HORIZONTAL, true,
➡75.0f, 100.0f);
add(meter);
```

This would work for the properties you modified, but what about inherited properties? For example, how would you alter the color of the meter bar without customizing the bean outside of the constructor? You wouldn't. The only way to modify inherited bean properties is by setting them with an accessor method, like this:

```
MeterBar meter = new MeterBar(HVOrientation.HORIZONTAL, true,
➡75.0f, 100.0f);
add(meter);
meter.setForeground(Color.red);
```

This code sets the foreground color of the meter bar to red, which draws in red the meter bar itself. As you can see, bean customization is a very straightforward process of calling the appropriate public methods (usually setter methods) to get the desired results.

Connecting the Beans

The last step in using beans directly in source code is connecting them together via events. JavaBeans fully supports the capability to connect beans together by responding to events that a bean fires. For example, the fancy button bean fires action events whenever it is pushed. If you are familiar with Java 1.1 event processing, you will notice that the approach used in JavaBeans is exactly the same due to the fact that JavaBeans uses the same event model as Java 1.1.

Connecting beans together using events is primarily a process of registering event listeners with a bean and then adding the necessary response code to respond to the event. The first step in this process is deciding which beans are generating events to which you want to respond. For each of these beans, you will need to call the appropriate event listener registration method for adding event listeners to the bean. For example, in the case of the fancy button bean you would call the addActionListener() method to register event listeners with the bean. The event listener passed into this method can be any class that implements the appropriate EventListener derived interface. In the case of the fancy button bean, the class would need to implement the ActionListener interface.

Implementing listener interfaces touches on a tricky problem with event handling in JavaBeans, as well as in Java 1.1. The problem is based on the fact that the event model in JavaBeans and Java 1.1 is based on event types, which are used as the basis for dispatching events to the appropriate event listener. This situation alone isn't the problem; the problem is that there is no clean way to distinguish between two beans dispatching events of the same type. In other words, there isn't a good way to distinguish between the source of events if the events are of the same type. As an example of this problem, consider an application that contains multiple fancy button beans. Regardless of which button you click, the same actionPerformed() method will be called on the registered class that implements the ActionListener interface.

The solution to the problem is to use different listener classes to respond to events for each button. However, this approach would quickly get annoying because it requires you to implement several little classes that do nothing more than respond to button events for an application. This solution not only is annoying, but it goes against object-oriented principles and ultimately results in a disorganized class structure. What should you do?

The architects at JavaSoft have managed to stay a step ahead of the game when it comes to dealing with problems like this. Their approach to solving this particular issue ended up requiring a change to the Java language syntax. The solution is to use *inner classes*, which are classes that can be defined in any scope, including within other classes. Inner classes are new to Java 1.1, which means that all classes in Java 1.1 can be defined in any scope. You probably are still wondering just how inner classes help solve the problem of responding to multiple events of the same type. Inner classes enable you to define small helper classes within the context of an application class for the express purpose of handling events.

It will be much easier for you to understand the benefit of inner classes if you see a practical example. Consider the scenario in which you have an application with two buttons: an OK button and a Cancel button. The following is the code that registers event listeners for each of these buttons in the constructor for the application:

```
okButton.addActionListener(new OKButtonAdapter());
cancelButton.addActionListener(new CancelButtonAdapter());
```

Notice in this code that the event listener classes passed into these methods are called OKButtonAdapter and CancelButtonAdapter. Adapter classes are classes that implement listener interfaces for the sole purpose of adding response code. These classes are the ones that are placed inline in the application class as inner classes. The following is the code for these classes:

```
class OKButtonAdapter implements ActionListener {
  public void actionPerformed(ActionEvent e) {
    System.out.println("You clicked OK!");
  }
}

class CancelButtonAdapter implements ActionListener {
  public void actionPerformed(ActionEvent e) {
    System.out.println("You clicked Cancel!");
  }
}
```

These classes each implement a single method, actionPerformed(), which responds to the event for each button separately. This approach to responding to events is very clean and still fits in well with the object-oriented design of the application because the event adapter classes are hidden within the application.

To connect beans to each other with this approach, you simply call the desired public methods on a bean within an event response method. For example, if you had a fancy button bean called playButton and an audio player bean called player, you could use the following code to cause the audio player to be played based on a button push:

```
class PlayButtonAdapter implements ActionListener {
  public void actionPerformed(ActionEvent e) {
    player.play();
  }
}
```

Of course, to use this code you must have registered the PlayButtonAdapter adapter class with the fancy button bean in the constructor for the application, like this:

```
playButton.addActionListener(new PlayButtonAdapter());
```

That wraps up the fundamental issues surrounding the direct use of beans in source code. Now move on to a complete example so you can put some of this newfound knowledge to work.

Designing the Bean Tester Application

The rest of this chapter is devoted to the design, development, and testing of the bean tester application, which uses all the beans you developed in the previous part of the book (Part III, "Creating Your Own Beans"). The design of the application is pretty straightforward because the goal is simply to test out all of the beans together using the hand-coded development approach about which you've learned throughout this chapter. Even so, you'll find that this application serves as a good example of how to use beans directly in source code.

Because the goal of the bean tester application is to test the beans, your most important design decision is figuring out how the beans should interact with each other. The fancy button bean is really the only user input bean in the group, so it makes sense to use it for the application's input needs. The LED display bean is an output bean that displays a numeric value. A good way to test it out would be to connect two buttons to it that increment and decrement its value. Similarly, the meter bar bean displays a fractional value in the form of a meter bar, which you could test using the same increment and decrement buttons. The only remaining bean is the audio player bean, which you could test with buttons that play and stop the player.

You can connect the buttons to the beans using the event adapter approach discussed in the previous section of this chapter, "Connecting the Beans." You then alter the beans in the event response methods by calling their public methods. Following is a list of the main functional requirements of the bean tester application:

- Two fancy button beans to increment and decrement the values of an LED display bean and a meter bar bean
- Two fancy button beans to play and stop an audio player bean
- An LED display bean
- A meter bar bean
- An audio player bean
- A constructor for the application which creates, customizes, and connects the beans
- Event adapter classes for responding to fancy button events

Developing the Bean Tester Application

The development of the bean tester application follows very closely the steps you learned earlier in this chapter to create, customize, and then connect the beans. These are the basic steps you will always follow when you use beans to hand code applications. As you work through the code for the application, you probably will notice that there is very little code beyond the maintenance of the beans. This fits in perfectly with the goal of JavaBeans, which is to keep all of a bean's functionality wrapped up tightly inside the bean.

> Note: The complete source code for the bean tester application is located on the accompanying CD-ROM. The main source code file is `BeanTester.java`, which contains the `BeanTester` application class.

The implementation of the bean tester application begins with the member variables, which are simply the bean instances used by the application. These member variables follow:

```
private FancyButton playButton,
                    stopButton,
                    incButton,
                    decButton;
private LEDDisplay  led;
private MeterBar    meter;
private AudioPlayer player;
```

No surprises here! All of the member variables are references to bean objects that are waiting to be created and used. The code that actually handles the creation of the beans is found in the `createBeans()` method, which follows:

```
private void createBeans() {
  // Create the beans
  try {
    playButton = (FancyButton)Beans.instantiate(null,
      "PJB.Source.Chap10.FancyButton.FancyButton");
    stopButton = (FancyButton)Beans.instantiate(null,
      "PJB.Source.Chap10.FancyButton.FancyButton");
    incButton = (FancyButton)Beans.instantiate(null,
      "PJB.Source.Chap10.FancyButton.FancyButton");
    decButton = (FancyButton)Beans.instantiate(null,
      "PJB.Source.Chap10.FancyButton.FancyButton");
```

```
    meter = (MeterBar)Beans.instantiate(null,
      "PJB.Source.Chap11.MeterBar.MeterBar");
    led = (LEDDisplay)Beans.instantiate(null,
      "PJB.Source.Chap12.LEDDisplay.LEDDisplay");
    player = (AudioPlayer)Beans.instantiate(null,
      "PJB.Source.Chap13.AudioPlayer.AudioPlayer");
  }
  catch (Exception e) {
    System.out.println(e);
  }

  // Add the beans
  add(playButton);
  add(stopButton);
  add(incButton);
  add(decButton);
  add(led);
  add(meter);
  add(player);
}
```

This method first creates the beans using the `instantiate()` method provided by the `Beans` class, and then assigns them to the appropriate member variables. Notice that the entire package name is used to refer to each bean when it is instantiated. The `createBeans()` method then systematically adds each of the new beans to the application by calling the `add()` method for each of them.

> Note: You might be wondering why the `Beans.instantiate()` method was used to create the beans instead of just using the new operator like when creating other Java objects. The reason is because `Beans.instantiate()` is capable of performing additional bean creation overhead as JavaBeans evolves over time. In other words, the JavaBeans architects acknowledge that JavaBeans is a young technology and suggest using `Beans.instantiate()` to create beans so that code is guaranteed to be compatible in future versions of JavaBeans.

That pretty well wraps up the creation and initialization of the beans. Let's move on to the customization of the beans! Following is the code for the `customizeBeans()` method, which handles customizing the beans:

```
private void customizeBeans() {
  // Customize the buttons
  Font f = new Font("Helvetica", Font.BOLD, 20);
  playButton.setLabel("Play");
  playButton.setFont(f);
```

```
    playButton.setForeground(Color.red);
    stopButton.setLabel("Stop");
    stopButton.setFont(f);
    stopButton.setForeground(Color.blue);
    f = new Font("Helvetica", Font.PLAIN, 16);
    incButton.setLabel("Increment");
    incButton.setFont(f);
    incButton.setForeground(Color.red);
    decButton.setLabel("Decrement");
    decButton.setFont(f);
    decButton.setForeground(Color.blue);

    // Customize the meter bar
    meter.setOrientation(HVOrientation.VERTICAL);
    meter.setForeground(Color.magenta);

    // Customize the audio player
    player.setLooping(true);
}
```

The customizeBeans() method takes care of customizing the button beans, along with the meter bar and audio player beans. The buttons are customized so that they use a different font and different colors for the label text. The meter bar is customized so that the foreground color is magenta, which results in a magenta colored meter bar. Finally, the audio player bean is customized so that the audio clip is looped when played.

The createBeans() and customizeBeans() methods take care of the first two bean development steps. The only remaining step is connecting the beans together, which is handled by the connectBeans() method, which follows:

```
private void connectBeans() {
  // Register the button action listeners
  playButton.addActionListener(new PlayButtonAdapter());
  stopButton.addActionListener(new StopButtonAdapter());
  incButton.addActionListener(new IncButtonAdapter());
  decButton.addActionListener(new DecButtonAdapter());
}
```

The connectBeans() method is perhaps the most important of the three because it takes care of registering event adapter classes with the button beans by calling the addActionListener() method on each. Of course, the event adapter classes are where the action is really taking place, so let's move on to them. Following are the event adapter classes, PlayButtonAdapter and StopButtonAdapter, for the Play and Stop buttons:

```
class PlayButtonAdapter implements ActionListener {
  public void actionPerformed(ActionEvent e) {
```

```
      player.play();
    }
}

class StopButtonAdapter implements ActionListener {
  public void actionPerformed(ActionEvent e) {
    player.stop();
    }
}
```

These classes are very similar to the sample classes you saw earlier in this chapter. They simply call the play() and stop() methods on the audio player bean to play and stop the audio clip whenever the buttons are pushed. The other two event adapter classes, IncButtonAdapter and DecButtonAdapter, are responsible for responding to action events fired by the Increment and Decrement buttons. These classes follow:

```
class IncButtonAdapter implements ActionListener {
  public void actionPerformed(ActionEvent e) {
    meter.incParts(5.0f);
    led.setValue(led.getValue() + 1);
  }
}

class DecButtonAdapter implements ActionListener {
  public void actionPerformed(ActionEvent e) {
    meter.decParts(5.0f);
    led.setValue(led.getValue() - 1);
  }
}
```

The IncButtonAdapter class increments the meter bar's value by calling the incParts() method on it. The value of the LED display is then altered by calling the setValue() method and passing the LED display's previous value incremented by one. The DecButtonAdapter class performs a very similar function, except it increments the values instead of decrementing them.

That just about finishes off the code for the bean tester application. The only thing missing is the code responsible for initializing the application, which is contained in the application's constructor. The code for the application's constructor follows:

```
public BeanTester(String title) {
  // Pass the title on to the parent
  super(title);
```

```
  // Change the background to light gray
  setBackground(Color.lightGray);

  // Change the layout
  setLayout(new FlowLayout());

  // Enable event processing
  enableEvents(AWTEvent.WINDOW_EVENT_MASK);

  // Create, customize, and connect the beans
  createBeans();
  customizeBeans();
  connectBeans();
}
```

The constructor first sets the background color of the application to light gray, which goes much better with the 3D look of the beans. The constructor then sets the layout of the application to a flow layout and enables window events so that it can detect when the main frame window has been closed. Finally, the constructor takes care of the three-step bean maintenance process by calling the createBeans(), customizeBeans(), and connectBeans() methods. These methods, as you've already learned, take care of everything in regard to getting the beans up and running together.

Testing the Bean Tester Application

After you have designed and developed the bean tester application, you're probably itching to see it in action. You can try out the application by executing the application class, BeanTester.class, within the Java 1.1 interpreter, like this:

```
java BeanTester
```

> Caution: Make sure the CLASSPATH environment variable is set so that the bean classes are accessible by the Java interpreter. This means that the root directory of the sample bean classes needs to appear in the listing of paths stored in CLASSPATH. If you installed the bean examples to your hard drive from the accompanying CD-ROM, then this directory will be the root directory of your hard drive.

When you execute the application in the Java interpreter, you'll see something similar to Figure 14.1.

Figure 14.1.
The bean tester application upon being executed.

Try pushing the different buttons to see how they impact the rest of the beans. Notice that both the LED display and the meter bar beans are impacted by the Increment and Decrement buttons. Figure 14.2 shows how the application looks after you try out these buttons.

You should also try pressing the Play and Stop buttons to see how they affect the audio player bean. Because the bean is set to looping, you'll have to press the Stop button to stop the playing after you press Play.

You've now tested out all your beans in a non-visual development environment, which is proof that JavaBeans components are as easy to use at a programmatic level as normal Java classes. In the process, you gained some extra insight about the internals of how beans are used together.

Figure 14.2.
The bean tester application after you push the buttons to interact with the beans.

Summary

This chapter focused on using JavaBeans in non-visual development environments where you have to do everything in straight source code. Although this isn't the recommended development approach in regard to JavaBeans, it is nevertheless a reality that you might have to use it at one time or another. Besides, reverting back to source code can often give you more insight about what is happening in an automated visual environment, which can come in handy. You began the chapter by learning about the primary issues involved in using beans at the source code level. You then moved on to design and develop the bean tester application, which used all the beans you developed in Part III of the book. The chapter finished up by testing out the bean tester application.

If nothing else, this chapter hopefully showed you that JavaBeans components are very similar to traditional Java classes, especially in how they are used at the source code level. This is an important realization because it highlights the fact that there is nothing secret or magical about the JavaBeans technology. Sure, some neat things go on behind the scenes when you use a bean with an application builder tool, such as automatic introspection, but when it comes down to it, a bean is really just a normal Java class with some extra component-related functionality. This chapter exposed this fact by using beans in a traditional hand-coded application.

The next chapter steps back from the coding a great deal by looking into some advanced JavaBeans concepts. Feel free to breathe a sigh of relief if you've felt overburdened by all the source code thrown at you in the past few chapters!

CHAPTER 15

Advanced JavaBeans

At this point in the book, you should be well on your way to being a proficient JavaBeans developer and user. You've learned all the conceptual basics and have even built some custom beans from scratch. However, there still are a few issues you haven't covered that are important as you move on to bigger and better JavaBeans things. This chapter addresses some of these advanced issues and gives you some perspective as to why they are important and what they mean in practical terms.

Unfortunately, this chapter isn't presented as a delicately flowing group of related information that ties together in a nice little package. Instead, it is a mixture of a wide range of issues; all they have in common is simply that you haven't learned much about them yet. In other words, this chapter takes a group of advanced JavaBeans issues and presents them to you in the most logical way possible. The goal of this chapter is mainly to tie up loose ends in regard to your knowledge of JavaBeans and address some important fringe issues.

You learn about the following topics in this chapter:

- Security
- Invisible beans
- Beans and multithreading
- Internationalized beans
- Beans in a windowing environment
- Inner classes

Security

Security has played a prominent role in the development of the Java programming language and runtime environment. This is primarily because Java has evolved as the programming environment of choice for the Internet, where security risks related to the online transfer of information are of great importance. It only stands to reason that the security issues relating to Java should transfer to JavaBeans, and in fact they do. JavaBeans components are subject to the same security model imposed on Java, which is very consistent with the positioning of JavaBeans as a logical extension of Java. The concerns related to Java security in no way change when it comes to JavaBeans.

More specifically, as far as security goes, beans are treated just like the applets with which they reside. A bean used within the context of an untrusted applet is considered just as untrusted as the applet. In practical terms, this means the bean isn't allowed to read or write files on a client or connect to arbitrary network hosts. To the Java runtime system, a bean that executes within an untrusted applet is no different than any other support class used by the applet. When a bean is associated with a trusted, or signed, applet, however, the whole scenario changes. Trusted applets are given full access to file manipulation and network host connections, just like full-blown Java applications. A bean that resides in a trusted applet or application is therefore given the same freedoms.

A simple rule to remember in terms of beans and security is that beans inherit the same security model as the parent applet or application within which they reside. It's important to note here that although many applets will be digitally signed, and therefore trusted, you should still assume the worst case when you design and develop beans. You should design beans in such a way that they can successfully function in an untrusted environment. In doing so, you are allowing the widest range of use for your beans. Of course, if your bean simply must perform file I/O or some other function that imposes security concerns as part of its core function, this guideline is impossible to meet.

When you are designing a bean, there are some steps you can take to minimize security concerns and allow the bean to perform in the most stringent of security environments. Following is a list of some of the areas in which security plays a role in the design of beans:

- Introspection
- Persistence
- Data transfer
- Menu merging

> Note: Keep in mind that none of these restrictions apply to beans running as parts of trusted applets or full-blown Java applications, because beans adhere to a relaxed security model in these scenarios.

Introspection

Recall from Chapter 5, "Introspection: Getting to Know a Bean," that there are two levels of functionality provided in the JavaBeans introspection services: low-level services and high-level services. The high-level services enable access to the publicly exported portions of a bean, and the low-level services are meant to be used primarily by application builder tools to assess the internal workings of a bean using reflection. Because of the access they provide to the internals of a bean, the low-level services raise some serious security concerns. It should come as no big surprise to find out that the low-level services are accessible only in a trusted environment, such as beans being used in an application builder tool. The high-level services, on the other hand, impose no security restrictions and are completely accessible in both trusted and untrusted environments.

Because of the security situation surrounding the introspection services, you should make sure you aren't relying on the low-level services in a bean that you intend to be used in untrusted environments. Instead, you should try to stick with using the high-level services, which are fully accessible across the board. Fortunately, the high-level services provide plenty of bean access for most situations through the publicly exported properties, methods, and events for a bean.

Persistence

Persistence doesn't seem like an area in which security would come into play in a big way. However, remember that beans are often serialized to and from files, which are extremely suspect when it comes to security. For bean developers, this doesn't mean you can't serialize a bean in an untrusted environment; it just means that you might not be able to have any direct control over the serialization stream itself. It is expected that the parent applet or application for a bean will provide the stream through which the bean is serialized. Depending on the security imposed by the parent applet or application, the bean might or might not be able to access the stream directly. As a bean developer, your safest bet is to peacefully read and write to streams through the standard serialization mechanism and not worry about directly modifying the stream from within your beans.

Data Transfer

The Java 1.1 AWT provides support for data transfer operations through extended windowing features such as the cut, copy, and paste clipboard functions. You learn a little more about the functional aspects of these additions to the AWT in the "Beans and Multithreading" section later in this chapter, but for now I want to focus on the security issues surrounding them and JavaBeans. Because clipboard services are based on the transfer of data over execution boundaries, you can't help but worry about the security implications involved.

This affects beans because they are fully capable of participating in clipboard operations and are therefore subject to the same security implications surrounding the operations. In general, clipboard operations aren't restricted by the default Java security model regardless of whether a bean resides in a trusted environment. However, there can be instances in which you will want to control the transfer of information in a clipboard operation, so you always have the option of altering the security model to be more strict in regard to data transfers. When it comes to data transfer, it is ultimately up to you as a developer to impose security restrictions based on the specific needs of the bean or parent applet or application.

Menu Merging

In Chapter 16, "The Future of JavaBeans," you will learn about future enhancements planned for the JavaBeans API. One of these enhancements involves the capability of beans to contain menu information that can be merged with the menu of a parent applet or application. Although menus themselves aren't typically considered at risk for security breaches, the capability of a bean to alter the parent applet in such a way is itself a risk to some degree. Understand that this risk exists only when an applet attempts to alter the menu of the containing Web browser. It's perfectly OK for a bean to alter the parent applet's menu, provided the applet doesn't propagate this change on to the containing browser menu. In other words, the browser menu is the one that is at risk in terms of security, so merging an applet menu with a browser menu is the real issue here.

This situation affects beans because they will eventually be able to alter their parent applet's menu in a future version of Java; these alterations can then be indirectly transferred to the browser menu. The simple solution imposed by the standard Java security model is to allow only trusted applets the capability to merge menus with a containing browser. Menu merging can occur between a bean and an applet in any security scenario, but the applet can merge menus with a browser only when it is trusted.

Invisible Beans

All the beans you built in Part III, "Creating Your Own Beans," are considered graphical beans because they have a graphical representation at runtime. This might seem like a prerequisite for all beans because the most practical application of beans is in user interface controls or as output displays, both of which are graphical in nature. However, it is perfectly acceptable for a bean to have no graphical representation at all. These invisible beans usually take the form of some support library that performs a function behind the scenes. A good example of an invisible bean is a timer bean, which sits in the background and fires timer events at regular intervals. This type of bean would be extremely useful for orchestrating animation frames or any other process that requires a periodic trigger.

> Note: In Chapter 13, "An Audio Player Bean," you learned how you can modify the audio player bean to act as an invisible bean. Although the task of actually converting the bean to an invisible bean was left as an exercise, you still got an idea about how the bean could be implemented and used invisibly.

Even though invisible beans have no visual representation in an executing applet or application, they have full access to all the services available to other beans, which makes them ideal for performing background functions. These beans have no visual representation at runtime, but they must be visible in some form at design time so that users can edit the properties of them inside an application builder tool. The typical approach is for an invisible bean to display a simple icon in design mode and then become invisible at runtime.

Another motivation for a bean to be invisible is so it can be used to build server applications, which typically aren't graphical. Knowing this, it is possible to design beans that are capable of being conditionally invisible depending on their use. This type of bean would be visible when used in an applet and invisible when used in a nongraphical server application.

Beans and Multithreading

JavaBeans components are designed as self-contained units that are accessible only through carefully constructed interfaces, so it's tempting to think that they are above some of the concerns that exist in other Java classes, such as applets. However, you can't lose sight of the fact that beans are really just normal Java classes with the capability to do some extra things such as export properties and support application builders. Therefore, beans are subject to all the same design concerns as Java classes. One of these concerns involves multithreading, which as you probably already know is the capability to enable multiple paths of execution to be taking place at once, potentially through the same piece of code. Multithreading is a fundamental part of Java and must be taken into consideration even with JavaBeans, just as it is for Java applets and applications.

Fortunately, the multithreading concerns relating to JavaBeans are relatively straightforward. Basically, you just have to consider the potential weaknesses a bean might have in regard to synchronization. You must question whether your bean has any code that could be problematic when multiple paths of execution are running through it. Because much of your bean's core functionality will be inherited from existing AWT classes that are highly thread-safe, you might not have to worry too much about how multithreading affects your bean. On the other hand, how you design your bean might mean you need to carefully evaluate how it will perform when it is multithreaded.

As an example, you learned while developing the fancy button bean in Chapter 10 that the event firing mechanism must be synchronized to avoid multithreaded problems. The problem involves the risk of an event listener being removed from the list by another thread while you are still moving through the list. If this situation occurred, you could feasibly end up firing an event to a nonexistent listener, which is a bad thing. Fortunately, a simple synchronization block fixes things and eliminates the risk. Although an in-depth discussion of synchronization problems and solutions is well beyond the scope of this book, I want you to be aware that multithreading and its related complexities must be addressed in JavaBeans.

Internationalized Beans

A new area in Java 1.1 that affects JavaBeans is internationalization, which enables Java applets and applications to be localized to a particular country or cultural region. International localization typically affects the representation of things such as dates, times, time zones, and text names. The internationalization APIs in Java 1.1 are based on Unicode 2.0 character encoding and include the capability to adapt text, numbers, dates, currency, and user-defined objects to any country's conventions.

Internationalization affects JavaBeans components just as it affects Java applets and applications. The burden of supporting localization is placed at the package level, meaning that each package is responsible for internally generating locale-dependent information. In this way, it is a bean developer's responsibility to provide localization information in the package that contains the bean. Before you get too discouraged, however, keep in mind that internationalization is only an issue for beans for which you expect to see a large amount of international use. Because many beans are being used on the Internet, supporting internationalization whenever possible certainly makes sense because the Internet is a worldwide medium. However, the Internet itself isn't very localized, so you must seriously evaluate the use of a bean before jumping into the work required to internationalize it.

Windowing Issues for Beans

Another area in which Java 1.1 has grown a great deal is the AWT, which includes a lot of enhancements and completely new additions. One of the new additions is support for advanced windowing features commonly found in graphical operating systems such as Windows and Macintosh. These windowing features involve data transfer services that are also new to Java 1.1. The data transfer services in Java 1.1 form a widely applicable underlying component of the AWT that opens the door for a lot of new functionality. The end goal of these additions is to bring the AWT up to par with other modern graphical programming environments.

The data transfer mechanism built into the Java 1.1 AWT provides the fundamental mechanism that enables the interchange of structured data among applets, applications, and beans. The significance of this mechanism to JavaBeans is that it provides a means of moving information among beans and other runtime objects in a highly structured fashion. The result is higher-level features such as drag-and-drop and clipboard functions, which support the cutting, copying, and pasting of information among beans, applets, and applications.

> Note: The drag-and-drop API actually did not ship with Java 1.1 due to development time constraints, but it is expected to materialize in the near future.

Inner Classes

As if Java 1.1 hasn't done enough for the cause of JavaBeans as it is, there is yet another topic I want to cover in regard to Java 1.1 and JavaBeans. I'm referring to inner classes, which is a surprising change to the Java language syntax that is largely responsible for making the Java 1.1 (and ultimately JavaBeans) event model possible. *Inner classes* basically refers to the capability to define a class in any scope. Previous versions of Java supported only top-level classes, which must be package members. Classes that weren't assigned a specific package were made members of a default global package.

> ### New Term
> *Inner classes* refers to a feature in the Java language that enables you to define classes at any scope.

In Java 1.1, this limitation has been lifted so that it is possible to define classes at any scope, including within other classes. You can even define classes within the scope of a block or expression. At first glance, this change might appear to be something done simply to appease the folks who have nothing better to do with their time but argue the fine points of language syntax. However, support for inner classes was added for a very practical reason: the Java 1.1 and JavaBeans event model would have gotten very messy without it because adapter classes, which form a major part of the event handling internals, are much easier to manage using inner classes.

The proof of the importance of inner classes is the simple fact that they required a change to the Java language syntax itself, which was frozen as of Java 1.0. However, because the Java architects were able to add inner classes without affecting any other parts of the language, they decided it was worth doing. Inner classes will go down as one of the least publicized but most critical changes made in Java 1.1, at least as far as JavaBeans is concerned.

> Note: For more information about inner classes or any of the other enhancements to Java 1.1, refer to the documentation that ships with the JDK 1.1.

Summary

This chapter brings some less obvious issues about JavaBeans to the forefront. Although most of these are advanced issues, it's still important for you to have at least a cursory understanding of them because they affect JavaBeans in a variety of ways. The first of these issues is security and how it relates to JavaBeans. Invisible beans are next on the menu, followed by multithreading and how it should be handled by beans. You then finished the chapter by learning about internationalization, windowing environment issues, and inner classes, all of which are additions to Java 1.1 that benefit JavaBeans.

This chapter is admittedly a jumbled group of seemingly misfit information, but there is a common thread: the issues covered are all important to your deep understanding of JavaBeans. Think of this chapter as a smoothing of the edges in terms of your JavaBeans knowledge, because it covers a wide range of topics that relate to concepts you've learned throughout the book. The purpose of presenting these advanced topics near the end of the book is to give you time to become more comfortable with JavaBeans.

Believe it or not, you will come across some of the information you learned today in practical JavaBeans development simply because software development inevitably requires you to dig around under the hood from time to time. Having an idea about some of the advanced issues of JavaBeans will make this process a little less painful. I encourage you to investigate some of these topics on your own, because I really only scratched the surface in this chapter.

The Future of JavaBeans

Throughout this book you've learned just about everything there is to know about the JavaBeans technology, at least in terms of what there is to know today. Like most software technologies, JavaBeans is rapidly growing and evolving to become more powerful and extensible. Because of this, it's only fitting that the last chapter of the book focuses on the future of JavaBeans. This chapter takes a look at what the future holds for JavaBeans from a few different perspectives.

You start off the chapter by learning about some of the enhancements planned for the bean component model. Few software technologies are perfect, and JavaBeans is no exception. Therefore, a few enhancements are already in the works for a future release. From there, you move on to learn about application builder tools that will support JavaBeans in the near future. These builder tools are expected to provide visual bean construction support similar to that provided by the BDK's BeanBox test container. You then turn your attention to JavaBeans and how it will integrate with other component models such as ActiveX and OpenDoc. Finally, you finish the chapter by taking a close look at how JavaBeans fits into the software component marketplace with ActiveX. These two technologies are being pitted against each other in many ways; you get the inside scoop as to how they really rate.

You learn about the following topics in this chapter:

- Enhancements to the bean model
- Application builder tool support
- Integration with other component models
- JavaBeans versus ActiveX

Bean Enhancements

This entire book so far discusses the JavaBeans technology with respect to version 1.0, which is the initial offering from JavaSoft. Although JavaBeans 1.0 implements a wide range of functionality that addresses and solves many problems inherent in component software, there are still a few areas in which it needs improvement. JavaSoft is fully aware of JavaBeans' shortcomings and is already working on enhancements that will solve many of them. In this section you learn about some of these new enhancements, which will appear in a future release of JavaBeans.

Keep in mind that everything you read about in this section, and in this entire chapter for that matter, is preliminary and therefore subject to change. The main goal here is to give you an idea about where JavaBeans is headed so you can start gearing up for the changes.

Menus

The primary usage of JavaBeans components is as building blocks of large, complex applications. It has become standard for applications to include a menu as part of the main application interface. It is fully expected that developers will want some beans to somehow alter the menu for an application, either to hide existing functionality or, more likely, to add new functionality. This extra menu information would be provided by the bean and would integrate directly with the parent application based on the bean's activation. The 1.0

release of JavaBeans provides no support for menus at the bean level, but JavaSoft is working on APIs to provide this functionality in a future release.

Externalized Persistence

The JavaBeans persistence support you learned in Chapter 7, "Persistence: Saving Beans for a Rainy Day," is directed toward providing an automated means of saving and restoring the internal state of a bean. More specifically, JavaBeans are currently automatically persistent based on their nontransient member variables. Even though this automatic approach to persistence is very nice for the vast majority of beans, there will certainly be situations in which bean developers will want fine control over how a bean is serialized at the binary level. This approach of using an external means of persistently storing and retrieving a bean is known as an *externalization mechanism*, or *externalized persistence*.

New Term

An *externalization mechanism* is a means of storing and retrieving an object through some type of custom, externally defined format.

JavaBeans 1.0 currently provides no direct facility for implementing externalized persistence. Recall that the automatic persistence functionality in JavaBeans 1.0 is really just the serialization support in Java 1.1. In other words, JavaBeans itself isn't responsible for implementing the automatic approach to persistence. However, support for externalized persistence will probably come in the form of a future JavaBeans release. Fortunately, the Java 1.1 serialization support is designed to enable an externalized approach, so the underlying mechanism is in place.

Multiple Bean Views

Many popular object-oriented programming class libraries are based on the concept of views. In these types of class libraries, one class represents the data for a conceptual object and another set of classes represents multiple views on that object. As a simple example, consider an object that models weather measurements made over a period of time. In a class library that supports multiple views, you could have different types of views on that object that graph the data in a variety of ways. In this way, a single conceptual object is modeled by a group of classes (a data class and multiple view classes).

In JavaBeans 1.0, beans map to classes on a one-to-one basis, which means that a bean is always represented by exactly one class. Of course, a bean can have an associated information class as well as a customizer class, but these are helper classes and don't directly affect the internal functionality of the bean itself. What I'm getting at is that JavaBeans 1.0 doesn't provide any support for multiple views on a bean. This is another area in which JavaSoft is working on enhancements for inclusion in a future release of JavaBeans.

Application Builder Tool Support

Much has been said throughout the book about application builder tools and the importance of them in terms of visually laying out and editing JavaBeans components. Even though JavaBeans provides comprehensive support for enabling the visual manipulation of beans, it is ultimately up to development tool vendors to directly add features to their tools that enable the visual integration of beans. Tool vendors must be willing to adopt the JavaBeans application builder support to their tools for users to benefit.

Fortunately, several development tool vendors have already pledged support for JavaBeans and have promised to integrate the application builder support provided by JavaBeans into their tools. Although none of the tools themselves were ready as of this writing, many were nearing completion. In fact, it is quite possible that some of them are available now as you are reading this. Following is a list of the development tool vendors that are planning an integration of JavaBeans into their visual environment:

- Symantec's Visual Café
- Borland's JBuilder
- Penumbra Software's Mojo
- SunSoft's Java Workshop
- SunSoft's Project Studio
- IBM's Applet Author
- IBM's Visual Age

Some of the development tools listed here will be available for download by the time you read this, so be sure to stop by their respective Web sites if you are interested in trying them out.

Visual Café

Symantec's Visual Café is slated to include full support for visually building beans, applets, and applications from a library of standard and third-party beans without writing any code. Visual Café will present beans to the user in the form of a tool palette, much like the one used in the BDK's BeanBox test container. For more information on Visual Café, check out Symantec's Web site at www.symantec.com.

JBuilder

Borland plans for JBuilder to integrate much of its Latte Java technology, including full support for visually constructing beans, applets, and applications using standard and third-party beans. The open and extensible development environment provided by JBuilder aims to give you complete flexibility in incorporating third-party beans and wizards. JBuilder is interesting in that several of its major subsystems are implemented as beans, meaning that the tool itself is designed around the JavaBeans technology. For more information about JBuilder, drop by Borland's Web site at www.borland.com.

Mojo

Penumbra Software's Mojo takes a little different approach than some Java development tools by providing two interfaces to the development process: a high-level visual interface and a lower-level coding interface. Mojo 3.0 will include complete support for JavaBeans, which means that you will be able to create and use JavaBeans components in the context of either of its two interfaces. For more information on Mojo, stop by Penumbra Software's Web site at www.PenumbraSoftware.com.

Java Workshop

SunSoft's Java Workshop is an interesting development tool because it is written entirely in Java. The result is a Web-centric tool that provides extensive Java support based on its being implemented in Java. A new release of Java Workshop will provide a host of new features, including full support for JavaBeans component development and use. In addition, Java Workshop will ship for the Solaris, Windows, and Macintosh platforms, which is a pretty big accomplishment for a development tool. For more information about Java Workshop, check out SunSoft's Web site at www.sun.com.

Project Studio

Beyond Java Workshop, SunSoft has another development tool that will fully support the JavaBeans technology: Project Studio, a visual application construction tool similar to an HTML authoring tool in that it is geared toward the completely graphical creation of Web content. Project Studio will ship with a rich set of reusable JavaBeans components that can be easily integrated with HTML content to enable a high-level development solution for the Web. Project Studio is geared toward Web developers who want to benefit from Java and JavaBeans without writing any code. To get the latest news on Project Studio, stop by SunSoft's Web site at www.sun.com.

Applet Author

Surprise—IBM is now in the Java development tool business. That's right, IBM's Applet Author, which is itself written entirely in Java, will give Web developers a visual development environment that boasts full support for JavaBeans. Applet Author is geared toward the visual construction of applets using JavaBeans components. For more information about Applet Author, take a peek at IBM's Web site at www.ibm.com.

Visual Age

If Applet Author doesn't quite suit your needs, IBM is also working on a new version of its Visual Age development tool that will integrate complete support for JavaBeans. Visual Age is geared more toward client/server enterprise development, an area of software development in which JavaBeans will eventually have a significant impact. Visual Age is scheduled to ship after Applet Author; for more information, visit IBM's Web site at www.ibm.com.

Note: You might be wondering where Microsoft stands in regard to JavaBeans, especially because it is the largest development tool vendor of them all. Because JavaBeans is a clear competitor of Microsoft's ActiveX component technology, Microsoft has been careful not to pledge any specific support for JavaBeans. Even so, I think the popularity of JavaBeans will be enough to persuade Microsoft to eventually support it in a future release of Visual J++, and potentially even Visual C++. Microsoft wants to protect ActiveX, but not at the risk of producing substandard development tools.

Integration with Other Component Models

One of the key concerns of the JavaBeans architects was how it relates to and integrates with existing component technologies. Although the JavaBeans technology is powerful in its own right, it is foolish to think it will replace existing technologies overnight, if ever. For this reason, JavaSoft specifically designed JavaBeans with the integration of other component models in mind. JavaSoft is currently in the process of working with industry partners to develop bridges that enable JavaBeans components to work seamlessly with other component architectures.

Following are the major component technologies JavaSoft is targeting with its initial JavaBeans bridge:

- ActiveX
- OpenDoc
- LiveConnect
- CORBA

ActiveX

ActiveX and its related technologies are quickly headed toward becoming a wide standard not just for the Windows world, but for computing in general. Microsoft has too much at stake and has a technology with too much clout to lose with ActiveX. For this reason, it is of utmost importance to JavaSoft that JavaBeans be interoperable with ActiveX. A bridge is in the works that will enable beans to act as first-class ActiveX components, which basically opens the door to using beans just as you would ActiveX components.

It's important to understand that part of the integration of JavaBeans with ActiveX is necessary to fulfill the requirement that JavaBeans reside as closely as possible to native APIs. JavaBeans is fully expected to rely on some native support in its implementation for each different platform. On platforms on which ActiveX is the dominant object model, JavaBeans will naturally rely on ActiveX to some degree under the hood. Beyond that, the ActiveX bridge will enable beans to be used as ActiveX components.

OpenDoc

Another important component technology is OpenDoc, which is an open, multiplatform architecture for component software heavily backed by Apple and IBM. JavaSoft is currently working with Apple, IBM, and Component Integration Laboratories to solidify the integration of JavaBeans with OpenDoc. With the OpenDoc bridge that is under development, beans will be able to be integrated as OpenDoc components inside OpenDoc containers such as CyberDog, Apple's integrated software suite that provides easy and intuitive access to Internet resources.

LiveConnect

JavaSoft is also working with Netscape to ensure that JavaBeans components will integrate with Netscape Navigator and the LiveConnect technology for interconnecting executable content. LiveConnect enables Web developers to use Java applets, JavaScript scripts, and Navigator plug-ins together. The successful integration of JavaBeans into this mix is an important one for JavaSoft.

CORBA

The last component model that is of great importance for JavaBeans to integrate with is CORBA (Common Object Request Broker Architecture), which is the industry standard for representing distributed objects. JavaSoft is working with SunSoft and other industry partners to provide full support for CORBA integration with JavaBeans.

JavaBeans Versus ActiveX

Even though JavaBeans will ultimately integrate peacefully with ActiveX as a component technology, don't be misled into thinking that JavaBeans and ActiveX have a truly peaceful relationship. It's true that concerns over ActiveX competing with Java were misplaced when ActiveX first hit the street, but this was because Java itself had no provision for components in any real sense. JavaBeans, on the other hand, is nothing but components. JavaBeans is JavaSoft's Java-enhanced answer to ActiveX, and as such it will be viewed in the software component market as a direct competitor of ActiveX. And make no bones about it, the mud is already slinging in terms of Microsoft and JavaSoft promoting their respective technologies.

Even though JavaBeans and ActiveX are competitors and ultimately aim to solve the same problem, they are very different technologies. ActiveX is a language-independent component technology based on Microsoft's popular OCX technology. ActiveX in its current implementation is entirely dependent on the Windows platform, which is a critical weakness, especially in regard to the Internet. Microsoft is busily working on versions of ActiveX for both UNIX and Macintosh, but it isn't clear when they will ship.

JavaBeans, on the other hand, is a component technology that is language-dependent in its current implementation. However, JavaBeans is platform-independent in that it will run on any platform that supports Java. The platform independence of JavaBeans makes it an ideal candidate for the Web because it is dangerous to handcuff Web content to a particular platform. The language dependency of Java might sound like a negative at first, but it really isn't simply because Java is becoming widely accepted as a powerful and useful programming language in its own right. There are no signs of Java losing ground as a programming language, which means that being forced to use it to create JavaBeans components isn't too much of a restriction. Even so, the bytecode nature of Java executables opens the door for supporting JavaBeans development in other programming languages in the future.

From the discussion thus far, it's clear that JavaBeans has a significant edge over ActiveX because it is cross-platform. This isn't to say that Microsoft can't release a cross-platform version of ActiveX in the near future, but the clock is ticking in a sense that JavaBeans will be gaining Internet market share until that day arrives. So, JavaBeans is the clear winner over ActiveX, right? Not quite.

The area in which Java and JavaBeans are both weak is the one area in which ActiveX shines: existing code base. ActiveX has a significant advantage over JavaBeans in this regard because its underlying OCX technology is widely used in the Windows software community. Granted, Windows is only one platform, but it is by far the dominant platform and one that drives the software market. So, JavaBeans is in for a fight when it comes to competing with the millions of lines of code out there that are heavily based on ActiveX-derived technologies.

Where this issue will come into play heavily is corporate intranets, which rely a great deal on existing ActiveX technologies such as Microsoft Office applications. It will be a tough pill to swallow for intranet builders to throw out all their existing code and switch to JavaBeans. The integration possibilities of JavaBeans and ActiveX muddy the water a little at this point, however, because who's to say you couldn't keep your ActiveX code base and still integrate new code that is based on JavaBeans?

To sum things up, the answer as to which technology is better or which technology will beat the other is a clear "I don't know." On one hand, Java has a clear advantage because it has a cross-platform design and is an ideal technology for the Internet. On the other, however, the sheer depth of the ActiveX code base makes it an ideal candidate in situations in which it just isn't feasible to develop everything new, such as corporate intranets. Based on these conflicting positives for each technology, it simply isn't clear which technology will emerge as the dominant one.

The fact that JavaBeans and ActiveX have their own unique advantages can be seen as a positive in some ways. Consider the likely outcome of neither technology dominating the other. If they are able to coexist with each other and integrate together, who cares which one wins? If you can leverage the use of each technology in situations that warrant their unique advantages, we all might be better off if both technologies succeed.

Summary

This chapter peers into the crystal ball and paints you a picture of the future of JavaBeans. Although the topics covered in this chapter vary considerably, they all somehow tie into the future of JavaBeans and what it means to JavaBeans developers and users. You started the chapter by learning about some of JavaSoft's planned enhancements to JavaBeans, which will appear in a future release. You then learned about some application builder tools that are adding support for the visual layout and editing of beans. From there, you shifted gears a little and looked at how JavaBeans is being integrated with other popular component models, which is critical to JavaBeans' success. Finally, you finished the chapter by learning about the differences between JavaBeans and ActiveX and where they fit into the future of component software.

This chapter marks the end of your foray into learning the JavaBeans technology. It should give you a few things to think about as you move on to use JavaBeans in your own development projects. Keeping tabs on the future of JavaBeans is a critical part of using the technology with success. I encourage you to check JavaSoft's Web site occasionally at www.javasoft.com to find out the latest information on JavaBeans. Good luck in your JavaBeans endeavors!

Appendixes

APPENDIX A

JavaBeans Online Resources

Perhaps the most important aspect of continued success in JavaBeans programming is keeping up with the latest trends and related technologies. Fortunately, there are plenty of online resources to help you keep your bean programming skills up-to-date. This appendix points you to some of the more useful resources, which you should use as often as possible.

JavaSoft's JavaBeans Web Site

JavaSoft's official JavaBeans site on the Web contains all the latest JavaBeans information and related tools. You'll definitely want to keep an eye on this site because it is the central location for obtaining the latest version of the Beans Development Kit (BDK). It also has an extensive set of online documentation. The JavaSoft Web site is located at `http://splash.javasoft.com/beans` (see Figure A.1).

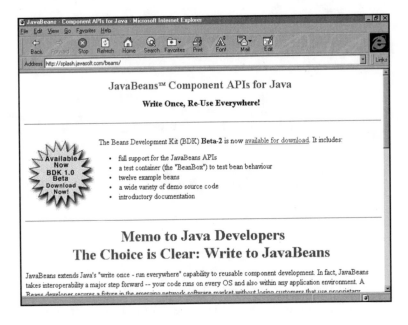

Figure A.1.
JavaSoft's JavaBeans Web site.

Gamelan Web Site

Gamelan is the end-all Java resource directory and will be adding more JavaBeans resources as they become available. Besides being possibly the official Java Web site at JavaSoft, Gamelan is by far the most useful and comprehensive source of Java information anywhere. It has Java conveniently divided into different categories, each leading to a wealth of information, source code, and sample applets. Check out Gamelan yourself and you'll see what I mean. It's located at `http://www.gamelan.com` (see Figure A.2).

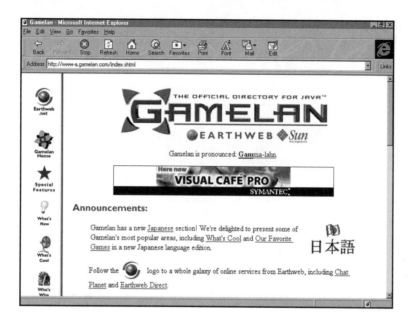

Figure A.2.
The Gamelan Web site.

JavaWorld Online Journal

The *JavaWorld* online journal is an excellent publication by IDG Communications that always has some interesting Java programming articles, including coverage of JavaBeans. You can even subscribe to *JavaWorld* and receive Java information by e-mail. The *JavaWorld* Web site is located at `http://www.javaworld.com` and is shown in Figure A.3.

ActiveXpress Web Site

The ActiveXpress Web site serves as an information source for ActiveX users and developers. Even though the site centers on ActiveX, it also contains a decent amount of information on JavaBeans. The site is located at `http://techweb3.web.cerf.net/activexpress` (see Figure A.4).

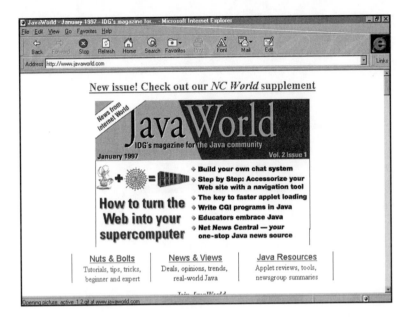

Figure A.3.
The JavaWorld *online journal Web site.*

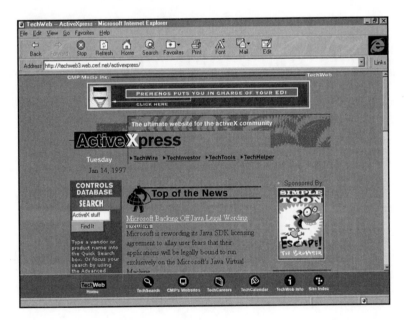

Figure A.4.
The ActiveXpress Web site.

Digital Espresso Online Summary

Digital Espresso is an online weekly summary of the traffic appearing in the various Java mailing lists and newsgroups. Digital Espresso is an excellent JavaBeans resource because it pulls information from a variety of sources into a single Web site. It is located at `http://www.io.org/~mentor/DigitalEspresso.html` (see Figure A.5).

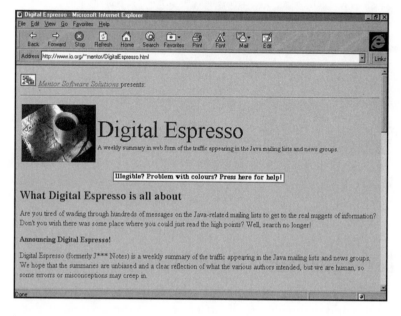

Figure A.5.
The Digital Espresso online summary Web site.

Java Developer Web Site

The Java Developer Web site is a good Web site for sharing information and finding answers to Java and JavaBeans programming questions. It has a section called "How Do I…" that lists common (and some not-so-common) Java programming questions and their corresponding answers, including sample source code. The Java Developer Web site is located at `http://www.digitalfocus.com/faq` (see Figure A.6).

Figure A.6.
The Java Developer Web site.

Nerdtalk Online Column

The Nerdtalk Web site is a biweekly online column that deals with technology issues in the world of distributed client/server computing. Topics include everything from distributed objects to database access to transaction processing. Although Nerdtalk admittedly isn't focused on JavaBeans, its current article as of this writing was solely about JavaBeans. The Nerdtalk Web site is located at `http://www.openenv.com/nerd/talk.htm` (see Figure A.7).

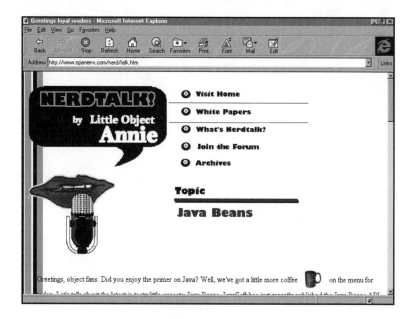

Figure A.7.
The Nerdtalk online column Web site.

JavaBeans API Quick Reference

The JavaBeans API package, also known as java.beans, provides the core classes and interfaces that make the JavaBeans technology possible. The API consists of interfaces, classes, and exceptions, which are covered in detail throughout the rest of this appendix.

Interfaces

The JavaBeans API consists of the following interfaces, which are described in detail throughout the next few sections:

- BeanInfo
- Customizer
- PropertyChangeListener
- PropertyEditor
- VetoableChangeListener
- Visibility

BeanInfo

Extends: `Object`

The `BeanInfo` interface defines a set of methods that can be used to find out information explicitly provided by a bean, such as lists of properties, methods, and events. Developers who want to provide explicit bean information must implement the `BeanInfo` interface and provide suitable information. It's important to note that any information not explicitly provided through the `BeanInfo` interface is determined by JavaBeans using the automatic introspection facilities of the JavaBeans API.

Member Constants

`public final static int ICON_COLOR_16x16`

This constant represents a 16×16-pixel color icon.

`public final static int ICON_COLOR_32x32`

This constant represents a 32×32-pixel color icon.

`public final static int ICON_MONO_16x16`

This constant represents a 16×16-pixel monochrome icon.

`public final static int ICON_MONO_32x32`

This constant represents a 32×32-pixel monochrome icon.

Methods

`public abstract BeanDescriptor getBeanDescriptor()`

This method gets the bean descriptor associated with a bean.

Returns:

A bean descriptor providing general information about the bean or `null` if the information should be obtained automatically.

`public abstract EventSetDescriptor[] getEventSetDescriptors()`

This method gets the array of event set descriptors associated with a bean.

Returns:

An array of event set descriptors describing the kinds of events fired by the bean or `null` if the information should be obtained automatically.

```
public abstract int getDefaultEventIndex()
```

This method gets the default event index for a bean, if it exists.

Returns:

The index of the default event in the event set descriptor array or -1 if there is no default event.

```
public abstract PropertyDescriptor[] getPropertyDescriptors()
```

This method gets the array of property descriptors associated with a bean.

Returns:

An array of property descriptors describing the editable properties supported by the bean or `null` if the information should be obtained automatically.

```
public abstract int getDefaultPropertyIndex()
```

This method gets the default property index for a bean, if it exists.

Returns:

The index of the default property in the property descriptor array, or -1 if there is no default property.

```
public abstract MethodDescriptor[] getMethodDescriptors()
```

This method gets the array of method descriptors associated with a bean.

Returns:

An array of method descriptors describing the externally visible methods supported by the bean or `null` if the information should be obtained automatically.

```
public abstract BeanInfo[] getAdditionalBeanInfo()
```

This method enables a bean information object to return an arbitrary collection of bean information objects providing additional information on the bean.

Returns:

An array of bean information objects or `null` if none exist.

```
public abstract Image getIcon(int iconKind)
```

This method returns an icon image object that can be used to represent the bean in application builder tools. There are four supported types of icons: 16×16 color, 32×32 color, 16×16 monochrome, and 32×32 monochrome.

Parameter

iconKind	The type of icon requested, which is one of the constant values ICON_COLOR_16x16, ICON_COLOR_32x32, ICON_MONO_16x16, or ICON_MONO_32x32

Returns:

An image object representing the requested icon or null if no icon is available.

Customizer

Extends: Object

The Customizer interface defines the overhead required to provide a complete visual editor for a bean. Classes implementing the Customizer interface are typically derived from the Component class so that they can be used in the context of a dialog box or panel.

Methods

`public abstract void setObject(Object bean)`

This method sets the object to be customized.

Parameter

bean	The object to be customized.

`public abstract void addPropertyChangeListener`
`➥(PropertyChangeListener listener)`

This method registers a listener for the PropertyChange event. The customizer should fire the PropertyChange event whenever it modifies the bean in a way that might require the displayed properties to be refreshed.

Parameter

listener	A listener to be notified by a PropertyChange event whenever the bean is modified.

`public abstract void removePropertyChangeListener`
`➥(PropertyChangeListenerlistener)`

This method removes a listener for the PropertyChange event.

Parameter

listener   The PropertyChange event listener to be removed.

PropertyChangeListener

Extends: EventListener

The PropertyChangeListener interface serves as the listener interface implemented by classes wanting to receive notifications about a bound property change. This interface consists of the propertyChange() method, which is called whenever the value of a bound property has changed on a bean for which the interface is registered.

Methods

public abstract void propertyChange(PropertyChangeEvent evt)

This method is called when a bound property has changed.

Parameter

evt   A PropertyChangeEvent object containing information about the event source and the property that has changed.

PropertyEditor

Extends: Object

The PropertyEditor interface defines a means of visually editing a single bean property of a given type. Because JavaBeans provides standard property editors for built-in data types, you are only required to develop property editors for custom data types.

Methods

public abstract void setValue(Object value)

This method sets the object that is to be edited.

Parameter

value   The target object to be edited.

public abstract Object getValue()

This method gets the object that is being edited.

Returns:

The object being edited.

```
public abstract boolean isPaintable()
```

This method determines whether the property can be painted.

Returns:

true if the property can be painted using the paintValue() method; false otherwise.

```
public abstract void paintValue(Graphics gfx, Rectangle box)
```

This method paints a representation of the property value into a given area on the screen.

Parameters	
gfx	The graphics object on which to paint
box	A rectangle within the graphics object that specifies the painting window

```
public abstract String getJavaInitializationString()
```

This method generates a fragment of Java code that can be used to initialize a variable with the current property value; this method is used when generating Java code to set the value of the property.

Returns:

A fragment of Java code representing an initializer for the current property value.

```
public abstract String getAsText()
```

This method gets the property value as a human readable string.

Returns:

The property value as a human readable string or null if the value can't be expressed as a human readable string.

```
public abstract void setAsText(String text) throws
➥IllegalArgumentException
```

This method sets the property value by parsing the string argument.

Parameter

text	The string to be parsed and set

`public abstract String[] getTags()`

This method returns an array of tagged values for the property, if they exist.

Returns:

The tagged values for the property or `null` if the property cannot be represented as tagged values.

`public abstract Component getCustomEditor()`

This method gets a custom visual property editor for the property.

Returns:

A custom editor that lets a human directly edit the property value or `null` if there is no custom editor for the property.

`public abstract boolean supportsCustomEditor()`

This method determines whether a custom editor is supported for the property.

Returns:

`true` if a custom editor is supported for the property; `false` otherwise.

`public abstract void addPropertyChangeListener`
`➥(PropertyChangeListener listener)`

This method registers a listener for the `PropertyChange` event.

Parameter

listener	A listener to be notified when a `PropertyChange` event is fired.

`public abstract void removePropertyChangeListener`
`➥(PropertyChangeListenerlistener)`

This method removes a listener from the `PropertyChange` event.

Parameter

listener	The `PropertyChange` listener to be removed.

VetoableChangeListener

Extends: `EventListener`

Similar to `PropertyChangeListener`, the `VetoableChangeListener` interface serves as the listener interface implemented by classes wanting to receive notifications about a constrained property change. This interface consists of the `vetoableChange()` method, which is called whenever the value of a constrained property has changed on a bean for which the interface is registered. The `vetoableChange()` method will throw a `PropertyVetoException` exception if it rejects the new value of the constrained property.

Methods

```
public abstract void vetoableChange(PropertyChangeEvent evt)
➥throws PropertyVetoException
```

This method is called when a constrained property has changed.

Parameter	
evt	A `PropertyChangeEvent` object containing information about the event source and the property that has changed.

Visibility

Extends: `Object`

The `Visibility` interface is used to determine whether a bean requires a graphical user interface and whether a graphical user interface is available for the bean to use.

Methods

```
public abstract boolean needsGui()
```

This method determines whether the bean needs a graphical user interface.

Returns:

true if the bean needs a graphical user interface available in order to function; false otherwise.

```
public abstract void dontUseGui()
```

This method instructs the bean that it should not use the graphical user interface.

```
public abstract void okToUseGui()
```

This method instructs the bean that it is okay to use the graphical user interface.

```
public abstract boolean avoidingGui()
```

This method determines whether the bean is avoiding using the graphical user interface.

Returns:

`true` if the bean is avoiding use of the graphical user interface; `false` otherwise.

Classes

The JavaBeans API consists of the following classes, which are described in detail throughout the next few sections:

- `BeanDescriptor`
- `Beans`
- `EventSetDescriptor`
- `FeatureDescriptor`
- `IndexedPropertyDescriptor`
- `Introspector`
- `MethodDescriptor`
- `ParameterDescriptor`
- `PropertyChangeEvent`
- `PropertyChangeSupport`
- `PropertyDescriptor`
- `PropertyEditorManager`
- `PropertyEditorSupport`
- `SimpleBeanInfo`
- `VetoableChangeSupport`

BeanDescriptor

Extends: FeatureDescriptor

The BeanDescriptor class provides global information about a bean, including the name of the bean and the bean's customizer.

Constructors

public BeanDescriptor(Class beanClass)

This constructor creates a bean descriptor for a bean that doesn't have a customizer.

Parameter	
beanClass	The Class object of the Java class that implements the bean.

public BeanDescriptor(Class beanClass, Class customizerClass)

This constructor creates a bean descriptor for a bean that has a customizer.

Parameters	
beanClass	The Class object of the Java class that implements the bean.
customizerClass	The Class object of the Java class that implements the bean's customizer.

Methods

public Class getBeanClass()

This method determines the bean's Class object.

Returns:

The Class object for the bean.

public Class getCustomizerClass()

This method determines the Class object for the bean's customizer.

Returns:

The Class object for the bean's customizer or null if the bean has no customizer.

Beans

Extends: `Object`

This class provides general-purpose bean utility methods.

Constructors

`public Beans()`

This constructor creates a default bean object.

Methods

`public static Object instantiate(ClassLoader cls, String name)`
`➡throws IOException, ClassNotFoundException`

This method reads a bean from a serialized object, where the serialized object is a named resource file available from a given class loader.

Parameters	
`classLoader`	The class loader from which the serialized object is read or `null` if the system class loader is to be used.
`name`	The name of the serialized object within the class loader.

`public static Object getInstanceOf(Object bean, Class targetType)`

This method gets an object representing a specified type view of a bean.

Parameters	
`bean`	The bean object from which a view is to be obtained.
`targetType`	The type of view to get.

`public static boolean isInstanceOf(Object bean, Class targetType)`

This method checks to see whether a bean can be viewed as a given target type.

Parameters	
`bean`	The bean from which to obtain a view.
`targetType`	The type of view to get.

Returns:

true if the given bean supports the given targetType; false otherwise.

```
public static boolean isDesignTime()
```

This method tests to see whether the bean is in design mode.

Returns:

true if the bean is in design mode; false otherwise.

```
public static boolean isGuiAvailable()
```

This method determines whether the bean is running in a graphical environment.

Returns:

true if the bean is in a graphical environment; false otherwise.

```
public static void setDesignTime(boolean isDesignTime) throws
➥SecurityException
```

This method is used to set whether or not the bean is running in an application builder tool.

Parameter	
isDesignTime	true if the bean is running in an application builder tool; false otherwise.

```
public static void setGuiAvailable(boolean isGuiAvailable) throws
➥SecurityException
```

This method is used to indicate whether the bean is running in a graphical environment.

Parameter	
isGuiAvailable	true if the bean is running in a graphical environment.

EventSetDescriptor

Extends: FeatureDescriptor

The EventSetDescriptor class represents a set of events that a bean is capable of generating. The events defined in an EventSetDescriptor class are all deliverable as method calls on a single event listener interface.

Constructors

```
public EventSetDescriptor(Class sourceClass, String eventSetName,
➥Class listenerType, String listenerMethodName) throws
➥listenerType, String listenerMethodName) throws
➥IntrospectionException
```

This constructor creates an event set descriptor based on the standard design patterns.

Parameters

sourceClass	The class firing the event.
eventSetName	The programmatic name of the event set.
listenerType	The listener to which events will be delivered.
listenerMethodName	The name of the method to be called when the event is delivered to its target listener.

```
public EventSetDescriptor(Class sourceClass, String eventSetName,
➥Class listenerType, String listenerMethodNames[],
➥String addListenerMethodName, String removeListenerMethodName)
➥throws IntrospectionException
```

This constructor creates a detailed event descriptor using string names.

Parameters

sourceClass	The class firing the event.
eventSetName	The programmatic name of the event set.
listenerType	The listener to which events will be delivered.
listenerMethodNames	The names of the methods to be called when the event is delivered to its target listener.
addListenerMethodName	The name of the method on the event source used to register event listeners.
removeListenerMethodName	The name of the method on the event source used to remove an event listener.

```
public EventSetDescriptor(String eventSetName, Class listenerType,
➥Method listenerMethods[], Method addListenerMethod, Method
➥removeListenerMethod)throws IntrospectionException
```

This constructor creates a detailed event set descriptor using `Method` and `Class` objects.

Parameters

eventSetName	The programmatic name of the event set.
listenerType	The listener to which events will be delivered.
listenerMethods	An array of `Method` objects describing each of the event handling methods in the event listener.
addListenerMethod	The method on the event source that is used to register an event listener.
removeListenerMethod	The method on the event source that is used to unregister an event listener.

```
public EventSetDescriptor(String eventSetName, Class listenerType,
➥MethodDescriptor listenerMethodDescriptors[],
➥Method addListenerMethod, Method removeListenerMethod)
➥throws IntrospectionException
```

This constructor creates a detailed event set descriptor using `MethodDescriptor` and `Class` objects.

Parameters

eventSetName	The programmatic name of the event set.
listenerType	The listener to which events will be delivered.
listenerMethodDescriptors	An array of `MethodDescriptor` objects describing each of the event handling methods in the event listener.

addListenerMethod	The method on the event source that is used to register an event listener.
removeListenerMethod	The method on the event source that is used to unregister an event listener.

Methods

`public Class getListenerType()`

This method gets the `Class` object corresponding to the registered event listener.

Returns:

A `Class` object for the event listener that is invoked when the event is fired.

`public Method[] getListenerMethods()`

This method gets the array of `Method` objects corresponding to the registered event listeners.

Returns:

An array of `Method` objects for the methods within the event listener that are called when events are fired.

`public MethodDescriptor[] getListenerMethodDescriptors()`

This method gets the array of `MethodDescriptor` objects for the methods within the event listener that are called when events are fired.

Returns:

An array of `MethodDescriptor` objects for the methods within the event listener that are called when events are fired.

`public Method getAddListenerMethod()`

This method gets the method used to register an event listener.

Returns:

The method used to register an event listener.

`public Method getRemoveListenerMethod()`

This method gets the method used to remove an event listener.

Returns:

The method used to remove an event listener.

`public void setUnicast(boolean unicast)`

This method sets an event as unicast.

Parameter	
unicast	true if the event is to be unicast; `false` if it is to be multicast.

`public boolean isUnicast()`

This method determines whether the event is unicast.

Returns:

`true` if the event set is unicast; `false` otherwise.

`public void setInDefaultEventSet(boolean inDefaultEventSet)`

This method sets an event set as being in the default set.

Parameter	
inDefaultEventSet	true if the event set is to be in the default event set; `false` otherwise.

`public boolean isInDefaultEventSet()`

This method determines whether an event set is in the default set.

Returns:

`true` if the event set is in the default set; `false` otherwise.

FeatureDescriptor

Extends: `Object`

The `FeatureDescriptor` class serves as a common base class for the `EventSetDescriptor`, `MethodDescriptor`, and `PropertyDescriptor` classes. It represents bean information that is common across these classes, such as the name of an event, method, or property.

Constructors

```
public FeatureDescriptor()
```

This constructor creates a default feature descriptor.

Methods

```
public String getName()
```

This method gets the programmatic name of the property, method, or event.

Returns:

The programmatic name of the property, method, or event.

```
public void setName(String name)
```

This method sets the programmatic name of the property, method, or event.

Parameter	
name	The programmatic name of the property, method, or event.

```
public String getDisplayName()
```

This method gets the localized display name for the property, method, or event.

Returns:

The localized display name for the property, method, or event.

```
public void setDisplayName(String displayName)
```

This method sets the localized display name for the property, method, or event.

Parameter	
displayName	The localized display name for the property, method, or event.

```
public boolean isExpert()
```

This method determines whether the expert flag is set for the property, method, or event. The expert flag is used to distinguish between features that are intended for expert users versus those that are intended for normal users.

Returns:

true if the expert flag is set for the property, method, or event; false otherwise.

```
public void setExpert(boolean expert)
```

This method sets the expert flag for the property, method, or event.

Parameter	
expert	true if this is an expert property, method, or event; false otherwise.

```
public boolean isHidden()
```

This method determines whether the hidden flag is set for the property, method, or event. The hidden flag is used to identify features that are intended only for application builder tool use and should not be exposed externally.

Returns:

true if the hidden flag is set for the property, method, or event; false otherwise.

```
public void setHidden(boolean hidden)
```

This method sets the hidden flag for the property, method, or event.

Parameter	
hidden	true if this is a hidden property, method, or event; false otherwise.

```
public String getShortDescription()
```

This method gets the localized short description for the property, method, or event.

Returns:

A string representing the localized short description for the property, method, or event.

```
public void setShortDescription(String text)
```

This method sets the localized short description for the property, method, or event.

Parameter	
text	The localized short description for the property, method, or event.

```
public void setValue(String attributeName, Object value)
```

This method sets a locale-independent named attribute for the property, method, or event.

Parameters

attributeName	The locale-independent name of the attribute to set for the property, method, or event.
value	The value of the attribute.

```
public Object getValue(String attributeName)
```

This method gets a locale-independent named attribute for the property, method, or event.

Parameter

attributeName	The locale-independent name of the attribute for the property, method, or event.

Returns:

The value of the attribute or null if the attribute doesn't exist.

```
public Enumeration attributeNames()
```

This method gets an enumeration containing the locale-independent names of any registered attributes for the property, method, or event.

Returns:

An enumeration containing the locale-independent names of any registered attributes for the property, method, or event.

IndexedPropertyDescriptor

Extends: PropertyDescriptor

The IndexedPropertyDescriptor class represents a publicly accessible indexed property. This class provides methods for accessing the type of an indexed property along with its accessor methods.

Constructors

```
public IndexedPropertyDescriptor(String propertyName, Class
►beanClass) throws IntrospectionException
```

This constructor creates an indexed property descriptor for a property that follows standard Java conventions by having getter and setter methods for both indexed and array access.

Parameters

propertyName	The programmatic name of the property.
beanClass	The Class object for the target bean.

```
public IndexedPropertyDescriptor(String propertyName, Class
►beanClass, String getterName, String setterName,
►String indexedGetterName, String indexedSetterName)
►throws IntrospectionException
```

This constructor creates a detailed indexed property descriptor based on the name of the property and method names for getting and setting the property, both indexed and nonindexed.

Parameters

propertyName	The programmatic name of the property.
beanClass	The Class object for the target bean.
getterName	The name of the method used for getting the property values as an array or null if the property is write-only or must be indexed.
setterName	The name of the method used for setting the property values as an array or null if the property is read-only or must be indexed.
indexedGetterName	The name of the method used for getting an indexed property value or null if the property is write-only.
indexedSetterName	The name of the method used for setting an indexed property value or null if the property is read-only.

```
public IndexedPropertyDescriptor(String propertyName, Method
➥getter, Method setter, Method indexedGetter,
➥Method indexedSetter) throws IntrospectionException
```

This constructor creates a detailed indexed property descriptor based on the name of the property and `Method` objects for getting and setting the property.

Parameters

propertyName	The programmatic name of the property.
getter	The method used for getting the property values as an array or `null` if the property is write-only or must be indexed.
setter	The method used for setting the property values as an array or `null` if the property is read-only or must be indexed.
indexedGetter	The method used for getting an indexed property value or `null` if the property is write-only.
indexedSetter	The method used for setting an indexed property value or `null` if the property is read-only.

Methods

```
public Method getIndexedReadMethod()
```

This method gets the method used to get an indexed property value.

Returns:

The method used to get an indexed property value or `null` if the property isn't indexed or is write-only.

```
public Method getIndexedWriteMethod()
```

This method gets the method used to set an indexed property value.

Returns:

The method used to set an indexed property value or `null` if the property isn't indexed or is read-only.

```
public Class getIndexedPropertyType()
```

This method gets the class type of the indexed properties.

Returns:

The class type of the indexed properties.

Introspector

Extends: `Object`

The `Introspector` class provides the overhead necessary to analyze a bean and determine its public properties, methods, and events. This class uses explicit bean information if it exists and relies on reflection and design patterns to automatically analyze a bean if not.

Methods

```
public static BeanInfo getBeanInfo(Class beanClass) throws
➥IntrospectionException
```

This method introspects a Java bean and learns about all its exposed properties, methods, and events.

Parameter	
beanClass	The bean class to be introspected.

Returns:

A bean information object describing the target bean.

```
public static BeanInfo getBeanInfo(Class beanClass, Class
➥stopClass) throws IntrospectionException
```

This method introspects a Java bean below a given stop point and learns about all its exposed properties, methods, and events.

Parameters	
beanClass	The bean class to be introspected.
stopClass	The base class at which to stop the introspection.

```
public static String decapitalize(String name)
```

This method converts a string name to standard Java variable name capitalization conventions, which usually means converting the first character from uppercase to lowercase.

Parameter

name   The string to be uncapitalized.

Returns:

A string representing the uncapitalized version of the string.

```
public static String[] getBeanInfoSearchPath()
```

This method gets an array containing the package names to be searched to find bean information classes.

Returns:

An array containing the package names to be searched to find bean information classes.

```
public static void setBeanInfoSearchPath(String path[])
```

This method sets the array of package names to be searched to find bean information classes.

Parameter

path   The array of package names to be searched to find bean information classes.

MethodDescriptor

Extends: `FeatureDescriptor`

The `MethodDescriptor` class represents a publicly accessible method. This class provides methods for accessing information such as a method's parameters.

Constructors

```
public MethodDescriptor(Method method)
```

This constructor creates a method descriptor based on the given `Method` object.

Parameter

---

method   An object containing low-level method information.

```
public MethodDescriptor(Method method, ParameterDescriptor
➥parameterDescriptors[])
```

This constructor creates a method descriptor based on the given `Method` object and parameter descriptors.

Parameters

---

method   An object containing low-level method
                        information.

parameterDescriptors   An array containing descriptive informa-
                        tion for each of the method's parameters.

Methods

```
public Method getMethod()
```

This method gets an object containing a low-level description of the method.

Returns:

The low-level description of the method.

```
public ParameterDescriptor[] getParameterDescriptors()
```

This method gets an array containing the locale-independent names of the method's parameters.

Returns:

An array containing the locale-independent names of the method's parameters or a null array if the parameter names aren't known.

ParameterDescriptor

Extends: `FeatureDescriptor`

The `ParameterDescriptor` class represents the parameters to a method, and is mainly provided as a means for bean developers to provide detailed parameter information beyond that obtained through the Java reflection services.

Constructors

```
public ParameterDescriptor()
```

This constructor creates a default parameter descriptor object.

PropertyChangeEvent

Extends: `EventObject`

The `PropertyChangeEvent` class is used to store information relating to a change in a bound or constrained property. This information consists of the name of the property, the old value of the property, and the new value of the property. `PropertyChangeEvent` objects are sent as notifications from a bean to registered listeners through the `PropertyChangeListener` and `VetoableChangeListener` interfaces, depending on whether the property in question is bound or constrained. More specifically, a `PropertyChangeEvent` object is sent as the only argument to the `propertyChange()` and `vetoableChange()` methods, which are called on the respective listener interfaces.

Constructors

```
public PropertyChangeEvent(Object source, String propertyName,
➥Object oldValue, Object newValue)
```

This constructor creates a property change event object based on information about the property and the source bean containing the property.

Parameters

source	The source bean that contains the property.
propertyName	The programmatic name of the property that has changed.
oldValue	The old value of the property.
newValue	The new value of the property.

Methods

```
public String getPropertyName()
```

This method gets the programmatic name of the property that has changed.

Returns:

The programmatic name of the property that has changed or `null` if multiple properties have changed.

`public Object getNewValue()`

This method gets the new value for the changed property.

Returns:

The new value for the property, expressed as an object, or `null` if multiple properties have changed.

`public Object getOldValue()`

This method gets the old value for the changed property.

Returns:

The old value for the property, expressed as an object, or `null` if multiple properties have changed.

`public void setPropagationId(Object propagationId)`

This method sets the propagation identifier for the event.

Parameter	
`propagationId`	The propagation identifier for the event.

`public Object getPropagationId()`

This method gets the propagation identifier for the event.

Returns:

The propagation identifier for the event.

PropertyChangeSupport

Extends: `Object`

The `PropertyChangeSupport` class is a helper class for managing listeners of bound and constrained properties. It primarily handles the chore of maintaining a list of listeners and firing property change notifications to each, which is often a nice convenience for beans with bound properties.

Constructors

`public PropertyChangeSupport(Object sourceBean)`

This method creates a default property change support object.

Methods

`public synchronized void addPropertyChangeListener`
`➥(PropertyChangeListenerlistener)`

This method registers a property change event listener.

Parameter	
listener	The property change event listener to be registered.

`public synchronized void removePropertyChangeListener`
`➥(PropertyChangeListenerlistener)`

This method removes a property change event listener.

Parameter	
listener	The property change event listener to be removed.

`public void firePropertyChange(String propertyName, Object`
`➥oldValue, Object newValue)`

This method fires a property change event to all registered event listeners.

Parameter	
propertyName	The programmatic name of the property that has changed.
oldValue	The old value of the property.
newValue	The new value of the property.

PropertyDescriptor

Extends: `FeatureDescriptor`

The `PropertyDescriptor` class represents a publicly accessed property. This class provides methods for accessing the type of a property along with its accessor methods and describes whether it is bound or constrained.

Constructors

```
public PropertyDescriptor(String propertyName, Class beanClass)
➥throws IntrospectionException
```

This constructor creates a property descriptor for a property that follows the standard Java convention of having getter and setter methods.

Parameters

propertyName	The programmatic name of the property.
beanClass	The Class object for the bean containing the property.

```
public PropertyDescriptor(String propertyName, Class beanClass,
➥String getterName, String setterName)
➥throws IntrospectionException
```

This constructor creates a property descriptor for a property by specifying the method names used for getting and setting the property.

Parameters

propertyName	The programmatic name of the property.
beanClass	The Class object for the bean containing the property.
getterName	The name of the method used for getting the property value or null if the property is write-only.
setterName	The name of the method used for setting the property value or null if the property is read-only.

```
public PropertyDescriptor(String propertyName, Method getter,
➥Method setter) throws IntrospectionException
```

This constructor creates a property descriptor for a property by specifying the methods used for getting and setting the property.

Parameters

propertyName	The programmatic name of the property.
getter	The method used for getting the property value or null if the property is write-only.
setter	The method used for setting the property value or null if the property is read-only.

Methods

`public Class getPropertyType()`

This method gets the class type for the property.

Returns:

The class type for the property or `null` if this is an indexed property that doesn't support nonindexed access.

`public Method getReadMethod()`

This method gets the getter method used to read the property value.

Returns:

The getter method used to read the property value or `null` if the property can't be read.

`public Method getWriteMethod()`

This method gets the setter method used to write the property value.

Returns:

The setter method used to write the property value or `null` if the property can't be written.

`public boolean isBound()`

This method determines whether the property is bound.

Returns:

`true` if the property is bound; `false` otherwise.

`public void setBound(boolean bound)`

This method sets the property as a bound property.

Parameter

bound   `true` if the property is to be bound; `false` if not.

`public boolean isConstrained()`

This method determines whether the property is constrained.

Returns:

`true` if the property is constrained; `false` otherwise.

```
public void setConstrained(boolean constrained)
```

This method sets the property as a constrained property.

Parameter

constrained   true if the property is constrained; false if not.

```
public void setPropertyEditorClass(Class propertyEditorClass)
```

This method sets the property editor used for editing the property.

Parameter

propertyEditorClass   The property editor used for editing the property.

```
public Class getPropertyEditorClass()
```

This method gets the property editor used for editing the property.

Returns:

The property editor used for editing the property or null if no special editor has been registered

PropertyEditorManager

Extends: Object

The PropertyEditorManager class is used to locate the property editor for a property of a given type. Property editors capable of being located by the PropertyEditorManager class must implement the PropertyEditor interface. The PropertyEditorManager class provides a means of registering property types so that their editors can be easily found. For property types that haven't been registered, the PropertyEditorManager class looks for property editors using the name of the property with Editor appended to the end.

Constructors

```
public PropertyEditorManager()
```

This constructor creates a default property editor manager object.

Methods

```
public static void registerEditor(Class targetType, Class
➥editorClass)
```

This method registers an editor class to be used to edit the property values of a given property class.

Parameters

targetType	The class type of the property to be edited.
editorClass	The property editor class to be used to edit the property values.

```
public static PropertyEditor findEditor(Class targetType)
```

This method finds a property editor for a given property class type.

Parameter

targetType	The property class type for the property to be edited.

Returns:

A property editor object associated with the given property class or `null` if no suitable editor can be found.

```
public static String[] getEditorSearchPath()
```

This method gets an array containing the package names that are searched in order to find property editors.

Returns:

An array containing the package names that are searched in order to find property editors.

```
public static void setEditorSearchPath(String path[])
```

This method sets the array of package names that are searched in order to find property editors.

Parameter

path	An array containing the package names that are searched in order to find property editors.

PropertyEditorSupport

Extends: `Object`

Implements: `PropertyEditor`

This class is a helper class that implements the `PropertyEditor` interface that is used to make the construction of custom property editors a little easier.

Constructors

`protected PropertyEditorSupport()`

This constructor creates a default property editor support object and is meant to be used by derived `PropertyEditor` classes.

`PropertyEditorSupport protected PropertyEditorSupport(Object`
`➥source)`

This constructor creates a property editor support object for use when another property editor is delegating information. This constructor is also meant to be used by derived `PropertyEditor` classes.

Parameter	
`source`	The source to use for any events fired by the property editor.

Methods

`public void setValue(Object value)`

This method sets the value of the property.

Parameter	
`value`	The new value of the property.

`public Object getValue()`

This method gets the value of the property.

Returns:

The value of the property.

`public boolean isPaintable()`

This method determines whether the property value can be painted.

Returns:

true if the property value can be painted; false otherwise.

public void paintValue(Graphics gfx, Rectangle box)

This method paints a representation of the property value into a given area on the screen.

Parameters

gfx	The graphics object to paint on.
box	A rectangle within the graphics object that specifies the painting window.

public String getJavaInitializationString()

This method generates a fragment of Java code that can be used to initialize a variable with the current property value; this method is used when generating Java code to set the value of the property.

Returns:

A fragment of Java code representing an initializer for the current property value.

public String getAsText()

This method gets the property value as a human readable string.

Returns:

The property value as a human-readable string or null if the value can't be expressed as a human-readable string.

public void setAsText(String text) throws IllegalArgumentException

This method sets the property value by parsing the string argument.

Parameter

text	The string to be parsed and set.

public String[] getTags()

This method returns an array of tagged values for the property, if they exist.

Returns:

The tagged values for the property or null if the property cannot be represented as tagged values.

```
public Component getCustomEditor()
```

This method gets a custom visual property editor for the property.

Returns:

A custom editor that enables a human to directly edit the property value or `null` if there is no custom editor for the property.

```
public boolean supportsCustomEditor()
```

This method determines whether a custom editor is supported for the property.

Returns:

`true` if a custom editor is supported for the property; `false` otherwise.

```
public void addPropertyChangeListener(PropertyChangeListener
➥listener)
```

This method registers a listener for the `PropertyChange` event.

Parameter	
listener	A listener to be notified when a `PropertyChange` event is fired.

```
public void removePropertyChangeListener(PropertyChangeListener
➥listener)
```

This method removes a listener for the `PropertyChange` event.

Parameter	
listener	The `PropertyChange` listener to be removed.

```
public void firePropertyChange()
```

This method fires a property change event to all registered event listeners.

SimpleBeanInfo

Extends: `Object`

`SimpleBeanInfo` is a support class designed to make it easier for bean developers to provide explicit information about a bean. This class basically implements every method in the `BeanInfo` interface but returns a value that triggers the automatic introspection services. This lets developers provide selective bean information by overriding specific methods, without having to implement every method in the `BeanInfo` interface.

Constructors

`public SimpleBeanInfo()`

This constructor creates a default simple bean information object.

Methods

`public BeanDescriptor getBeanDescriptor()`

This method denies explicit knowledge of a bean descriptor for the bean, resulting in JavaBeans relying on automatic introspection.

Returns:

A bean descriptor for the bean.

`public PropertyDescriptor[] getPropertyDescriptors()`

This method denies explicit knowledge of property descriptors for the bean, resulting in JavaBeans relying on automatic introspection.

Returns:

An array containing property descriptors for the bean.

`public int getDefaultPropertyIndex()`

This method denies explicit knowledge of a default property for the bean, resulting in JavaBeans relying on automatic introspection.

Returns:

The default property for the bean.

`public EventSetDescriptor[] getEventSetDescriptors()`

This method denies explicit knowledge of event set descriptors for the bean, resulting in JavaBeans relying on automatic introspection.

Returns:

An array containing event set descriptors for the bean.

```
public int getDefaultEventIndex()
```

This method denies explicit knowledge of a default event for the bean, resulting in JavaBeans relying on automatic introspection.

Returns:

The default event for the bean.

```
public MethodDescriptor[] getMethodDescriptors()
```

This method denies explicit knowledge of method descriptors for the bean, resulting in JavaBeans relying on automatic introspection.

Returns:

An array containing method descriptors for the bean.

```
public BeanInfo[] getAdditionalBeanInfo()
```

This method denies explicit knowledge of any other bean information objects for the bean, resulting in JavaBeans relying on automatic introspection.

Returns:

An array containing other bean information objects for the bean.

```
public Image getIcon(int iconKind)
```

This method denies explicit knowledge of any icons for the bean, resulting in JavaBeans relying on automatic introspection.

Returns:

The icon for the bean corresponding to the given icon type.

```
public Image loadImage(String resourceName)
```

This method is a utility method that loads icon images for a bean based on the name of a resource image file.

Parameter	
resourceName	A path name for the icon image relative to the directory holding the class file for the bean.

Returns:

An icon image or null if the load failed.

VetoableChangeSupport

Extends: `Object`

Implements: `Serializable`

Similar to `PropertyChangeSupport`, the `VetoableChangeSupport` class is a helper class for managing listeners of bound and constrained properties. It primarily handles the chore of maintaining a list of listeners and firing property change notifications to each, which is often a nice convenience to beans with constrained properties.

Constructors

`public VetoableChangeSupport(Object sourceBean)`

This method creates a default vetoable change support object.

Methods

`public synchronized void addVetoableChangeListener`
`➥(VetoableChangeListenerlistener)`

This method registers a vetoable change event listener.

Parameter

listener	The vetoable change event listener to be registered.

`public synchronized void removeVetoableChangeListener`
`➥(VetoableChangeListenerlistener)`

This method removes a vetoable change event listener.

Parameter

listener	The vetoable change event listener to be removed.

`public void fireVetoableChange(String propertyName, Object`
`➥oldValue, Object newValue) throws PropertyVetoException`

This method fires a vetoable change event to all registered event listeners.

Parameters

propertyName	The programmatic name of the property that has changed.
oldValue	The old value of the property.
newValue	The new value of the property.

Exceptions

The JavaBeans API consists of the following exceptions, which are described in detail throughout the next few sections:

- IntrospectionException
- PropertyVetoException

IntrospectionException

Extends: Exception

The IntrospectionException exception class signals that an error has occurred during introspection. Examples of situations in which this exception is thrown include not being able to map a string class name to a Class object, not being able to map a string method name to an existing method, and specifying a method name that has the wrong type of signature for its intended use.

Constructors

public IntrospectionException(String s)

This constructor creates an introspection exception with the specified detail message, which contains information specific to this particular exception.

Parameter

s	The detail message.

PropertyVetoException

Extends: Exception

The PropertyVetoException exception class signals that a veto has occurred on an attempt to change a property value; this exception is thrown only for constrained properties.

Constructors

`public PropertyVetoException(String s, PropertyChangeEvent e)`

This constructor creates a property veto exception with the specified detail message, which contains information specific to this particular exception.

Parameters	
s	The detail message.
e	A property change event indicating the vetoed change.

Methods

`public PropertyChangeEvent getPropertyChangeEvent()`

This method gets the property change event describing the vetoed change.

Returns:

A property change event indicating the vetoed change.

What's on the CD-ROM?

On the *Presenting JavaBeans* CD-ROM, you will find all the sample files which have been presented in this book along with a wealth of other applications and utilities.

> Note: Please refer to the `readme.wri` file on the CD-ROM (Windows) or the Guide to the CD-ROM (Macintosh) for the latest listing of software.

Windows Software

The following is the Windows software that appears on the CD-ROM.

Java

- Sun's Beans Development Kit for Windows 95 and NT 4/3.51 (Solaris version included)
- Sun's Java Developer's Kit for Windows 95 and NT (Solaris versions included)
- Sample Java applets
- Sample JavaScripts
- Trial version of Jamba for Windows 95/NT
- JPad IDE
- JPad Pro Java IDE demo
- Kawa IDE
- Studio J++ demo
- Javelin IDE demo
- JDesigner Pro database wizard for Java

HTML Tools

- W3e HTML Editor
- CSE 3310 HTML Validator
- Hot Dog 32-bit HTML editor demo
- HoTMetaL HTML editor demo
- HTMLed HTML editor
- Spider 1.2 demo
- Web Analyzer demo

Graphics, Video, and Sound Applications

- Goldwave sound editor, player, and recorder
- MapThis image map utility
- Paint Shop Pro 3.12 graphics editor and graphic file format converter for Windows
- SnagIt screen capture utility
- ThumbsPlus image viewer and browser

Utilities

- Microsoft Viewers for Excel, PowerPoint, and Word
- Adobe Acrobat viewer
- Microsoft PowerPoint Animation Player and Publisher
- WinZip for Windows NT and 95
- WinZip Self-Extractor

Macintosh Software

The following is a list of the Macintosh software available on the CD-ROM.

Java

- Sun's Java Developer's Kit for Macintosh v1.0.2
- Sample applets
- Sample JavaScripts

HTML

- BBEdit 3.5.1 freeware
- BBEdit 4.0 demo
- HTML edit
- HTML Editor
- HTML Web Weaver
- HTML Markup
- WebMap
- Web Painter

Graphics

- Graphic Converter
- GIFConverter

Utilities

- Adobe Acrobat reader
- SnagIt Pro
- SoundApp
- Sparkle
- ZipIt 1.3.5 for Macintosh

About Shareware

Shareware is not free. Please read all documentation associated with a third-party product (usually contained with files named `readme.txt` or `license.txt`) and follow all guidelines.

Glossary

accessor method   A public method defined in a bean that reads or writes the value of a property.

ActiveX   A family of technologies developed by Microsoft to combine computing capability with Internet connectivity.

ActiveX control   A software module with OLE capabilities that can easily be embedded within Web pages or programs.

applet   A Java program that can be embedded within an HTML page with the APP element and run within a Java-enabled browser.

bound property   A property that provides notifications to an interested party based on changes in its value.

browser   A computer program used to view Web pages written in HTML and other languages. Also referred to as a client.

bytecode   An intermediate form of a Java program that's between the source code and a native executable. Bytecode Java programs are interpreted by the Java runtime system.

COM (Component Object Model)   A binary standard developed by Microsoft for representing software components in a distributed environment.

constrained property   A property that enables an interested party to perform a validation on a new property value before accepting the modification.

container   A context in which components can be grouped together and interacted with.

CORBA (Common Object Request Broker Architecture)   The industry standard for representing distributed objects.

cross-platform   A term used to indicate that a piece of software can run on any operating system platform.

customizer   A user interface that provides a specialized means of visually editing bean properties.

design patterns   Rules used to determine information about a bean from its reflected method names and signatures.

digital signature   A security technique that consists of attaching a code to a software component that identifies the vendor of the component.

event   Something that happens within a component that an application or other component might want to know about and possibly react to.

event adapter   An intermediary placed between an event source and a listener that provides additional event delivery behavior.

event listener   An application or bean capable of responding to events.

event source   A bean capable of generating events.

event state object   An object used to store information associated with a particular event.

externalization mechanism   A means of storing and retrieving an object through some type of custom, externally defined format.

getter method   An accessor method that reads, or gets, the value of a property.

indexed properties   A property that represents an array of values.

inner classes   Refers to a feature in the Java language that enables you to define classes at any scope.

interface   A set of public methods used to interact with a component.

Internet   The global "network of networks" that communicates through the suite of protocols encompassed by the TCP/IP specification.

introspection   The mechanism that exposes the functionality of a component to the outside world.

language-independent   A term used to indicate that a piece of software can be developed in any programming language.

LiveConnect   A technology included with Netscape Navigator that provides a means of interconnecting different types of executable content.

low-level events   Events that correspond to a low-level input or visual interface interaction.

method   Similar to properties in an object-oriented world; however, instead of merely setting the characteristics of an object, methods invoke an action for that object. For example, a Web browser object can have a method you invoke for connecting to and displaying a Web site.

multicast event source   An event source capable of generating events for retrieval by any number of listeners.

object-oriented   A term specifying that a piece of software is composed of objects, which are self-contained modules that contain both data and procedures that act on the data.

OLE (Object Linking and Embedding)   A COM-based technology developed by Microsoft that provides a wide range of services including application automation, reusable controls, version management, standardized drag-and-drop, documents, object linking and embedding, and visual editing.

OpenDoc   An open, multiplatform, component software architecture heavily backed by Apple and IBM.

persistence   The means by which a component is stored to and retrieved from a non-volatile location.

platform   A term referring to a particular operating system and runtime environment, such as Windows 95 or Solaris.

property   A discrete, named attribute of a bean that determines its appearance and behavior.

property editor   A user interface enabling the visual editing of a particular property type.

property sheet   A user interface that contains property editors for all the exported properties of a bean.

reflection   The process of studying a bean to determine information about its functionality and public facilities.

semantic events   Events that correspond to high-level visual interface actions that are based more on the semantics of a particular bean.

serialization   The process of storing or retrieving information through a standard protocol.

setter method   An accessor method that writes, or sets, the value of a property.

software component   A piece of software isolated into a discrete, easily reusable structure.

unicast event source   An event source capable of generating events for retrieval by only one listener.

URL (Uniform Resource Locator)   The site and file-addressing scheme for the World Wide Web.

versioning   The inevitable tendency for an object to evolve over time and gain new functionality.

visual component   A type of software component that has a visual representation that requires physical space on the display surface of a parent application.

wizard   A user interface that uses multiple-step questionnaires to gather information from the user.

WWW (World Wide Web, or simply "the Web")   A popular hypertext-based system of transmitting textual and multimedia-based information through the Internet.

Index

E

MACMILLAN COMPUTER PUBLISHING USA

A VIACOM COMPANY

Technical Support:

If you cannot get the CD-ROMs to install properly, or if you need assistance with a particular item in the book, please feel free to check out the Knowledge Base on our Web site at **http://www.superlibrary.com/general/support**. We have answers to our most Frequently Asked Questions listed there. If you do not find your specific question answered, please contact Macmillan Technical Support at **(317) 581-3833**. We can also be reached by e-mail at **support@mcp.com**.

Teach Yourself Java in 21 Days, Professional Reference Edition

Laura Lemay and Michael Morrison

Introducing the first, best, and most detailed guide to developing applications with the hot new Java language from Sun Microsystems. Includes coverage of browsing Java applications with Netscape and other popular Web browsers.

CD-ROM includes the Java Developer's Kit.

Price: $59.99 USA/$84.95 CDN   *Casual—Accomplished—Expert*
ISBN: 1-57521-183-1   *1,296 pp.*

Teach Yourself JavaScript in a Week, Second Edition

Arman Danesh

Teach Yourself JavaScript in a Week, Second Edition, is a new edition of the best-selling JavaScript tutorial. It has been revised and updated for the latest version of JavaScript from Netscape and includes detailed coverage of new features such as how to work with Java applets with LiveConnect, writing JavaScript for Microsoft's Internet Explorer, and more!

Price: $39.99 USA/$56.95 CDN   *Beginning—Intermediate*
ISBN: 1-57521-195-5   *600 pp.*

Java Developer's Reference

Mike Cohn, et al.

This is the information- and resource-packed development package for professional developers. It explains the components of the Java Developer's Kit (JDK) and the Java programming language. Everything needed to program in Java is included within this comprehensive reference, making it the tool developers will turn to over and over again for timely, accurate information on Java and the JDK.

Price: $59.99 USA/$84.95 CDN   *Accomplished—Expert*
ISBN: 1-57521-129-7   *1,296 pp.*

JavaScript Developer's Guide

Wes Tatters

The *JavaScript 1.1 Developer's Guide* is the professional reference for enhancing commercial-grade Web sites with JavaScript. Packed with real-world JavaScript examples, the book shows the developer how to use JavaScript to glue together Java applets, multimedia programs, plug-ins, and more on a Web site.

Price: $49.99 USA/$70.95 CDN   *Accomplished—Expert*
ISBN: 1-57521-084-3   *600 pp.*

Teach Yourself SunSoft Java WorkShop in 21 Days

Rogers Cadenhead, Laura Lemay, and Charles E. Perkins

Written in Java itself, the Java WorkShop included with this book is a cross-platform tool that provides a rich set of tools for the beginner or professional Java programmer. The workshop enhances the book to provide the most comprehensive way to learn SunSoft Java WorkShop.

Price: $39.99 USA/$56.95 CDN *Casual—Accomplished*
ISBN: 1-57521-159-9 *656 pp.*

Web Programming with Java

Michael Girdley and Kathryn A. Jones, et al.

This book gets readers on the road to developing robust, real-world Java applications. Various cutting-edge applications are presented, allowing the reader to quickly learn all aspects of programming Java for the Internet.

Price: $39.99 USA/$56.95 CDN *Accomplished—Expert*
ISBN: 1-57521-113-0 *500 pp.*

Web Programming with Visual Basic

Craig Eddy and Brad Haasch

This reference quickly and efficiently shows the experienced developer how to develop Web applications using the 32-bit power of Visual Basic 4. It includes an introduction and overview of Web programming and then quickly delves into the specifics, teaching readers how to incorporate animation, sound, and more into their Web applications.

Price: $39.99 USA/$56.95 CDN *Accomplished—Expert*
ISBN: 1-57521-106-8 *400 pp.*

HTML 3.2 & CGI Unleashed, Professional Reference Edition

John December and Mark Ginsburg

Readers will learn the logistics of how to create compelling, information-rich Web pages that grab attention and keep readers returning for more. This comprehensive professional instruction and reference guide for the World Wide Web covers all aspects of the development processes, implementation, tools, and programming.

Price: $59.99 USA/$84.95 CDN *Accomplished—Expert*
ISBN: 1-57521-177-7 *1,376 pp.*

Add to Your Sams.net Library Today
with the Best Books for Internet Technologies

ISBN	Quantity	Description of Item	Unit Cost	Total Cost
1-57521-183-1		Teach Yourself Java in 21 Days, Professional Reference Edition (Book/CD-ROM)	$59.99	
1-57521-195-5		Teach Yourself JavaScript in a Week, Second Edition (Book/CD-ROM)	$39.99	
1-57521-129-7		Java Developer's Reference (Book/CD-ROM)	$59.99	
1-57521-084-3		JavaScript Developer's Guide (Book/CD-ROM)	$49.99	
1-57521-159-9		Teach Yourself SunSoft Java WorkShop in 21 Days (Book/CD-ROM)	$39.99	
1-57521-113-0		Web Programming with Java (Book/CD-ROM)	$39.99	
1-57521-106-8		Web Programming with Visual Basic (Book/CD-ROM)	$39.99	
1-57521-177-7		HTML 3.2 & CGI Unleashed, Professional Reference Edition (Book/CD-ROM)	$59.99	
		Shipping and Handling: See information below.		
		TOTAL		

Shipping and Handling: $4.00 for the first book, and $1.75 for each additional book. If you need to have it NOW, we can ship product to you in 24 hours for an additional charge of approximately $18.00, and you will receive your item overnight or in two days. Overseas shipping and handling adds $2.00. Prices subject to change. Call between 9:00 a.m. and 5:00 p.m. EST for availability and pricing information on latest editions.

201 W. 103rd Street, Indianapolis, Indiana 46290

1-800-428-5331 — Orders   1-800-835-3202 — FAX   1-800-858-7674 — Customer Service

Book ISBN 1-57521-287-0